SAN FRANCISCO

Magic City

SAN FRANCISCO

Magic City

by

MRS. FREMONT OLDER

(Cora Older)

LONGMANS, GREEN & CO.

NEW YORK · LONDON · TORONTO

1961

91880

LONGMANS, GREEN AND CO., INC.
119 WEST 40TH STREET, NEW YORK 18, N.Y.

LONGMANS, GREEN AND CO., LTD.
48 GROSVENOR STREET, LONDON W 1

LONGMANS, GREEN AND CO.
137 BOND STREET, TORONTO 2

SAN FRANCISCO

PUBLISHED SIMULTANEOUSLY IN THE DOMINION OF CANADA BY
LONGMANS, GREEN AND CO., TORONTO

FIRST EDITION

LIBRARY OF CONGRESS CATALOG CARD NUMBER 61-10953

Printed in the United States of America

Contents

Illustrations

(*between pages* 88 *and* 89)

CHAPTER 1

Earthquake and Fire

ON THE summery night of April 17, 1906, San Franciscans heard Caruso and Fremstad sing *Carmen*—farewell to the old city. My husband, Fremont Older, and I returned to the Palace Hotel at midnight with the Toreador song in our ears.

I left a six-o'clock call at the desk. I wished to catch the seven-o'clock train for William James's lecture on Philosophy at Stanford University. At 5:13 what my sleepy mind mistook for my call began like the roaring of a monstrous train. The Palace Hotel turned on its axis; the building twisted and moaned. The sound of the earth grew louder and more ominous, then in the living room of our suite a crash as if the walls had collapsed. I found myself out of bed and kneeling in the passageway between the bedroom and the living room. A marble bust of our friend, the San Francisco novelist Gertrude Atherton, had been thrown from its pedestal to the floor and lay in fragments. I was praying, my husband told me later, a loud, indignant prayer in which I kept protesting, "I'm too young to die!"

We didn't speak. What was happening was too terrifying. The violent opening temblor seemed to last forever but actually lasted only forty-eight seconds.

Then hysterical voices sounded in the hallway. We were not alone. We put on our dressing gowns and went into the hall. People in night attire were standing in their doorways in states of shock, and a wrinkled woman with peroxide hair was dashing from one to another, crying, "Save me! Save me!" All were as terrified as she, but her panic was so grotesque that it calmed us and we returned to our rooms and dressed, putting on the oldest garments we could find.

1

When we came into the hall again the elevators were not running and people in various states of undress were scrambling down the stairs. As we walked down we met sculptor Waldo Story panting and puffing to the gallant rescue of Bessie Abbott, who had sung the role of Micaela at the Opera House a few hours earlier.

As we left the Palace we did not know we were taking leave forever of Ralston's "largest hotel in the West," with its balconies, braziers, its Palm Court, and its dramatic history and romance. The world-famous hostelry had survived the quake. It would not survive the fire.

A few people, aimless and disheveled, were in the streets, which showed little evidence of destruction. We went to the *Bulletin* office on Bush street, Older's first thought being to get out an edition concerning the tragedy that had come to the city. He found no power to turn the presses.

We encountered there the earthquake's first tragedy.

Opposite the *Bulletin* office, in the building of Engine Company Number Two, lay Chief Dennis T. Sullivan, fatally mangled by a falling chimney. The chief and his wife had occupied adjoining rooms in the firehouse, which a cupola crashing down from the adjoining California Theater had cut in half. The chief, rushing to his wife's room to rescue her, fell into the chasm. With his skull fractured and the ribs of his left side stabbing his lungs, he lay atop the debris in the basement. Three days later he died at Letterman Hospital. Mrs. Sullivan, protected by bed and mattress, survived.

At first, like everyone else in San Francisco that morning, we did not realize the gravity of our situation. We did not know we were homeless refugees. We met the Republican orator, George Knight, driving along Bush Street in his car and he offered to drive us out to the ocean beach where we had a small bathing house. There we were joined by friends who straggled out by various means from the city and brought us word of what was happening in San Francisco.

Small fires were breaking out in various places south of Market Street. First Assistant Chief John Dougherty and his men fought the first few. Then in a hundred spots flames were doing a devil dance and it was learned that the water mains were broken. The exhausted firemen, unable to check the advance of the holocaust, fled for their lives. The panic was on.

Martial law in the form of General Funston's Presidio soldiers took charge of the burning city.

Mayor Eugene Schmitz assembled a Committee of Fifty to determine a course of action. Flames drove them from building to building. Finally they took refuge in the half-finished Fairmont Hotel on Nob Hill. All day long the earth shook the city. Flames gnawed up Third Street toward Market. The *Call* was the first newspaper building to go, the *Examiner* went next. The Chronicle Building was doomed by falling sparks. The Emporium Building succumbed.

Dynamiters took over, trying to blow up the Monadnock Building in order to save the adjoining Palace Hotel, which was fighting for survival with its own artesian well. Finally the well gave out, and the hotel's myriad bay windows on both sides shot out flames at once like a last blaze of glory. The Fairmont went the second day, but the St. Francis held out till the third.

People at the beach where we were feared a tidal wave. They cried, "One always follows a big earthquake." That night, with other refugees, we slept on sand dunes at a safe elevation from the dreaded wave.

As we walked three miles through Golden Gate Park next morning, we realized that our sole possessions consisted of our oldest clothes, which we were wearing. Why, I mourned, hadn't I saved my new dress, my silly new hat, the manuscript of the book I had been writing? In the park we rushed into the arms of weeping friends who had spent the night sleeping in a carriage. We ate the food they offered. We ate wherever we went, fearing that we could never again have food. Golden Gate Park was filled with refugees who had slept on rugs, overcoats, often without covering. That night a baby was born in the park.

The dynamite blasts grew more deafening. Could any of San Francisco be saved? Van Ness Avenue was the new battlefront. Flames must not pass that 125-foot thoroughfare where many beautiful residences were situated. In the ruins below the avenue we met by chance my brother, Hiland Baggerly, and some of the *Bulletin* staff. They had rushed to the Palace Hotel, gathered up our clothing and buried it in a vacant lot above Van Ness Avenue, opposite the Holluschickie Club, where they lived. As a result of their thoughtfulness, we found ourselves embarrassed by our good clothing when so many others had little to wear.

We read the *Call-Chronicle-Examiner* published in Oakland, four pages, seven columns each, no advertisements, all devoted to fire news. "San Francisco seems doomed to entire destruction," was the first sentence. Distributed from automobiles, the paper sold at inflated prices.

The wharves had been saved and ferries were still running. We walked down Market Street to the Ferry Building. Everyone spoke to everyone else. Wild rumors were exchanged. Communication with the East was severed and imagination ran riot. It was reported that Vesuvius had erupted, that Pelée had burst forth again, that Chicago was again in ruins, and that entire cities on the Atlantic Coast had been swallowed up by a tidal wave. Millionaire John D. Spreckels heard that the Hotel Coronado and all his San Diego possessions had dropped into the sea. Mr. Spreckels faced pauperism bravely and decided he would become a chauffeur. Mrs. Spreckels said she would sell embroidery.

We crossed the bay to Oakland where the *Bulletin* and *Call* issued their papers from a local newspaper office.

Mayor Schmitz issued a proclamation, "The Federal troops and members of the Police Force have been authorized to kill any or all persons who engage in looting, or in the commission of any other crime . . . All the gas and electric companies must not turn on the electricity until I order them to do so. All citizens must remain home from darkness to daylight every night until order is restored."

There was little looting. Doors and windows of houses were left wide open in an effort to keep glass from being broken by dynamite blasts. Furniture and belongings were unprotected. Crime ceased, for liquor had been emptied into the streets. There was no temptation to go out. Trolley-car lines were down. Powerhouses of cable companies were burned, their machinery disabled. Many tracks were twisted and impassable. All automobiles were turned over to the city.

Curious incidents of the Fire: a man dragging his trunk along the street; men wearing several hats, one above the other; man bumping a piano along; woman carrying an empty birdcage; woman rolling a sewing machine along the sidewalk with bedding lashed to it. Mrs. Will Tevis casually strolled down the street, carrying her jewels in a pillow slip. Ex-Mayor Phelan in his Valencia Street garden picked up a cancelled check that had been blown from his office in the Phelan Building on Market Street, nearly two miles away.

That morning a telegram came to Governor Pardee:

IT WAS DIFFICULT TO CREDIT THE NEWS OF THE CALAMITY THAT HAD BEFALLEN SAN FRANCISCO. I FEEL THE GREATEST CONCERN FOR YOU AND THE PEOPLE, NOT ONLY OF SAN FRANCISCO BUT OF CALIFORNIA IN THE TERRIBLE DISASTER. YOU WILL LET ME KNOW IF THERE IS ANYTHING THAT THE GOVERNMENT CAN DO. THEODORE ROOSEVELT

During the second day fire fighters depended upon dynamite, blowing up most buildings below Van Ness Avenue. Only once did the flames cross Van Ness, but they were soon extinguished. James B. Stetson related how, after having been ordered out of his house by soldiers, he went back and saved the building with wet blankets.

Enormous effort was put forth to save the old Montgomery Block on Montgomery Street, built in 1853, San Francisco's first four-story brick building. Firemen laid charges of powder to demolish it in order to halt the devouring flames, but Dr. Emma Sutro Merritt and friends of the Sutro Library pleaded that the building containing her father's $2,500,000 library be spared. The powder was removed. Captain Thomas R. Murphy, later chief of the Fire Department, led firemen inside the building. They went from window to window, with fire roaring around them on three sides, and used wet sacks to beat out flames creeping in at the windows. The brick walls withstood the fire, and nearly 100,000 books were saved. In 1959 the historic Montgomery Block was razed to build a garage.

Captain Murphy and his crew also saved the Custom House and the Appraiser's Building. Although all structures surrounding it burned, historic Mission Dolores, the oldest building in the city, came through the earthquake without a crack or a scar.

Anxious relatives in the East and in Europe flooded telegraph offices with messages of inquiry that could not be delivered.

On the fourth day the flames were under control, and on Saturday night Fillmore Street cars ran. The following Sunday thousands attended Mass celebrated on the steps of St. Mary's Cathedral. That Sunday was also a day of marriages.

On the day following the shock Governor Pardee declared the 19th, 20th, and 21st days of April legal holidays. The thirty days following were later similarly declared to protect banks from *runs*. Insurance Commissioner Myron Wolf announced that most of the losses would be paid, but German companies largely defaulted. Losses reached a half billion dollars.

The Committee of Fifty, with ex-Mayor James D. Phelan as chairman, virtually became the city government, meeting in Franklin Hall on Fillmore Street. There were committees of relief for the hungry, housing the homeless, sick and wounded, guards for medical supplies, restoration of water supply, lights, telephones, transportation, and sanitation.

Food could not be purchased and use of stoves was prohibited. Women cooked on bricks or stones in the street. Outlying food stores were stripped of candy, groceries, anything to appease the appetite. Even the wealthy stood in bread lines. Trainloads of supplies arrived. Volunteers assisted in relief work. Physicians donated their services. People moved from parks into tents. Soldiers served milk, crackers, and corned beef to women and children.

Congress authorized relief expenditure of $2.5 million. Secretary Taft sent a million dollars' worth of supplies and army tents. Within a few days, more than $9 million were subscribed by churches, corporations, banks and clubs. Railroads carried supplies free, giving relief trains right-of-way over all regular trains.

The Chicago fire covered only three and one-third square miles. In San Francisco 4.7 square miles were burned over; 28,188 buildings destroyed. Within the burned district were saved 283 wooden buildings, thirteen of brick, four of brick and wood, three of corrugated iron. On Telegraph Hill tugs pumping water from the bay and the pumps of a cold-storage plant saved warehouses. Two blocks near the Custom House and two blocks of frame and plaster houses on Russian Hill escaped in the same manner. The United States Mint at Fifth and Mission Streets was protected from flames by a local well and pump. The Western Electric Building near Folsom came through because of its own supply. Owing to Class A construction—fireproof steel frame with structural parts of incombustible material—the Atlas Building on Mission near Second withstood the fire. The Kohl Building luckily was protected by small buildings nearby. Woodwork on the upper floors was metalsheathed, saving the upper portion of the building from destruction. The Call Building with its exposed woodwork was gutted.

A survey of the ruined buildings revealed that graft in construction and incompetent workmanship had caused the greatest earthquake losses. One side of the City Hall, completed under an honest administration, stood but the other side, built by grafters, fell into the street. The Hall of Justice, Girls' High School, St. Dominic's Church, Beth Israel Synagogue, Scottish Rite's Temple, and Knights' Templar Asylum suffered heavily because of poor construction. On Willow Creek, where soil had been filled in, there was much destruction, including the Valencia Street Hotel. Water pipes, 45 inches in diameter, were torn apart on filled ground. Both the Post Office and the Ferry Building were on made ground, but they had been expertly built, with solid foundations, and so withstood the shock. Geological surveys revealed that defective construction of Spring Valley Water Company's pipeline across the region of the "fault" precipitated the disaster. Scientific laying of pipelines would have assured the water supply and saved the city.

Sensationalists have written that thousands died in the Earthquake, describing miles of dead bodies piled up like cordwood, but the coroner's office handled only 315 dead. Six were shot for crime, and one was killed by mistake. Two hundred fifty-two were reported missing or unaccounted for. Some may have perished in the flames.

The Earthquake was caused by cooling and contracting of earth from Point Arena above Point Reyes through Bolinas, San Francisco, and Wright's—a part of the San Andreas fault.

Although much of the city was in ruins, San Franciscans were not cast down. Clubman Lawrence W. Harris expressed the spirit of the city:

From the Ferry to Van Ness you're a God-forsaken mess,
But the damndest finest ruins, nothing more and nothing less . . .

Prizefighter Willie Britt seconded Harris's verse with, "I'd rather be a busted lamp post on Battery Street, San Francisco, than the Waldorf-Astoria!"

The newspapers came back from Oakland. The *Chronicle* and the *Call* moved into hastily refitted offices in their former buildings. The *Bulletin* published on the roof of a cold-storage plant. The *Examiner* occupied a one-story shack on Folsom Street near the waterfront. One week after the Earthquake, the Orpheum had a matinee at the Chutes. The City of Paris opened in the Hobart mansion on Van Ness Avenue, the first department store to revive. Tait's new restaurant was in Judge William T. Wallace's house on Van Ness Avenue. The St. Francis Hotel erected Little St. Francis on Union Square. Banks built sheds over their vaults and did business in their old locations. Bank clearings soon surpassed those of the previous year.

At the time of the Earthquake and Fire assessed property valuations of the city and county of San Francisco were $524,230,947. For the 1959–60 tax year they were $1,391,454,204.

Within three months of the catastrophe 6,600 new buildings were undergoing construction in the city and fireproof buildings were being repaired. San Francisco, the phoenix city, had always ridden triumphant over flames. After the five great fires of the early 1850's San Franciscans had pledged themselves to build better and stronger buildings. Now the pioneers of 1906 made a new promise:

"We are going to build the most beautiful city in the United States."

The memory of horror lingered. It would be many years before the last of the charred ruins would be gone from San Francisco's streets and the reminiscences of that morning in April grew with the years. Those who had slept in parks and on beaches and hills and watched their city shaken into ruins had asked questions on that morning. Would their beautiful magic city ever again be as it was before? What would become of the romance and legends it had known? How much would be forgotten, and what remembered?

The pioneers of 1906 asked these questions while starting again.

CHAPTER 2

The Railroad Kings

SAN FRANCISCO had grown from the Mexican village of Yerba Buena, nourished by the avalanche of gold flowing down from the high Sierras. From its beginning the city's pioneers had dreamed of a railroad from the Mississippi River to the Pacific Ocean.

The first step toward its realization was made by engineer Theodore Dehone Judah, son of an Episcopal clergyman of Bridgeport, Connecticut, and a graduate of Troy Polytechnic Institute, who was one of the engineers of the Erie Canal and also of the Niagara Gorge Railroad. After coming to California in 1854 he became a flaming missionary for the transcontinental railroad. While the project was being discussed in Congress, he built a short line at Sacramento in 1855 and rode on a handcar over four hundred feet of track. He was enjoying the first railroad ride in California.

Enthusiasts fancied a California netted with rails, but when the placer output fell railroad building ceased, until May 1, 1861, when ground was broken for the San Francisco Railroad to San Jose. Peter Donahue, H. M. Newhall, Charles Mayne, and others began the enterprise. San Francisco opened its purse for $300,000, and the road was built without state or federal aid, but not completed for three years.

Judah held to his dream. At the Pacific Railroad Convention in San Francisco, September 20, 1859, he presented his idea to delegates from the Coast states. San Francisco capitalists refused to invest in such a crackpot venture, but Judah continued to plan a route for the rails. He virtually lived in the Sierras. In a one-horse wagon, equipped with barometer, compass and odometer, he crossed the mountains seventy-three times. Finally, merchants realized that

9

a railroad would enable them to sell more goods to the roaring Nevada towns where silver mines were paying a million dollars a month in dividends.

In the spring of 1861 Judah called a meeting at the St. Charles Hotel, Sacramento, and on June 28 the Central Pacific Railroad Company of California was organized. Ten days previously Leland Stanford had been nominated for governor, and he was elected president of the new company; Collis P. Huntington, vice-president; his partner, Mark Hopkins, treasurer; Theodore D. Judah, chief engineer; James Bailey, secretary. E. B. Crocker, John F. Morse, D. W. Strong, and Charles Morse were directors.

Charles Crocker canvassed San Franciscans to sell shares. Banker D. O. Mills wrote the promoters, praising their enterprise—that was all. Wholesale drygoods merchant Adam Grant replied, "Why, Crocker, you're crazy, talking about building a railroad over the mountains." "We're going to build a railroad." "You think the road will pay two per cent a month?" "No, but we're going to build the road."

Even those who had subscribed for stock paid only 10 per cent of its supposed value; total assets were less than $100,000 and that would not build two miles of road. Undaunted, Judah, as agent for the company, set out to appeal to Congress for aid.

He arrived in Washington at a propitious moment, just after the battle of Bull Run, when the capital was in the gloom of defeat. Luckily the government needed California's gold and Nevada's silver to maintain the currency in wartime. Should there be a foreign attack by way of the Pacific, the railroad would bind the Atlantic and Pacific states together.

Judah aided Congressman Aaron A. Sargent in molding the bill to be introduced in the House in January of 1862. Senator James A. McDougall fathered the Senate bill. Midsummer saw the measure enacted. President Lincoln affixed his signature on July 1, 1862. San Francisco bells rang and newsboys shouted "EXTRA! EXTRA! THE PRESIDENT SIGNS THE RAILROAD BILL!" Stanford predicted that the road would be running by 1870, but it was in operation in 1869.

The Big Four—Leland Stanford, C. P. Huntington, Charles Crocker, and Mark Hopkins—would bring new momentum to San Francisco. They were like Horatio Alger heroes. Crocker came up the hardest way. After his father failed in the liquor business in Troy, New York, twelve-year-old Charles quit school to become a newsboy with his own route for the *Transcript*. He told George Bancroft that he had a wonderful schooling in experience. He could always swap knives with boys and win. After his father and the four boys settled on a farm in Marshall County, Illinois, Charles worked on the farm and in a sawmill and became a blacksmith. At age seventeen he rose at four o'clock, split a hundred rails a day—doing chores afterward. Such toil made him appreciate money; he never paid $1.50 for a carriage when he could ride on a streetcar for 5 cents. At twenty-eight, he and his brother tried their luck in California. When the wagon train had to ford rivers in crossing the plains, Charles carried the rope. He arrived in 1850 but had no luck in the mines.

With his brother he opened a camp store in El Dorado County, another in a neighboring town, and finally in Sacramento he sold dry goods. "One man works hard all his life and ends up a pauper," he said. "Another man, no smarter, makes twenty million. Luck has a hell of a lot to do with it."

Tall and imposing, thirty-nine-year-old Stanford treasured the memory that when Lafayette visited this country he, as a lad, had sat on the knee of the great Frenchman when he stopped at the Stanfords' Bullhead Tavern near Albany, New York. Summers he worked on his father's farm, attending common school in winter. Later he went to Cazenovia Seminary. After being admitted to the bar, he married well-to-do Jane Lathrop of Albany. Briefly he practiced law at Port Washington, Wisconsin.

His five brothers had gone to California, and the loss of his law library by fire in 1852 decided him to venture with them. He came alone, his wife remaining with her family for a year. At Michigan Bluff, Placer County, he dealt in groceries, sleeping on the counter with his boots as a pillow. He became the head of the Sacramento firm of Stanford Brothers.

Vice-president Collis Potter Huntington, aged forty-two, a commanding giant from Oneonta, New York, was the son of a wool merchant at Harvington, Connecticut. Even as a child he earned money, receiving only rudiments of education. His spelling always remained that of a grammar school boy. Huntington called toil a privilege. Chopping down trees and sawing wood kept him in good condition. With pleasure he recalled peddling throughout the South, carrying a heavy pack on his back. En route to California in 1849, while crossing the Isthmus of Panama, he traded in mining tools, and arrived in San Francisco with several thousand dollars added to his slender fortune. At Sacramento he opened a store to sell hardware and supply miners with tools. His wife, Elizabeth, did not venture with her husband, but remained in the East till 1851 when he went to fetch her. They lived over the hardware store in San Francisco.

Mark Hopkins, a bachelor, spare and tall, seemed older than his fifty years. Charles Crocker said that anything "Uncle Mark was interested in must be all right." From Henderson, New York, Hopkins' birthplace, the family moved to St. Claire, Michigan. At his father's death Mark became a clerk at age sixteen.

He studied law briefly with his brother at Lockport, New York, and arrived in California in August, 1849.

From Sacramento, Hopkins transported supplies to a store in Placerville, using an ox team. He established a grocery with his friend and fellow passenger E. H. Miller, afterward secretary of the Central Pacific Company. Hopkins's partnership with C. P. Huntington was begun in 1850 and continued until his death.

These merchants were insignificant financially when they embarked on the railroad project, but Crocker said to Bancroft, "We had faith that if anyone could build a railroad it was us, and we built it." They helped make history in San Francisco and were listed among the world's richest men.

CHAPTER 3

Transcontinental Railroad
Enters San Francisco

WHILE MEN were dying at Vicksburg and Gettysburg the Big Four battled mountains, snow, and heat. Soon they discovered that the cost of the Central Pacific Railroad as estimated by the government would be doubled. At times there was not a dollar in the treasury. Charles Crocker said that he would have been glad to take a clean shirt and get out. Huntington went east to obtain material for the first fifty miles of road.

Friction arose between Judah and the Big Four when he refused to certify to federal authorities that the line entered the mountains twenty miles sooner than was actually the case. State geologist Professor J. D. Whitney "moved the Sierras" into the middle of the valley, enriching the Big Four by $640,000.

Judah sold his interest for $100,000 and took an option to buy out the Big Four at $100,000 each, planning to sell to the Vanderbilts. While crossing the Isthmus of Panama the thirty-seven-year-old genius was stricken with fever and on November 2, 1863, he died in New York when most needed by the railroad.

Huntington expertly prodded Congress into supplying more construction funds, resorting to the old argument that California might be lost to the Union if the railroad was not built. Public relations man Stanford, in California, met fresh opposition in collecting funds. All steamship lines and toll roads that might be injured by competition chorused that the railroad was "crazy, impracticable, the Dutch Flat swindle." Stanford induced the city and county of San Francisco to subscribe for $600,000 worth of stock. So many pro-

13

tests were made against this transaction that the purchase was reduced to a gift of $400,000. Other counties subscribed, and at this critical moment Stanford collected $1.5 million.

From Promontory Point, Utah, on May 10, 1869, President Leland Stanford sent President U. S. Grant this telegram:

The last rail is laid! The last spike is driven! The Pacific Railroad is completed! The point of junction is 1086 miles west of the Missouri River and 690 miles east of Sacramento City.

The magnetic ball dropped from its pole above the Capitol and with a whistle that could be heard for miles the East saluted the West. Fire alarms sounded in Chicago, Cincinnati, St. Louis, and Milwaukee. While officials banqueted in the Stanford car at Promontory Point, workmen drew out the gold and silver spikes and removed the polished laurel tie. The San Francisco Fire of 1906 burned the tie. The gold spike was for years in the custody of the Wells Fargo Bank, San Francisco, but recently was transferred to the museum at Stanford University, still carefully guarded in a special case. On May 10, 1959, a special luncheon for five hundred persons at the Palace Hotel was held to commemorate the ninetieth anniversary of driving the gold spike at Promontory, Utah. It was sponsored by the Society of Pioneers and the major speaker was D. J. Russell, president of the Southern Pacific. On display at the head table was the original gold spike which had been brought from the Stanford Museum to the hotel under armed guard. The Stanford Museum also is custodian of the silver spike and silver shovel.

On the day the gold spike was driven, San Francisco heard booming cannons, artillery salvos, clanging fire bells, screeching steam whistles. The 21st Infantry band played "America." A procession of ten divisions made the jubilee complete. The city was swathed with flags. At Mechanics' Pavilion Mayor Frank McCoppin presided and Judge Nathaniel Bennett delivered an oration to the vast cheering crowd.

For several months the transcontinental run ended at Sacramento. Between Sacramento and San Francisco Bay the Central Pacific line passed through Stockton and Niles Canyon, to a connection with San Francisco at Alameda and the San Francisco and

Oakland Railroad Company. These lines were independently owned and served Oakland, Alameda, San Leandro, and Hayward. The two properties were acquired by the Stanford-Huntington group about 1868, and over these lines the Oakland trains first reached San Francisco Bay by connecting with the line from Sacramento to Stockton. The first through-train service was to the Alameda Wharf, September 6, 1869, but the Oakland Wharf became the transcontinental terminal on November 8, 1869.

Cost of building the Central Pacific Railroad was about $40 million. The Big Four received $55,711,000: $360,000 in bonds, besides the road, all equipment, and 32,931,091 acres of land. The four builders left fortunes estimated at from $40 to $50 million each. The greater part of the Stanford and Huntington fortunes has been returned to the public in Stanford University and the Huntington Library at San Marino. Large bequests from the Hopkins estate were made by Mr. Searles, widower of Mrs. Hopkins, to the University of California. That institution, the Episcopal Church, and many museums, have received large benefactions from the Crocker family.

Like many who acquire power, the railroad builders at times abused theirs. They shut out competitors, discriminated in freight rates, repudiated obligations to the government that had created them, corrupted legislators and the press. The nation's highway, however, has been of vast benefit to California and the world, sometimes inspiring poets like Joaquin Miller: "There's more poetry in the single rush of a railway train across the continent, than in all of the gory stories of the burning of Troy."

CHAPTER 4

Spectacular Nevadans in San Francisco

THE "SILVER kings" added glamour and growth to the city. After fortunes came from Washoe's silver ledges a get-rich-quick fever afflicted San Francisco, resulting in the creation of the Stock Exchange Board, September 8, 1861. Gould and Curry, Ophir, Savage and Hale, and Norcross mines produced large amounts of silver, but assessments were often more than dividends. Gambling-crazed San Franciscans were victims of manipulators, who in advance found the real value of the mine and knew how to bull and bear the market, water stock and sell at the same price as the original stock. The gamblers never suspected "marked" cards, but played on, buying and selling on margin.

Most highly regarded of San Francisco's silver kings was Ireland-born John W. Mackay, who in 1853 was a placer miner near Downieville. There he married Marie Louise Hungerford Bryant, daughter of Major Hungerford. With carefully saved earnings he purchased a small interest in the Kentuck Mine before he met James Graham Fair, a forty-niner, also from Ireland.

After quartz mining in the Feather River country, at Angels Camp, Fair met pretty Theresa Rooney, whose mother, a boarding-house keeper, had sent her to New York to be educated in a convent. She became Fair's wife. His mechanical ability, coupled with a knowledge of quartz mining, made him superintendent of the Ophir and Hale and Norcross mines.

Mackay and Fair met two other Irishmen, James Clair Flood and William S. O'Brien, who kept a saloon on Washington Street, San Francisco. Following customers' "tips," they bought and sold with much profit and induced Mackay and Fair to become their part-

16

ners. For $80,000 the new company bought some unproductive ground near the north end of the Comstock lode—the Consolidated Virginia Mine.

At this time the two most powerful men in the mining district were William C. Ralston and William Sharon. Ralston lent Sharon $500 and appointed him agent of the Bank of California at Virginia City. Shrewd, small, wiry, well-educated Sharon was an Ohio-born lawyer. He bought mining stock, forming the Union Mill and Mining Company, with Ralston and D. O. Mills; they monopolized mining mills. After building the Virginia and Truckee Railroad, Sharon became Nevada's richest man.

Most spectacular of the San Francisco-Nevadans was William C. Ralston, San Francisco's magnificent Medici. As clerk on a Mississippi steamboat this Ohioan set out for San Francisco in 1850. His attractive personality and ingratiating manner obtained for him the position of agent at Panama for Garrison and Morgan. Soon he represented them in San Francisco, and in 1853 he became a partner in their banking house. He withdrew and established the firm of Fretz and Ralston. Joseph A. Donahoe and Eugene Kelly became their partners in 1861. Three years later the Bank of California opened at Washington and Battery Streets. It was capitalized at $2.5 million and led in financial affairs. D. O. Mills, Sacramento banker, was president, but cashier Ralston succeeded him.

Superpromoter Ralston contributed to the building of the dry dock at Hunter's Point, to reclamation works, and to the San Joaquin irrigation canal. He built the magnificent California Theatre for John McCullough, advancing Bret Harte $2,000 for a play he never wrote. Ralston built the Grand Hotel, but it was not large enough. Then he planned the Palace, largest hotel in the world, seven stories high, with 800 rooms, walls two and a half feet thick and a marble-paved courtyard. He paid $400,000 for the two and a half acres on which the hotel stood. He bought a ranch to obtain oak planks for the Palace, but used none of the oak. Instead, wood was brought from India and Mexico.

When Ralston bought the Kimball Manufacturing Company to make furniture for the Palace, Sharon protested, "If you're going to buy a foundry for a mill, a ranch for a plank, and a factory to make furniture, where is it going to end?"

Ralston pitied Sharon's lack of imagination. He caused New Montgomery Street to be cut through the sand hills and he became a member of the New Montgomery Realty Company. Three-fifths of the Spring Valley Water Company was Ralston's. He was also interested in the Cornell Watch Factory and San Francisco Sugar Refinery. He organized the state-legalized million-dollar lottery, to pay debts on the new Mercantile Library Building. He spent $225,-000 on his Pine Street residence, which was supposed to cost $25,000.

In 1865 Ralston began his ducal country seat at Belmont, where twenty gardeners tended the flowers. He remodeled the old residence of Count Cipriani, an Italian exile, twenty miles down the peninsula, in the Cañada del Diablo.

Ralston was not astonished when approached by his friend Asbury Harpending, who introduced two embarrassed workers from the Rockies, Philip Arnold and John Slack. "Confidentially" they had found a mine of diamonds, rubies and emeralds in the Wyoming mountains. They wouldn't sell their claim, they would dispose of just enough to start opening it up.

Diamonds dazzled and fascinated Ralston. Mining engineer Henry Janin was given a few thousand dollars to pass on the mine. Even more stones were found than Ralston had expected and Tiffany lapidaries declared them genuine. Ralston and friends invested several hundred thousand dollars in the diamond mine. Even Rothschild agents begged to buy a share.

Investigating for the United States government, geologist Clarence King revealed the terrible truth—the mine had been "salted." The stones, really from South Africa, had been bought by Arnold and Slack in London. Princely Ralston assumed his friends' losses.

San Franciscans talked in millions. Stock gambling became so prevalent that in 1872 the California Stock Exchange Board was organized with forty members. In his message, Governor Newton Booth warned the public against stock buying, but San Francisco was too busy "getting rich quick." Real estate sales trebled. Mining stock exchanges were crowded. Mackay, Fair, Flood, and O'Brien uncovered a bonanza in a new ledge in the Consolidated Virginia which produced $137 million on an $80,000 investment. Montgomery Street brokers were ordered to buy and buy. They had to be escorted by officers to places of business. Crowds roared around the brokerage houses like wolves fighting over carrion. Police had to clear the streets. The Big Four—Mackay, Fair, Flood, and O'Brien—fought for control.

In less than thirty days in November, 1874, the California, a portion of Con-Virginia, advanced from 90 to 480, top price being 790. By February 18 it had fallen to 50. Con-Virginia and Ophir had similar fluctuations. Only the mining ring knew what was going on. Millions were lost by San Franciscans, although before ceasing to be profitably worked the Con-Virginia, California, Gould and Curry, Savage, Hale and Norcross, Chollar, Potosi, Imperial, Kentuck, Yellow Jacket, Crown Point and Belcher, produced $338 million. Most of this flowed into San Francisco. Comstock money erected the Nevada Block, Dividend Block, Arizona Block, the Stock Exchange at 310 Pine Street, the Hobart Building, Union Block, and the Palace Hotel.

During the shrinkage of Comstock values of more than $40 million in a week, rumors were afloat of overissued stocks on which Ralston had borrowed enormous sums for his own use. Instead of two millions cash in the Bank of California's vaults, there was only half a million. Ralston had deposited cash tags for a million and a half. He had also disposed of bullion in the refinery and appropriated the funds. The directors asked Flood and O'Brien to liquidate the bank. They refused, as they were about to establish the Bank of Nevada.

Vainly Ralston tried to get the money from other banks, and he did not appear at the directors' meeting. He transferred all his possessions to Sharon. The directors demanded his resignation. He signed it, put on his hat, left by the side door, and went to swim at his usual North Beach bathing place. At three o'clock word was brought that San Francisco's most fabulous citizen was dead from drowning, whether by intent or by accident has never been determined.

After nine years of commercial and political leadership, on August 26, 1875, the Bank of California closed its doors. To protect themselves from runs by depositors, other banks did not open. Excitement was intense. Ralston left unsecured liabilities of $5,419,616.93. Of this he owed the bank $4,655,907.50. The capital of the corporation was engulfed. Everyone connected with the bank was plunged into the abyss.

William Sharon subscribed $1 million to reorganize the bank, asking D. O. Mills to do the same. Mills refused, saying he had owned no stock in the bank for two years. Sharon informed him that his stock had never been transferred on the books. As stockholder, director and partner, Mills was responsible for irregulartities occuring prior to his retirement. Mills subscribed a million.

Reluctantly James R. Keene came in. Sharon guaranteed Peter Donahue's subscription. Michael Reese was warned that his large claim would not be paid unless he subscribed.

An especially difficult task was that of obtaining 13,180 shares of overissued stock in the hands of lenders of collateral for loans. To the most menacing and insulting Sharon paid close to par. More docile debtors received only sixty cents on the dollar.

Sharon manipulated Ralston's debt with 20 per cent of the syndicate's funds, reopening the Bank of California and all banks that had closed on the same day. D. O. Mills accepted the presidency of the bank, and then sold all his stock. This time he saw that it was recorded on the books, and then he moved to New York. William Alvord was chosen president, and the institution became one of the great American banks.

On October 14, two months after Ralston's death Sharon, the new lord of Belmont, opened the Palace Hotel, which covered more than two acres of land, had 9,000 cuspidors, and was four times too large for the city. Sharon presided at the great celebration: "In the crowning hour of victory . . . I experience a sense of almost overwhelming sadness. I miss, as you do, the proud and manly spirit of him who devised this magnificent structure, and under whose direction and tireless energy it has been mainly reared. I mourn, as you do, that he is not with us to enjoy this scene of beauty, and I offer here, with you, the incense of respect and affection for his memory."

One of the anomalies of life is that Sharon, who had rehabilitated the Bank of California, was one of the city's least popular rich men, while Ralston, who wrecked the institution, was often lauded. San Francisco liked Ralston's warm humanity, his dazzling showmanship, and shed tears when he died. General Sherman, who arrived shortly after Ralston's death, expressed the city's spirit: "No matter what Billy Ralston did, I hope he has gone to Heaven."

Another San Franciscan whose fortune was founded in Nevada was Adolph Sutro, builder of the Sutro Tunnel. A youth of twenty, he arrived in 1850, from Aix-la-Chapelle, Prussia. After dealing in cigars and tobacco, he joined the Washoe Rush, establishing his family in Virginia City and operating a small quartz mill on the Carson River. Lives of miners were often threatened by tapping water pockets underground, which caused work to be suspended. Sutro planned a tunnel at 2,000 feet depth, 10 by 12 feet wide, that would drain and ventilate the Comstock lode and eliminate ore hoisting.

At first he was loudly acclaimed by mineowners. In 1865 the Tunnel Company was incorporated by Adolph Sutro, William M. Stewart, D. E. Avery, Louis Janin, and H. K. Mitchell. Congress granted them right-of-way, fixing the rate at $2.00 a ton for ore extracted.

The Bank of California owners realized that their own mill monopoly would be rendered obsolete by the tunnel, and Sutro found himself without support. He spoke against the "Bank Crowd," attacking them for destruction of forests, extortionate water rates, and their "crooked railroad—no more crooked than the management." In turn the Bank Crowd denounced the tunnel as a "coyote hole."

Miners came to Sutro's support, subscribing $60,000. He broke ground for the tunnel on October 19, 1869. London and eastern cities invested $2 million. Not until April, 1887, could the drillers reach the Comstock mineral belt, for they advanced only 300 feet a month. The temperature rose to 114 degrees. Sutro worked half naked in heat, smoke and slush, with the laborers. He performed a great service for the Comstock, because billions of gallons of water annually were carried away from the mines at comparatively small expense.

Sutro returned to San Francisco a multimillionaire during the late 1870's and bought a part of the 12,000-acre Rancho San Miguel, covering one-tenth of the area of the city and county of San Francisco.

He called the 920-foot elevation Mount Parnassus, now known as

Mount Sutro, and named the highest hill, 938 feet, for the scientist George Davidson. When Davidson surveyed it in 1862 he called it Blue Mountain for its blue lupine, flag and violets.

On Mount Davidson a giant concrete cross, 103 feet high, was erected, following the suggestion of James G. Decatur. At its base is a crypt brought from the Holy Land, including a jug of water from the River Jordan. The cross was first lighted March 24, 1934, when President Franklin D. Roosevelt pressed a gold telegraph key in the White House. It is kept lighted every night. The $1,400 annual expense is met by the Lakeside Church and friends.

James G. Decatur and the Rev. Homer K. Pitman organized a citizens' committee which sponsored the Easter Sunrise Service at the foot of the cross. Thousands assemble at the base of the cross and the Sunrise Services are broadcast to the nation by radio. This yearly service is now arranged by the San Francisco Council of Churches.

When Sutro acquired his wide acreage the land was almost devoid of trees, but in 1887 he employed gardeners to plant Monterey cypress and eucalyptus. He also gave school children thousands of trees to plant on the first Arbor Day.

Attracted by the possibilities of the Cliff House property, he purchased it from Samuel Tetlow, former owner of the Bella Union, and erected a dwelling which became his home. Here he spent more than a million dollars, collecting rare plants, importing statuary for the garden from Europe, and acquiring a stable of thoroughbred horses. On one occasion a performance of *As You Like It* was given on the lawn by the Daly Company. The seals on the rocks seemed a part of the family, and the Sutro children, famed swimmers, often swam to the rocks. A walk on a tightrope over the waves to Seal Rocks was made in the 1860's by tightrope walkers James Cooke and Rose Celeste.

On Christmas Day, 1894, the Cliff House burned to the ground, frightening the seals so that they retreated to the Farallones and did not return for several years. Now the seals are wards of the city of San Francisco. Sutro rebuilt the Cliff House. Here lunched and dined Presidents McKinley, Roosevelt and Taft. After withstanding the Earthquake, it burned the following year, but was again rebuilt by Sutro.

For a time it was unoccupied, but in 1929 it was rejuvenated by the Whitney brothers. Their cable-car route from the Cliff House to Inspiration Point was completed and opened May 3, 1955. It cost $150,000 and was constructed by Roebling & Sons, who built the Brooklyn Bridge. The 1,000-foot ride to Seal Rocks takes about three or four minutes each way. A passenger may stay as long as he likes on the twenty-seater. About 135,000 people enjoy the ride annually.

First of Sutro's many interests was his collection of books, and by 1885 he had assembled 60,000. His library was especially notable for 4,000 volumes printed before the year 1500. He bought Bibles in every language and in every country, ancient manuscripts of Spanish and Mexican literature, and classics in all languages, but especially in English. At the time Sutro's library was completed it numbered 250,000 volumes and was the largest private library in the United States. It had a narrow escape in the Fire of 1906 when it was housed in the Montgomery Block and at 107 Battery Street. The Battery Street books were lost, but Dr. Emma Sutro Merritt and a caretaker at the Montgomery Block appealed to the firemen and the block and books were saved.

After he died in office as mayor, August 8, 1898, the Sutro heirs offered their father's library to California on condition that a San Francisco branch of the State Library be established to house and care for the books. The State Library has done so without any increased appropriation of funds. In 1959 the Board of Supervisors appropriated $50,000 to house the Sutro Library in the Public Library building in the Civic Center. In 1961 for convenience it is housed by the University of San Francisco.

Dr. Emma Sutro Merritt purchased the 20-acre Sutro Heights property from other heirs, and deeded it to San Francisco as a public park, retaining only the right to reside on it until her death. She died in 1938.

CHAPTER 5

Fashion Moves to Nob Hill

NOB HILL became the residential section of the rich city. Yerba Buena's villagers had called it "Fern Hill." In Fern Hill days Arthur M. Ebbetts pioneered present-day Taylor Street by having a wagon road graded around what he called the "Hill of Golden Paradise." As fashion's center, it was renamed "Snob," or "Knob," or "Nob" Hill.

The James Ben Ali Haggins erected the city's first mansion on Taylor Street: fifty rooms, nine baths, and an 86-foot observatory tower. The terraced garden, with exotic flowers and shrubs, occupied the entire block between Washington and Clay Streets. Stables accommodated 40 horses and 19 carriages. Colorful, dark-bearded, Kentucky-born "J. B." had Turkish blood. His hobby was horses, and often he drove on the Point Lobos Road in his four-horse English coach with a pair of bays and iron-grays, and a handsome coach dog. One of his horses, Salvator, was made famous by Ella Wheeler Wilcox in her poem "How Salvator Won."

The Lloyd Tevises lived near the Haggins. Mrs. Haggin and Mrs. Tevis were sisters. The Tevis house was more modest, with only nine bedrooms. Haggin and Tevis were lawyers, also business partners, with immense landholdings in Kern County. The Homestake Mine in North Dakota and the Cerra de Pasco Mine in Peru were theirs. Senator George Hearst was their partner in many projects. The Homestake was bought on his advice. When he was asked to investigate the mine, Mrs. Hearst said to her husband, "I hope this mine will be our homestake." He said, "We will call it 'The Homestake'."

The Hearsts lived at Taylor and Sacramento Streets in the late 1870's. This was not, however, the Taylor Street section that is usually called Nob Hill, but the abrupt rise from Kearny Street

24

up California and Sacramento. It was so precipitous that only a lover of solitude, like Dr. Arthur P. Hayne, would chop his way through brush and venture up its slope to build a house of wood and clay, on the southwest corner of California and Powell Streets. With him was his beautiful actress wife, Julia Dean.

Shortly after the Central Pacific offices were moved to San Francisco from Sacramento in 1873, ex-Governor and Mrs. Leland Stanford lived at the Palace Hotel with their son, Leland Jr. When Stanford paid $60,000 for two acres of land on Nob Hill as a building site, he heard "Folly! $60,000 for two acres of sand; no one can go up that precipice without two horses." Having helped build the railroad over the Sierras, Stanford was not intimidated by the California Street hillock. Fascinated by machinery, he became interested in the cable car, a novelty invented by the Britisher Andrew S. Hallidie, which made "vertical real estate" practicable.

Hallidie had seen cars in British coal mines ascend and descend by gravity, but the method had never been applied in transporting passengers. Devices for taking hold and letting go of the cable and bringing the car to a stop were his own invention. William Eppelsheimer was engaged for the Nob Hill project.

On January 28, 1873, the first cable car moved from Clay and Kearny Streets six short blocks to Jones, an elevation of 307 feet. Cable cars doubled real estate values on the hills. Now the city could move westward toward the Presidio. Tourists delighted in America's first cable-car system and still find it thrilling to ride on a cross between an elevator and a roller coaster. Since buses have been much used in recent years, the cable-car system has become controversial. Mrs. Hans Klussman and friends became their champions, delaying their removal, but all lines have been replaced by buses, except No. 59 Powell, No. 60 Jackson, and No. 61 California, which are still a highly popular tourist novelty. A gay Cable-Car Festival is held annually in Union Square.

While the Stanford residence was building, openhanded Stanford annoyed realistic Huntington by buying Mrs. Stanford a $100,000 diamond necklace with earrings. At the great Stanford housewarming, guests were dazzled by the frescoed Pompeian reception room, its furniture upholstered in cream satin; the onyx-slab table cut from St. Peter's, Rome; the conservatory, with its playing fountain and its wide windows overlooking the city. Here the Stanfords expected to be happy with their son, Leland, born at Sacramento on May 14, 1868, after eighteen years of marriage.

Stanford's hobby was fast horses and fast driving. Once when he and Charles Crocker, driving through Golden Gate Park, were accosted by a policeman for speeding, the dignified Stanford joked, "Officer, let's compromise. Arrest Charlie."

The Stanford stables on Nob Hill were on the site of the present University Club. From that stable came horses of world fame. They were the nucleus of the great Stanford sires that helped attract attention to "the Farm" at Palo Alto that later became the Stanford University Campus.

Stanford sold half of his California Street lot to "Uncle Mark" Hopkins, who a few years after coming to the state married his cousin, Mary Sherwood of Massachusetts. Uncle Mark was quite content in the Sutter Street cottage at the base of Nob Hill, for which he paid $35 a month rent. At times he was alarmed when he saw his wife's wooden castle with towers and gables being reared on the Hill. The tall, frail, bearded man, working among his vegetables, asked neighbors and friends if they thought the "Hotel de Hopkins" would pay dividends.

Before the mansion was completed, Hopkins died at 65. After placing his remains in a handsome mausoleum at Sacramento, America's richest widow moved into the castlelike building, with galleried courts of carved Italian marble and murals of Venetian scenes between the arches. The drawing room was like a chamber in the Doges' Palace. Bedrooms finished in ebony and inlaid with ivory and semiprecious stones delighted beauty-loving Mary Sherwood Hopkins.

She closed the house and built a New York dwelling. At Great Barrington, Massachusetts, the home of the Hopkins forebears, another great mansion became hers. She married Edward T. Searles, interior decorator, twenty-two years her junior.

After Uncle Mark's death she legally adopted Timothy Nolan, son of her maid, who married her niece, Clara Crittenden. At her death in 1891, Mrs. Hopkins left her millions to Searles, disinheriting her adopted son, but the will contest was compromised. Searles turned over the California Street mansion to the University of California and the San Francisco Art Association.

At Searles's death most of his fortune was left to an art teacher named Walker. The site of the Hopkins dwelling was sold by the Art Association for $350,000, and the 20-story Mark Hopkins Hotel, standing on the site of the mansion, offers the most magnificent view of the city.

Next to build on Nob Hill were the Charles Crockers, the only ones of the Big Four with a large family: three sons, Frederick, George, William, and a daughter, Harriet. Their house was on an even higher elevation than those of Stanford and Hopkins, a block bounded by California, Sacramento, Taylor, and Jones Streets.

Undertaker Nicholas Yung owned forty feet on Sacramento, but he spiraled Crocker's $6,000 offer to $40,000. "Extortion!" claimed Crocker, and built a "spite" fence 30 feet high, completely shutting off light and air from the neighbor's house except on Sacramento Street. Yung threatened to turn his house into an undertaking establishment; he and the city joined in a suit against Crocker, who would not remove the fence. The spite fence became a greater attraction to tourists then the imposing dwelling. At the turn of the century the Yung lot was acquired by the family. William H. Crocker erected his residence on a portion of his father's lot. Both houses were destroyed by the Fire in 1906. The family then gave the site to the Episcopal Diocese of San Francisco and the cathedral has been reared thereon.

At first C. P. Huntington would not live in San Francisco. "The mild California climate produces weaklings." New York was his home. The childless Huntingtons adopted Clara Prentice, Mrs. Huntington's attractive Sacramento niece.

After his wife's death he married handsome Arabella Duval Arrington of Alabama, widow of one of his employees. He paid Henry Ward Beecher $4,000 to perform the ceremony, an unexpected gesture from a man who boasted that his personal expenses were only $200 a year. He adopted the new Mrs. Huntington's 16-year-old son, Arthur Worsham. After he remarried, Huntington's New York mansion became more luxurious than those of his partners. He bought tapestries and paintings by the truckload, and made a $3 million settlement on spendthrift Prince Paul de Wildenberg Hatzfeldt, who married Clara. Several years later, Huntington acquired the chaste white dwelling on Nob Hill erected by David D. Colton, Charlie Crocker's attorney, whose blonde daughter, Caroline, was a beauty of the eighties.

The Huntington property was acquired by the A. N. Townes. After the Fire the classical columns at the entrance of the dwelling, "Portals of the Past," were placed in Golden Gate Park. Widowed Mrs. Huntington presented the site of the house to the city of San Francisco for a park. It is now a children's playground.

Among Nob Hill's earliest residents were the cultured Richard Tobins. Tobin, a lawyer and one of the founders of the Hibernia Bank, had a three-story house, with observation tower, conservatory, and private chapel. Each morning a priest came from St. Mary's to say Mass. A forty-niner, with a knowledge of Mexican and Spanish law, Tobin was often retained by the United States government as an expert in interpreting Mexican and Spanish laws. His son, Richard M. Tobin, patron of the arts, served as minister to the Netherlands during the Harding administration. When he died in 1952 he was president of the Hibernia Bank.

Next door to the Tobins lived E. B. Pond, merchant and banker— mayor from 1886 to 1890. His son, the late Samuel Pond, recalled the miniature farm on the Benchley property, purchased by his father, with apple trees, a stable for saddle horses, and even a cow. Sam Pond and neighborhood boys appeared Saturday mornings at the Crocker house for holiday money. Jolly Charles Crocker tossed them handfuls of coins, chuckling as they scrambled for quarters for their weekly excursion on the Mission Street horse car running to Woodward's Gardens. Most of the boys attended Dr. Spaulding's Trinity School, but they also enjoyed shooting quail in the brush at Van Ness Avenue.

Pond remembered when Mason Street was cut through, at the time the Flood house was erected. The James C. Floods chose the highest part of Nob Hill, but it was leveled, and load after load of yellow dirt was carted away to make room for an impressive brownstone dwelling. It has been said that the Flood fence railing was of bronze and kept a man busy polishing it, but Pond declared it was always the same color as it is today. After the Fire the Pacific Union Club purchased the gutted building, restored the roof, adding two small wings, and has been housed therein for many years.

The family of James G. Fair of Comstock fame lived on the lower part of Nob Hill, at the corner of Jones and Pine Streets. They had a gay, well-cared-for garden. Virginia Fair became Mrs. William

K. Vanderbilt, Jr., of New York and Theresa Fair married Herman Oelrichs. Charles Fair, who had San Francisco's first imported automobile, was killed in an accident in France, and Jimmy Fair also died young.

Fair had planned to build a residence on the David Porter property purchased by him. After his death in 1894 Mrs. Oelrichs bought her sister's share of the Nob Hill lot and began the Fairmont Hotel, with Reid Brothers as architects. The hotel was gutted in the Fire of 1906, and Herbert E. and Dr. Hartland Law bought the property before the hotel was completed. Upon the roof was placed the time ball, originally on Telegraph Hill. The Law Brothers celebrated the earthquake anniversary, April 18, 1907, by opening the Fairmont Hotel—a $3 million investment. The hotel is owned by the Benjamin H. Swig Company.

Neither San Francisco nor Nob Hill attracted Mrs. John W. Mackay. Perhaps because her life had been spent largely at Downieville and Virginia City, she longed for the great world. With her daughter, Eva Bryant, and her sons, William and Clarence Mackay, she left for Europe to entertain kings and princes.

John W. Mackay spent most of his time at the Palace Hotel, but he visited his family annually. Little Eva Bryant married Prince Ferdinando Galatro-Colonna, who annoyed the Comstock millionaire by insisting on alimony when after a brief marriage he and Eva were divorced. Mackay died during one of his annual visits to his family in London. Before dying he saw the shore end of the first transpacific cable laid in San Francisco by the Commercial Pacific Cable Company, December 13, 1902.

William S. O'Brien, the jolly bachelor of Comstock's Big Four, had a dwelling on Sutter Street near Mason, afterward owned by the Parrott family. O'Brien died young at San Rafael and his millions were divided among near relations. A sister, Mrs. Kate McDonough, built the new California Theatre and Hotel, and her son, William, owned the great horse Ormonde for which he paid $150,-000, at that time a record price.

San Francisco celebrated its hundredth birthday in 1876, but few tourists came. During the ensuing year there was a drought, resulting in a large army of unemployed, led by Dennis Kearney, who harangued workmen gathered on sand lots with "The Chinese must go!" He said unemployment was caused by the Central

Pacific's importing Chinese who worked for 65 cents a day. California had 116,000 Chinese, San Francisco's Chinatown had 32,000. His agitation resulted in Chinese property being sacked and burned, while from his drayman's truck Kearney shouted, "Drive out the Chinese, or burn the city! The rich have ruled us until they've ruined us! I want everyone within the hearing of my voice to own a musket and a hundred pounds of ammunition! Make the thieves give up the plunder! Burn the Pacific Steamship dock where Chinamen are being landed! I'll make a burning Moscow of this city! Who will follow me up Nob Hill?"

Kearney led a mob of two or three thousand up Nob Hill to tear down Crocker's spite fence. At California and Mason Streets he built a large bonfire, and was crowned with a wreath of flowers by his admirers. He denounced the mansion owners as "thieves." "If you don't take down that spite fence within a month, the working men will tear it down!"

Young Will Crocker came home from Andover and found the hall of the family residence filled with guns. Fifteen hundred of the Vigilante police had been called out to guard the Hill. The *Pensacola* steamed in from Mare Island to protect the city. Kearney heard that the legislature might proceed against him. "If they do, then I say, Hemp! Hemp! Hemp!"

Kearney was arrested while making a speech near Kearny and Washington Streets and charged with misdemeanor. He was tried and released. One week later Kearney led his followers through the streets carrying banners demanding work. No reference was made to the Nob Hill millionaires nor did Kearney demolish the spite fence. In his *American Commonwealth* James Bryce stated that the magnates bought Kearney a new dray. Samuel Pond said that his father contributed, as did many other Nob Hill residents.

Kearney lost power with his own Working Men's Party. He toured the state, but farmers had little faith in the Sandlotter. Agitation against the Chinese continued, however, until the Chinese Exclusion Act was signed by President Theodore Roosevelt on April 2, 1902.

Kearney became a grain speculator. Before his death in 1907 he said, "Watching the wheat game is harder than trying to exclude the Chinese."

CHAPTER 6

Education

THE FIRST institution of higher learning in the San Francisco area began in 1851, when Archbishop Joseph Sadoc Alemany gave $100 to the Rev. John Nobili, S.J., to establish a college in abandoned Mission Santa Clara. Squatters were ejected from the cloistered gardens, and among Castilian roses, orange, olive and fig trees, professors opened classes with twelve boys seated on tree trunks.

Santa Clara has produced many able attorneys and public speakers, among them United States Senator Stephen M. White, Delphin M. Delmas, playwright Clay M. Greene, and film actor Edmund A. Lowe. The college received its charter in 1855, and is now the University of Santa Clara, with enrollment approximating 2,000. It is the only university located on a California mission property.

San Francisco's earliest institution of learning began when the Rev. Anthony Maraschi, S.J., in 1855 applied to Archbishop Alemany for permission to erect a college and church. "Yes," said His Grace. Father Maraschi asked, "Where?" The archbishop waved a hand toward the sand hills at the corner of Market and Stockton Streets. "Over there."

Father Maraschi borrowed $11,500 to buy an acre of sand dunes, in order to build a small church and the Academy of St. Ignatius. Today he would not recognize its offspring, the University of San Francisco, with its 22-acre campus, "The Hilltop."

Father Maraschi paid his entire borrowed portion for a lot on the south side of Market, between Fourth and Fifth Streets, in a hollow between two sand hills, then called St. Ann's Valley.

On July 15, 1855, four hundred of the faithful trudged over sand hills for the dedication of the small wooden gable-roofed building, its altar bright with wildflowers. Happy Father Maraschi was able to forget that the building was mortgaged to Marzion and Company, with interest at 18 per cent a year.

The academy opened on October 15 of that year in a frame building, 40 by 30 feet, erected behind the church. John Haley, a young Irishman, was teacher and Richard McCabe was the first pupil. Haley lived in the schoolroom with Fathers Maraschi and Bixio, Brother Isabella resided in two rooms, with the kitchen nearby. Pierre, an old soldier of Napoleon's army, occupied the attic. Father Maraschi's bed was a mattress which he rolled up in the daytime and slept on at night. He cultivated wildflowers. One day Brother Isabella brought him what he thought a rare specimen and planted it beside the church—poison oak.

During the first year tuition was only $106, but the founders established a library association and contributed to the plank sidewalk from Stockton to Montgomery Street, borrowing $3,100 to meet expenses. Four years later the academy's professors numbered six, and were teaching sixty-five pupils ancient and modern languages, history, rhetoric, elocution, geography, vocal music, drawing, with a night school projected.

When a new building with two classrooms was erected, the debt grew to $24,000, but St. Ignatius Academy became St. Ignatius College. In 1859 the college received a charter empowering the institution "to confer degrees with such literary honors as are granted by any university in the United States."

In the year of the Sacramento flood a torrent poured down Stockton Street, forming a lake around church and college. Although Father Maraschi could not make ends meet, he solicited funds for new buildings. More land was bought for $84,056, a continuous stretch from Market to Jessie Street. Contributions of $5 and $10 were usual, but D. J. Oliver gave $100. In the rear a chapel and study hall were erected, costing $102,500 of which only $5,300 had been donated. The debt mounted to $139,714 with interest at 12 per cent a year, but St. Ignatius College and Church were the finest in the city. At the end of the year 459 pupils thrilled to the sound of the six-foot steel bell, costing $1,350, set on timbers 30 feet high in the garden, the pride and delight of San Francisco.

At the first college commencement exercises, Augustus Bowie

received the first Bachelor of Arts degree. During this historic year the debt increased $18,000. In 1867 Stephen M. White, later United States senator, began his distinguished career as St. Ignatius' orator, but he received his Bachelor of Science degree at Santa Clara. Another United States senator, James Duval Phelan, was a graduate of St. Ignatius. California's Chief Justice Matt I. Sullivan, class of 1879, served as dean of the University's Law School. John J. Montgomery, the "father of aviation," was graduated with the B.S. degree in 1880.

During the earthquake of 1868, St. Ignatius shook for forty-two seconds and the falling chimney caused the ceiling plaster to crash upon the priest saying Mass. Wooden ceilings replaced plaster. The interior was repainted. Of five hundred students, not more than half paid tuition, and in 1870 the college debt mounted to $175,524.

St. Ignatius focused all eyes on San Francisco on the evening of April 29, 1874, when the Rev. J. M. Neri, who taught physics, displayed the mammoth electromagnetic machine purchased by Tiburcio Parrott, costing $5,000. It had been used in the siege of Paris by the defenders and was the first of its kind in America. Mounted on a rotating table, placed atop St. Ignatius Tower, it lighted not only all San Francisco, but the countryside for 200 miles around as well.

Taxes on Market Street property increased so rapidly that Father Maraschi decided that both college and church should be removed. He borrowed $200,000 in 1877 and bought a lot bounded by Van Ness Avenue, Hayes, Franklin and Grove Streets. When buildings were completed, the debt had grown to $862,510, interest to $42,492. School furniture was transferred, January 21, 1880, but pupils decreased because the college was "too far out."

John Parrott, a graduate of St. Ignatius, and his bride, Minnie Donohoe, were the first couple married in the church in 1882; the second couple were Frank Sullivan and Alice Phelan.

After years of struggle with debt and exorbitant interest, light shone for Father Maraschi when Mrs. Abby Parrott bought the Market Street property for $900,000. Father Maraschi's borrowed $11,500 increased fiftyfold and he was called "a worker of miracles." Businessmen asked his advice. His counsel was: "Never be cast down by difficulties. Never lose faith."

The debt was not entirely liquidated when he died in 1897, but four years later it was wiped out; 802 acres of the San Pablo Ranch near Oakland, which had been bequeathed to him by friends, sold for $200,000. After fifty-six years St. Ignatius was free of debt.

The Earthquake and Fire of 1906 completely destroyed the buildings at Van Ness Avenue, and temporary wooden structures were taken over on Hayes Street near Golden Gate Park. Students called the college "the shirt factory." Plans were made for a new St. Ignatius, and in 1912 the cornerstone of the present church was laid on Ignatian Heights. Classes opened on the "Hilltop" in 1927. During the Diamond Jubilee celebration in 1930, in recognition of the link between the city and its first university, St. Ignatius became the University of San Francisco. Although founded in 1855, its Charter Centennial Commemoration Week was celebrated in 1959, because when the charter was granted in April, 1859, there was some doubt about whether the tiny college was worth $20,000. Today the university is a multimillion-dollar institution.

Through the generosity of friends, in 1931 twelve acres were added to the campus and a School of Law was established. All courses are restricted to men, except the School of Law, the evening division and the summer sessions, both of which are coeducational. Women are also students at the School of Nursing, founded in 1954. Eighteen-year-old Ellen Tully, a nursing student, in 1955 made history when she was elected secretary of the student body, the first woman to hold a student office at the Hilltop school. St. Ignatius emphasizes that it was the first, and currently the only, school to make the study of communism a required course.

The University of San Francisco has had no spectacular bequests, but Senator James D. Phelan left $100,000 to his Alma Mater. In 1955 Phelan Hall, the university's new seven-story $1.5 million residence building, was dedicated to him. Mrs. Bertha Welch contributed the Faculty Building. The Richard A. Gleason Library was erected in 1952 at the cost of $500,000. In 1959 the university dedicated two new buildings: the Memorial Gymnasium (dedicated to World War II men) and Xavier Hall, the new residence hall for the Jesuit faculty.

The pride of the University of San Francisco is that it has trained several generations of men in morality and Christian living, as well as having imparted sound education. Present enrollment is approximately 4,000.

Although no longer in San Francisco, St. Mary's College was established there in 1863, as a little school by the Rev. John T. Harrington, in the basement of Old St. Mary's. It was the third college suggested by Archbishop Alemany, who dedicated it the following year.

St. Mary's was incorporated as a college in 1872, its students being accredited to the University of California. The college campus was transferred to Oakland in 1889. For this occasion, Cardinal John Gibbons arrived and with Archbishop P. W. Riordan presided at the dedication.

Again seeking breathing room, St. Mary's moved in 1928 to its beautiful 420-acre site in Moraga Valley.

The state's first normal school, which began as Minns' Evening Normal School, was founded in San Francisco in 1857. Sessions were held weekly, and attendance of San Francisco's teachers was compulsory. Harvard graduate George Washington Minns was the principal. He was assisted by John Swett, who later became state superintendent of public instruction, Thomas S. Myrick and Ellis H. Holmes, all members of the city school staff. Harvard records show that Minns was "rusticated" for two years for exploding a bomb in the dormitory. He returned, however, to receive his degree in 1836. For five years Minns' Evening Normal School kept its teachers abreast of the latest methods of teaching.

Andrew J. Moulder, John Swett, and other educators went before the legislature and brought about establishment of the first state normal school, with the appropriation of $3,000 for five months' support. Opening day was July 21, 1862, with Ahira Holmes as principal. The school functioned without apparatus, equipment, or faculty. It was quartered on the ground floor of the high school building on Powell Street, offered by the City Board of Education. Candidates for admission signed a statement obligating themselves to teach permanently in common schools. Those unwilling to make common teaching a career were to pay $5 a month tuition.

A large enrollment was expected, but only five young women appeared: Augusta Fink, Emily L. Hill, and Nellie Hart of San Francisco. From Nevada County came Ellen Grant, and Contra Costa sent Ellen S. Baldwin. One lone man arrived, Frank G. Randle, of San Francisco. By August the class had grown to twenty-one students. Enrollment increased and other cities sought to have the normal school. San Jose offered Washington Square as a building site, and the school was formally opened in San Jose on June 14, 1871.

In the first class to graduate in 1872 was Edwin Markham, whose oration at the commencement exercises was entitled "Genius in Ruins." Markham later attained world fame as author of "The Man with the Hoe." Among distinguished normal school graduates were Mrs. Herbert Hoover; Dr. Henry Suzzalo—later president of the University of Washington; Governor James H. Budd; Dr. Philip Justin Newlon, dean of Graduate School of Education at Harvard; Dr. Elmo Stevenson, president of the Southern Oregon College of Education; and Eleanor Calhoun, the actress, who became Princess Lazarovich.

By an act of legislature, July 30, 1921, normal schools became known as teachers' colleges.

San Francisco State College began as a second normal school in 1899, opening in a building on Powell Street near Clay, formerly belonging to the City School Department. In 1899 it was transformed by an act of the legislature into the San Francisco State College. Its first president was Frederick L. Burk, a graduate of the University of California and of Stanford, who secured his Ph.D. at Clark University under the tutelage of G. Stanley Hall. Dr. Burk received $10,000 for the first year of operation.

Within ten days after the great Fire in 1906, Dr. Burk had the school in session in Oakland. Renting a temporary building on Waller Street, he continued classes and in June, 1906, opened the first public school after the Fire. To make up for time lost, there was no vacation that year.

Dr. Burk built an institution that received world-wide attention. A faculty of men and women made educational history. After Burk's death in 1924, he was succeeded by vice-president Archibald B. Anderson, who served as acting president until his death in 1927, when Alexander C. Roberts, of the University of Washington, became president. Under his leadership the Anderson Hall of Science and Frederick Burk Elementary School were finished. In 1935 the name of the institution was changed to San Francisco State College. Dr. Roberts retired in 1945, and did not live to see the 94-acre $13 million campus dedicated in October, 1954. Today's president is Dr. Glenn Dumke, formerly of Pomona College.

About 61 per cent of the students hold jobs. Three hundred come from forty-two foreign countries. Current enrollment, including limited and extension students, is 11,183.

In 1929 Archbishop Edward J. Hanna suggested that a Roman Catholic Women's College be opened in San Francisco. The Lone Mountain site was purchased by the Society of the Sacred Heart, which had come to America from France in 1818, and established an academy for women in San Francisco with another at Menlo Park. On the crest of historic Lone Mountain, the geographic center of San Francisco, a Spanish Gothic building with an iron cross, was erected 115 feet above the mountaintop. Bishop Alemany purchased Lone Mountain in 1860 when a giant wooden cross had been fixed thereon, but a storm in 1900 toppled it. The cross remained fallen until grading for the campus began in 1930.

Upon the recommendation of professors from the University of California and Stanford, a charter was obtained empowering the college to grant academic degrees. Its first degrees were conferred in May, 1952.

On the crest of Lone Mountain, where the students have a panoramic view of the Pacific Ocean, the Marin hills, the bay, and the bridges, the students enjoy basketball, tennis, volleyball, and archery. In the east wing is a notable oak beam library with 100,000 volumes, mostly donated by Monsignor Joseph M. Gleason. It contains an unpublished and autographed poem by Henry Wadsworth Longfellow, letters written by Presidents Grant, Jackson, and Johnson, and what is probably the most complete collection of book plates in the United States. There are also sermons by Pope Leo the Great, wills and indentures covering the reigns of English sovereigns from James I to George I, and several papal bulls.

Students are first trained in liberal education, studying theology, science, languages, mathematics, literature, art and music. Financial assistance for students is possible by obtaining work at the library, office, or laboratory. Scholarships are also awarded through the generosity of alumnae. Nearly eight hundred women are enrolled.

"The Truth Shall Make You Free" is the inscription above the entrance to the main building of the City College in San Francisco, the new name of the city's infant seat of learning. Established by the Board of Education in 1935 as San Francisco Junior College, with tuition free, it accents community service and confers a degree of Associate in Arts. The college began in the University of California Extension Building at the Galileo High School, with 1,400 students immediately enrolled. Soon classes were held in fourteen widely separated areas. Then came the acquisition of the 65-acre campus in Balboa Park at Ocean and Phelan Avenues where once had stood the Ingleside jail. A huge carved ram, the mascot, stands on the campus.

In 1960 the City College constructed a new auditorium with a Little Theatre. Here President Louis G. Conlan placed the famed 22-by-73-foot mural by the late Diego Rivera which was stored at the college for twenty years.

City College enables graduates to take up business careers, follow courses leading to medicine, dentistry, engineering, law, journalism, radio, accounting, and floriculture. One quarter of all the cut-flower industry of the United States is within fifteen miles of San Francisco, giving many opportunities to those following floriculture. The institution is unique in being the only college training its students to become chefs and bakers. Hotelmen eagerly employ its graduates. Curricula have expanded until the City College course compares favorably with most of those offered by four-year colleges and universities. Enrollment approximates 7,500.

Golden Gate College, at 220 Golden Gate Avenue, is one of eighteen American colleges originating in educational programs of the Young Men's Christian Association during the late nineties. In 1901 here was established the first evening Law School on the Pacific coast. When fire destroyed the building in 1906, classes were continued in an old mansion on Geary Street and in a tent. In 1923 all work was on a college level, and Golden Gate College was incorporated. The college offers instruction in law, business administration, traffic, advertising, and insurance, as well as general studies. Approximately 2,000 part-time and full-time students are enrolled. Russell T. Sharpe is president.

Many generations of San Franciscans owe their higher learning to two great centers outside the city. The University of California at Berkeley and the Leland Stanford Junior University at Palo Alto began as San Francisco projects.

The Rev. Henry Durant came to San Francisco in 1853 with the intention of building a university in or near the new golden city.

He was Massachusetts born and a graduate of Yale. He finally found a roof for his planned institute in a thirteen-room house at the corner of Fifth Street and Broadway in Oakland.

He opened the Contra Costa Academy with an enrollment of three pupils, under the auspices of the Congregational Association of California and of the Presbyterian Church. That was in 1853.

The academy soon became a college. Its trustees were able to buy four lots as a building site, bounded by 12th, 14th, Franklin, and Harrison Streets. Squatters living on the land tried to drive away the academy people. Dr. Durant went down among the squatters, obtained their attention and announced that negotiations were pending for securing four blocks for the purpose of building a college. There was much discussing, haranguing, and fighting. Colt revolvers were displayed, but finally the squatters gave three cheers for the coming college. After the skirmish ended, the legislature was asked for a charter and on April 13, 1855, the College of California became an established fact.

Among its thirteen trustees were the founder, Durant, and the Rev. Samuel Willey, a missionary-minister who had arrived in San Francisco in 1849. Both were talented fund raisers.

The college began its formal career in 1860, with a faculty of six and a freshman class of eight. Durant, Martin Kellogg, and I. H. Brayton were the first professors, assisted by three instructors. Expenses for rent and salaries were $300 a month. The college acquired 158 acres of the Peraltas' beautiful, many-leagued Rancho San Antonio. Frederick Billings suggested that the area be named "Berkeley." Today the Berkeley campus covers more than 900 acres. Added to this acreage is that of the other six campuses and land-holdings which are 25,877 acres.

Trustees of the College of California bought the land in Berkeley with the hope of developing their institution into a university. They saw the way open when the legislature passed a bill on March 30, 1866, establishing "The Agricultural, Mining and Mechanics Arts College." The newly created institution had no land, and the College of California offered to disincorporate and give all its land and buildings to the state provided the legislature would retract the establishment of "The Agricultural, Mining and Mechanical Arts College" and pass a new bill which would establish a true university. This offer was accepted. On March 23, 1868, Governor Haight signed the bill creating the University of California.

Doors were opened September 23, 1869, at the College of California site in Oakland, with forty students and ten professors. Following the suggestion of Regent Samuel F. Buttermouth, tuition was free. Women suffragists won a victory by insisting that the institution be coeducational. Professor John LeConte was the first member of the faculty appointed by the Regents. His brother, Joseph LeConte, was the fourth member chosen. Both spent their lives at Berkeley, adding much distinction to the university.

General George B. McClellan of Civil War fame, was first offered the presidency, but he declined, as did Professor Daniel C. Gilman. John LeConte served as temporary president until founder Henry Durant was given the honor. After serving two years, Durant resigned. Gilman accepted, but two years later departed to found the Johns Hopkins University at Baltimore.

At the turn of the century Benjamin Ide Wheeler became president; for twenty years his rich scholarship and attractive personality made him a notable figure in the state. He was chosen as a Roosevelt professor at the University of Berlin. Dr. Wheeler's successors were Dr. David Prescott Barrows and Dr. William Wallace Campbell.

In 1930 Robert Gordon Sproul was the first native-born San Franciscan to become president of the University of California, from which he had graduated. For sixteen years he had served as Comptroller and Secretary of the Regents and he became president without ever having taught a class. Under his direction, the university became world-famed, with campuses at San Francisco, Davis, Santa Barbara, Los Angeles, Riverside, and La Jolla, plus six experimental stations and laboratories throughout the state. He declined many high-salaried positions, including the presidency of Columbia University, and remained president until he retired in 1958, having served longer in that office than any of his predecessors.

Dr. Sproul was succeeded by Clark Kerr, a forty-one-year-old Pennsylvanian who had served as chancellor at Berkeley since 1952. Kerr, a graduate of Swarthmore, had received his Ph.D. in economics at Berkeley in 1939 and brought his abilities as an internationally-known labor mediator to the task of doubling the size of the statewide university. After President Kerr was installed on the seven California campuses, he planed from one to the other.

Two more campuses will soon be developed—Orange County and the Santa Cruz area. Also, a general campus—San Diego—will be built up near the present site of the university's Scripps Institution of Oceanography.

Although its scientists have made the university celebrated throughout the world, lovers of California history revere Hubert Howe Bancroft's Library at Berkeley, center of Pacific coast historical research, long directed by Dr. George P. Hammond. Beginning in 1859 as a San Francisco bookseller, Bancroft employed agents who within a few years collected, in England and on the Continent, 10,000 volumes concerning the Pacific slope. By 1890 they had gathered more than 125,000 manuscripts. Bancroft and his assistants obtained interviews and recollections from Spanish-Californians and English-speaking pioneers. He sent copyists to record state and mission archives and transcribe important documents. With the aid of writers, interviewers, and clerks Bancroft produced thirty-nine volumes on the history of the Pacific slope from Alaska to Panama, and as far east as the Rockies.

With his publishing program completed, Bancroft sought a home for his collection. President Benjamin Ide Wheeler and Professor Henry Morse Stephens urged its purchase for the university, and it was acquired in 1905 for $250,000, the historian donating $100,000 of the amount. Professor Stephens became the library's first director, and under this guidance it published translations of the diaries of Portolá, Vila, Costansó, Fages, Durán, Font, also a Donner Party diary and papers of the San Francisco Vigilance Committee of 1851. Dr. Herbert Eugene Bolton, nationally known historian of Stanford University, became professor of history at the University of California and curator of the library. Herbert I. Priestley and Charles E. Chapman also did important work in the Department of History. Dr. Priestley was for many years librarian, under the direction of Dr. Balton who has since passed away.

Largely through assistance of the Native Sons, the library acquired transcripts and photo copies of 200,000 pages of manuscript material from foreign archives. Since World War I, the library's foreign microfilm project has brought in material from the principal archives of Mexico, Spain, portugal, France, England and the Netherlands, amounting to more than two and a half million film exposures. During the past fifty years so many large collections and individual items of importance have been added that the library now has nearly four million manuscripts. Among them are the minutes of the San Francisco Board of Alderman for 1852–1855, the papers of Chester H. Rowell, Senator James D. Phelan, Governors Olson and Pardee, and a collection of John Muir letters.

Recently published by the library are the papers of U.S. Consul Larkin under the editorship of George P. Hammond. The Friends of the Bancroft Library, an active organization, have sponsored the publication of half a dozen books. Dr. Bolton asserted that the collection could not be replaced with $10 million and twenty years' time.

The library of the University of California, including its seven branches, has been ranked as the nation's third best in quality, surpassed in the United States only by that of Harvard and the Library of Congress. It contains 4,702,842 volumes.

Showpiece of the university is the cyclotron, created by the most famed of all the university's scientists, the late E. O. Lawrence, who helped usher in the atomic age and change history. He realized the 2,400-year-old dream of Democritus: transmutation of the elements by bombarding them with the atom smasher.

Ernest Orlando Lawrence, grandson of a Norwegian immigrant, arrived at the university and began work in LeConte Hall in 1928. The twenty-seven-year-old scientist had helped pay his own expenses at the University of South Dakota, by clerking in hotels and selling aluminum utensils. After doing graduate work at the Universities of Minnesota and Chicago, he became assistant professor of physics at Yale. His aides in building the first 60-ton cyclotron were Neils Edlefsen, Stanley Livingston, and David Sloan. Assistance was given by Leonard Fuller of the Electrical Engineering Department, who supplied a powerful magnet, and Gilbert Lewis, professor of chemistry, who furnished heavy hydrogen or deuterium. For this achievement the National Academy of Sciences, America's lordliest band of scholars, in 1937 gave Lawrence its highest scientific award, the Comstock Prize of $2,500 and a certificate bestowed only once every five years. In 1939 he received the Nobel Prize.

Twenty-one years later he was given the Enrico Fermi Award created by Congress in 1954 in honor of the late scientist. It consisted of a gold medal, a citation, and $50,000. Shortly before receiving that award, he was one of three top scientists who assured President Eisenhower that it was possible to make a hydrogen bomb that would eliminate 95 per cent of radioactive fallout, "the clean bomb." Dr. Lawrence's other honors included, besides the Comstock Prize, National Academy of Sciences, 1937: the Hughes Medal, Royal Society, 1937; the Duddell Medal, American Physicians Society, 1940; the Faraday Medal, 1952; and an award from the American Cancer Society, 1954.

The California physicist was an officer of the French Legion of Honor and an honorary member of the Academy of Sciences of the Soviet Union, as well as of the Royal Swedish Academy and the Royal Irish Academy.

Lawrence's first cyclotron was succeeded by others, including the huge 184-inch cyclotron which required financing to the extent of $1,150,000, provided by the Rockefeller Foundation, with additional funds supplied by the John and Mary Markel Foundation, bringing the total cost to about $1.5 million. Through gifts of the Rockefeller Foundation, the university erected a building to house the huge instrument of steel, copper, and aluminum to study the nucleus of the atom. Men work behind thick concrete shields as protection against radiation and, while the cyclotron is running, barriers keep the crew at a safe distance. Cyclotrons are being built in the United States, England, Canada, and the Orient. The Crocker Laboratory, financed by the late W. H. Crocker, houses a 220-ton instrument built in 1938 and developed by Lawrence for research in medical physics and the medical application of radioactivity.

Completed on the Berkeley campus in March, 1954, was a new atom smasher, the bevatron, which is, temporarily at least, man's mightiest destructive force. Lawrence and his colleagues made a major contribution to the development of the atom bomb during World War II, and the Livermore Laboratory, which he founded in 1952, is one of the nation's two nuclear weapons research laboratories.

Great was the shock to the university, and to the world, when in August, 1958, a force mightier than any created by man, struck down Ernest Orlando Lawrence. University flags were at half-mast as telegrams of sympathy arrived from distinguished world figures. The following day President Eisenhower ordered creation of an annual Ernest Orlando Lawrence Award to honor the scientist.

In eulogizing Dr. Lawrence, President Kerr said, "We may take comfort in the assurance that his work goes on in the exciting pursuit of knowledge in the great laboratory he created. I once asked Ernest, 'What new there was yet to be discovered?' He laughed —a thing he did readily and often—and said: 'If I knew, I would discover it.'" President Kerr concluded by calling Lawrence "an extraordinary leader of men, a giant of our time and of history."

In 1959 President Kerr headed a committee planning to build the Ernest Orlando Lawrence Hall of Science as a memorial to the great scientist. High in the Berkeley hills above the Lawrence Radiation Laboratory the memorial hall will be erected with laboratory facilities and a complete science library for junior scientists and inventors. Lectures and demonstrations for the public will be part of this great science education center.

Dr. Lawrence's close collaborator and adviser, Dr. Edwin M. McMillan, was selected as a director of the University of California Radiation Laboratory. In 1951 McMillan, professor of physics, shared the Nobel Prize in chemistry with Professor Glenn T. Seaborg, professor of chemistry. Professor McMillan and P. H. Abelson discovered element 93, neptunium, the first element heavier than uranium, "a new cosmic brick." This was followed by the discovery by Professor Seaborg and others of plutonium, element 94. Later Professor Seaborg and his colleagues brought forth elements 95, 96, 97, 98 and 101, or Americum, Curium, Berkelium, Californium, Mendelevium, and participated in the discovery of elements 99 and 100, or Fermium and Einsteinium. These revelations were important in understanding nuclear reaction. Element 102 is still unnamed.

As professor of chemistry, William F. Giauque won the 1949 Nobel Prize for devising a technique to study substances at a temperature a few thousandths of a degree above absolute zero, using this technique to elicit important, new information on thermodynamics.

Harold C. Urey, professor of chemistry, became a Nobel Laureate in 1934 for his discovery of heavy hydrogen. Drs. Wendell M. Stanley, now professor of biochemistry and director of the Virus

Laboratory, and John H. Northrop, professor of bacteriology, already were Nobel Laureates when they joined the faculty in 1948. Dr. Stanley had shared the Nobel Prize in chemistry in 1946 with Professor John H. Northrop and Professor James B. Sumner of Cornell, for the preparation of pure crystalline viruses, and his elucidation of their chemical nature, opening the way to better understanding of infection. In 1960 came the announcement that two members of the faculty were to be added to the Nobel laureates. Dr. Willard F. Libby was given the award in physics for the development of the bubble chamber. Dr. Donald A. Glaser received his honor in chemistry for the carbon 14 radioactive dating technique.

Seven of the thirty-five living American Nobel laureates have earned degrees from the University of California. They represent nearly 40 per cent of the entire number of Nobel winners graduated from American state universities. Ten of the Nobel laureates are on the faculty at the University of California: Professors Owen Chamberlain, William F. Giaque, Donald A. Glaser, Willard F. Libby, Edwin M. McMillan, John H. Northrup, Glenn T. Seaborg (recently appointed a member of the Atomic Energy Commission), Emilio Segre, Wendell M. Stanley, and Harold C. Urey. Ralph Bunche, winner of the Nobel Peace Prize, received his A.B. from the University of California at Los Angeles in 1927.

Other Berkeley scientists of distinction are Drs. H. Fraenkel-Conrat and Robley C. Williams who in 1955 took an infectious virus apart and reduced it to a mixture of apparently inert chemicals, then put it together and made it infectious again. They hope that this will be an important step in creating vaccine against disease.

In 1955 a team of Berkeley scientists, physicists Segre, Chamberlain, Wiegand, and Ypsilantis, discovered antiprotons, creating them artificially and identifying them. Antineutrons were revealed a year later by physicists Cork, Lambertson, Piccioni, and Wenzel. They worked with the bevatron. Antiprotons have no practical use for the present, but the scientists think that study of them and experiments may lead to new discoveries.

In 1956 Dr. Luis W. Alvarez and his colleagues discovered a third type of energy-yielding nuclear reaction to add to the two already known—fission and fusion. Alvarez, born in San Francisco, and son of the widely syndicated medical columnist, Dr. Walter Alvarez, was winner of the $5,000 Albert Einstein Award and Gold Medal for 1961.

In a new era of cancer research, the University of California scientists have developed a method of keeping fragments of the human lung alive after their removal from the body by surgery. Dr. T. Timothy Crocker, age thirty-nine, head of the Cell Research Laboratory of the University's Cancer Research Institute, and ten other California scientists have been awarded $79,500 from the American Cancer Society for the project.

On Parnassus Heights stands the University of California San Francisco Medical Center. Here are the Schools of Medicine, Dentistry, Pharmacy, together with the Langley Porter Neuropsychiatric Institute maintained by the California Department of Mental Hygiene.

Since 1950, a $24 million building program has put into operation the Herbert C. Moffitt Hospital and the Medical Sciences Building.

The George Williams Hooper Foundation and the Francis I. Proctor Foundation for Research in Ophthalmology and various research institutes, among them the Metabolic Unit for Research in Arthritis, are likewise housed on this campus.

A similarly extensive medical center is maintained on the Los Angeles campus.

The Hastings College of the Law and the California School of Fine Arts, both located in San Francisco, are affiliated with the University of California.

Until 1940 more than half the cost of university buildings and land was met by agencies other than the state of California. Since its inception in 1868, the university has received gifts exceeding $1 billion besides hundreds of donations of books, manuscripts, paintings, and scientific collections.

The university has two extension services. One serves all types of citizens, but Agricultural Extension serves the farmer primarily and has sponsored meetings and demonstrations attended by more than five million persons. University extension centers for the armed forces were operated for several years in Japan, Guam, Okinawa and the Philippines. One hundred forty-two communities are now served by the university extension service.

Responsibility for and administration of intercollegiate athletics were transferred from the students at Berkeley and Los Angeles to Departments of Intercollegiate Athletics officially established on those campuses by the Regents in 1960.

Originating as an academy with three pupils, the university's total registration for 1960 was 49,169, the largest full-time enrollment of any in the United States. The teaching staff of all seven campuses totals 4,321. The operating budget of the University of California for 1960 was $170,039,359 with more than 1,100 donors recorded for the same time.

University alumni are high in quantity as well as quality. Since 1873 the university has granted approximately 260,670 degrees.

Among alumni who have been distinguished in state and national life are Chief Justice Earl Warren, former governor of California; James Black, board chairman of the Pacific Gas and Electric Company; King Wilkin, president of Zellerbach Paper Company; John McCone, chairman of the Atomic Energy Commission. In the entertainment world are Gregory Peck and Ralph Edwards. Military heroes include General William F. Dean and General Jimmy Doolittle.

With California's rapidly increasing population, the University of California doubtless will have, when its centennial arrives in 1968, the highest attendance of any university in the world.

CHAPTER 7

In Memoriam—A Great Seat of Learning

STANFORD UNIVERSITY is another nearby seat of higher learning that began as a San Francisco project. It is a memorial to a happy boy's life spent mainly on Nob Hill.

Leland Stanford, father of the lad, made a many-sided impact on San Francisco. He helped build the railroad; he was the first man to live on Nob Hill, the first to ride on a San Francisco cable car. He served as governor of California and United States senator before culminating his active life in the founding of a great university in memory of his only son.

Leland Stanford, Jr., born late in his parents' lives, was at fifteen a tall, dark-eyed, narrow-shouldered youth, gentle in manner, always pale. The lives of his elderly parents centered in this delicate boy.

In 1876 Stanford bought Mayfield Grange owned by George Gordon near Menlo Park where he planned to breed and raise horses. He rechristened it Palo Alto Farm, because of its historic redwood tree with a 9-foot base which he admired. The farm, later the Stanford campus, became the favorite family dwelling, enjoyed especially by young Leland, who had there his own driving horse, Cheetem.

Stanford horses broke records. Stanford would sit for hours in a sulky, watching them being trained. At the farm 115 employees looked after 60 stallions, 250 brood mares, and a 60-acre trotting park. A 60-acre carrot field supplied food for young horses. President Franklin Delano Roosevelt's father bought Stanford's Gloucester, the first trotter to cover a mile under 2:2. In *The Roosevelt I Knew*, Frances Perkins wrote: "The President was so devoted to the

48

horse that even in the White House, he had 'Gloucester's' tail hanging on the wall in his bedroom."

On the Stanford University campus, there is a statue of the great Sherwood for whom Stanford refused $100,000 after he made the trotting record of 2:08¾, a gift to the university from Timothy Hopkins. The bones of Electioneer, his other world-famous stallion whose offspring sold for as high as $50,000, have been assembled and placed in the University Museum.

Stanford's interest in horses caused him to wonder if all four feet of an animal left the ground at the same time. He engaged British-born Eadweard Muybridge of the Morse Gallery, San Francisco, to photograph running horses. "Impossible," said Muybridge, but Stanford insisted, agreeing to pay all expenses.

On the Palo Alto Farm, in 1877, Muybridge's experiments proceeded. Twenty-four cameras were placed a foot apart, in a long building which stood parallel with the one-mile training track near Stanford stables. Instantaneous pictures were made with an exposure of only 1/50,000 part of a second, showing the complete stride of the horse. Wet plates were used, but later came the films. Stanford gave Muybridge permission to copyright the photographs, which had cost him $40,000. Muybridge was the world's first movie cameraman. Afterward Muybridge claimed the idea as his own, but finally turned over to his employer an album of two thousand pictures with this letter:

Honorable Leland Stanford, Sir: Herewith please find the photographs illustrating the attitude of animals in action, executed by me according to your instructions, at Palo Alto, in 1878 and 1879.

(signed) Muybridge, Menlo Park, 15th May, 1881.

In 1929 Stanford University set aside a day commemorating the development of the motion picture on what is now the campus. Early films were shown and addresses given, including one by Louis B. Mayer of the Metro-Goldwyn-Mayer Corporation. One of the original cameras, #5, used in the Stanford-Muybridge battery of twenty-four, was shown as well as his celebrated album of pictures, which is now kept in the Stanford Museum.

This was followed by the unveiling of the tablet in the inner quadrangle, near the site of the Muybridge studio, inscribed:

In Commemoration of
the Motion Picture Research Conducted
in 1878 and 1879 at the Palo Alto Farm
now the site of Stanford University
this Extensive Photographic Experiment
Portraying the Attitudes of Men and
Animals in Motion was Conceived
by and Executed under the Direction
and Patronage of
Leland Stanford
Consecutive and Instantaneous Exposures
Were provided by a Battery of Twenty-
Four Cameras fitted with Electro Shutters
. . . .
This tablet erected by Stanford University

In 1883 Stanford was ordered to European baths for the "cure."
Before the family left, a dancing party was given for Leland Jr. and
his friends at the Nob Hill place. It was the only time the youth
used the ballroom.

At Kissingen, Mrs. Stanford became anxious not only about her
husband but about her tall, pale son. She was anxious when he
waded in snow knee-deep in Athens, in his excitement over Dr.
Heinrich Schliemann's archaeological discoveries. At Florence ty-
phoid fever developed. The boy was wrapped in icy wet blankets
to reduce the fever. He died at the Hotel Bristol, March 13, 1884,
aged fifteen years and ten months. Stanford Sr. fell unconscious, but
when he could speak, his first words are said to have been "The
children of California shall be our children." With those words a
university would be born.

The grief-stricken parents returned to California on a special train
with the remains of Leland Jr. The family proceeded to San Francisco, where memorial services were held on November 30, 1884,
at Grace Church, which was walled with flowers. Burial was at the
"farm."

Mrs. Stanford, longing for word from her son, sought an honest
demonstration of spiritualism, although friends strove to dissuade
her. Governor Stanford urged her to take refuge from grief in founding the university as a memorial to Leland on their acreage at Palo
Alto. Stanford's first Palo Alto property consisted of the Spanish

grants on which the university stands: Rancho de San Francisquito and Rancho del Rincon de San Francisquito. Later he bought the Matadero Ranch, the Rancho de los Trancos, and the Coon Farm —in all, 8,940 acres. On the anniversary of Leland's nineteenth birthday, May 14, 1887, the cornerstone was laid.

Plans were made for erecting mission-style, buff-colored sandstone buildings of New Almaden stone around two quadrangles with arcades, both to recall the Spanish origin of California, and to protect students in going from class to class. The buildings were to cover three and a half acres.

At first, a university for boys was planned, but it was decided to have a coeducational institution, with women students limited to five hundred. While the buildings were being erected, Mrs. Stanford opened a kindergarten at Palo Alto, built a new house for the Presbyterian minister and repaired his church, and organized singing and night school for the people at the stock farm. Once a week she and her guests attended classes.

On the 11th day of November, 1885, Leland Stanford and Jane Lathrop Stanford formally established the endowment of the Leland Stanford, Jr., University. The estate was valued at $20 million.

In this same year Stanford entered the United States Senate, and this caused a breach with his partner, Huntington, who called the university "a circus" and compared the founder to a clown painting himself red and climbing a pole. Huntington intimated that Stanford bought the office—"A damn fool!" Stanford would "trust Huntington only as far as he could throw Trinity Church up the side of Mt. Shasta." After Stanford entered the Senate, the partners met only when necessary. Huntington decided to succeed Stanford as president of the Southern Pacific.

When the university buildings were ready, Senator and Mrs. Stanford made a tour of America's seats of learning in their private car seeking a president. They offered $10,000, at that time a large salary for a college president. At Ithaca, New York, they asked President Andrew D. White of Cornell University to accept the position. White suggested a Cornell graduate, Dr. David Starr Jordan, president of the University of Indiana.

The forty-year-old president, six feet tall, arrived in California the following June with his wife. Jordan was carrying an infant son in one arm, and two pieces of luggage in the other. Dr. David Starr

Jordan was to become a leader in biology and education and a world figure in the advocacy of peace.

Stanford University opened its doors on the hot afternoon of October 1, 1891. In his speech to 1,500 listeners, Jordan said the university was "hallowed by no traditions and hampered by none, the finger posts all pointing forward . . . the Golden Age of California began when its gold was used for purposes like this."

Aside from the death of his son, Senator Stanford's greatest heartbreak occurred a year after the university was opened. Pale, silent, he returned from the railroad office in San Francisco and lay down on the couch looking years older than when he had left in the morning. "What is the matter?" asked Mrs. Stanford. When he did not reply, she was alarmed. Slowly came the words, "I'm no longer president of the Southern Pacific. Huntington has taken my place." Since the railroad's organization Stanford had been president, but now he had been driven out. Mrs. Stanford could not forgive Huntington for humiliating her husband. The Huntington victory was a headline sensation.

From that day Stanford walked more slowly. He began to realize that he was living on borrowed time. He explained stock-farm management to his wife, as well as that of the Vina Ranch. Early on the morning of June 21, 1893, Leland Stanford's life ended at the Palo Alto residence.

Open air-exercises were held in the completed inner quadrangle of the university. Bishop Nichols, the Rev. Dr. Foute, and the Rev. Horatio Stebbins presided. The senator's coffin was carried by eight Southern Pacific engineers to the family mausoleum.

For the first time Mrs. Stanford realized what responsibility meant. "Mother of the University," she called herself. When founded, Stanford University was the most highly endowed in the United States, but during the panic of 1893 the United States government attached all its assets to settle a government claim of $57 million against the railroad. Resources were sold, the Vina Ranch was shut down, and expenses were slashed. At one time Dr. Jordan had only $1,500 to dole out to professors for salary claims of $15,000 a month.

"Stop the circus!" jeered Huntington, working double time. A businessman would have followed his expert advice, but a mother was fighting for her dead son. Mrs. Stanford dismissed her servants and paid visits on foot: "I can't afford a carriage." She made a trip to Washington to close their house there, and by living in her car spent only $160. She sold some of her jewels. "I'll live on bread and water, if necessary. Every dollar that I can rightly call my own is sacredly laid on the altar of my love for the university. I would lay down my life for it."

She said that Huntington and his friends manipulated Southern Pacific stock and sold her third at a low figure. The $57 million debt was later settled by the railroad owners by paying it in ten years with interest. University finances improved, and once more Mrs. Stanford enjoyed life among the students: "My boys and girls." She relinquished control of the university on June 1, 1903.

When Mrs. Stanford and Huntington were both past seventy, realizing that they were the only two left of the original railroad group, she sent her secretary to request an appointment with him at his office. "I'll call on Mrs. Stanford," he gallantly replied. "No, Mrs. Stanford wishes to call." Her face was chalk-white, as she entered the Southern Pacific offices. "Mr. Huntington, I've come to make peace with you." He took both her hands, bade her be seated, wiping his brow. "Well, I declare!" "We're both getting old, Mr. Huntington. We shouldn't harbor thoughts inimical to peace." "Of course, of course." Tears were in the eyes of both. They never met again.

Senator and Mrs. Stanford had planned that there should be a nonsectarian church at the university, but it was not begun until after the senator's death. Mrs. Stanford erected it as a chapel memorializing her husband. Its stained-glass windows and mosaic murals were made by R. Salviati and Company of Venice. The façade picture of Jesus delivering his Sermon on the Mount expressed Mrs. Stanford's devotion. The chapel was dedicated on January 23, 1903, at a ceremony performed by clergy of all denominations. She said to friends, "While my whole heart is in the university, my soul is in that church." She died a year before the great Earthquake that toppled the church steeple and pushed the façade into the quad. Seven years later it was reconstructed, this time with earthquake-proof methods, and the church was rededicated.

On January 15, 1905, Mrs. Stanford gave a dinner for about

twenty guests at the long-silent Nob Hill house. After dinner she
retired to her private suite on the second floor and poured herself a
customary glass of Poland water, placed there as usual by her maid.
Finding it intensely bitter, she thrust her fingers into her throat to
cause vomiting. Immediately she telephoned Dr. Jordan, "What is
the bitterest thing in the world?" "Strychnine."

On being analyzed, the water showed undissolved crystals of
strychnine. Detectives questioned servants. Everyone was under
suspicion. For some weeks there had been friction in the Stanford
household. One simple-minded maid had been notified that her
services would not be required at the close of the month. Mrs.
Stanford left the house with her secretary, Miss Berner, and went
to the Hotel Vendome at San Jose. All medicine bottles were thrown
away, but by a mistake the bicarbonate of soda was kept.

From San Jose, Mrs. Stanford went with Miss Berner to Honolulu to recover from the shock of the attempt upon her life. While
stopping at a hotel she died of a "heart ailment" following indigestion. Her bicarbonate bottle was found to contain powdered
strychnine, but not in sufficient quantity to cause death. Miss Berner
said that the bottle had been supplied by a physician while they
were in India in 1903, who thought strychnine a good remedy for
indigestion. Perhaps it was a carelessly prepared prescription.
Although there was an investigation, no evidence was produced
against any one person.

Stanford was especially fortunate in its first president, David
Starr Jordan. He was not only a leading educator and biologist, but
a world figure in efforts to bring about international peace. From
1910 to 1914, he was chief director of the World Peace Foundation,
and in 1915 president of the World Peace Congress. After having
been president of the university from 1891, he retired to serve as
chancellor, from 1913 to 1916, becoming president emeritus,
and dying in 1931. In 1951 his hundredth birthday was observed
at the university.

A giant in the field of ichthyology, Dr. Jordan assembled one of
the four most important fish collections in the world. In the Natural
History Museum on the campus is the fish collection of more than
half a million specimens which he began. Many ichthyologists in the
United States and other countries are Stanford-trained or taught by

Stanford-trained experts. The George Vanderbilt Foundation, a newly formed scientific research organization primarily engaged in fish studies, is now established in the Natural History Museum.

Iowa-born Dr. Ray Lyman Wilbur succeeded Dr. Jordan. Four years of his administration were passed in Washington, as President Hoover's secretary of the interior. After Dr. Wilbur became chancellor, he turned over the presidency to Dr. Donald B. Tresidder, a Stanford graduate. Tresidder was greatly beloved for his democracy and reforms, such as abolishing sororities. Death suddenly took him in January, 1948.

Like his predecessors, Dr. Wallace Sterling, who became president on April 1, 1949, is more than six feet tall. Although Canadian-born, he spent two years at Stanford as a graduate student, history instructor, and research assistant in the Hoover Library, receiving his Ph.D. from the university. From the directorship of the Huntington Art Gallery at San Marino he came "home to Stanford." The Sterling family occupy the Lou Henry Hoover house given by the ex-president to the university in memory of his wife.

Two Stanford presidents, Dr. Day Lyman Wilbur and Dr. Donald B. Tresidder, were physicians, and it was their thought that the Stanford School of Medicine should be moved from San Francisco to Palo Alto. This was accomplished in 1959. New buildings were constructed in the area of the museum, so that the School of Medicine would be in closest possible physical and intellectual relationship to the entire university.

Stanford's Medical Center has an initial cost of $22 million. Included in the program, aside from the hospital, is a rehabilitation center, and several medical school buildings. Edgar D. Stone of New York City, whose American Pavilion at the Brussels Fair received wide acclaim, was the architect of the new buildings, which were dedicated in September, 1959.

Senator and Mrs. Leland Stanford originally gave $20 million to found the university, but in 1959 President Eisenhower at a press conference proposed that a $105 million linear accelerator be built in the hills behind the university. Fifteen Midwestern universities competed for the distinction of having the huge atom smasher, but Stanford was selected. Although the project will be built by Stanford scientists, it is being financed by the federal government and will be at the disposal of scientists from other universities and from governmental agencies. When completed in six years it will be the largest scientific instrument ever erected. Congress has yet to approve the measure.

Dr. L. I. Schiff, executive head of the Stanford Physics Department, stated that "The Monster"—as it already has been nicknamed —will be rated far more powerful than Russia's newest 10 BEV machine. At present the largest in the world is the 35 BEV device at Brookhaven, New York.

Stanford's museum was the first steel-reinforced concrete building in the United States, railroad rails being used for reinforcing. This central building suffered little in the Earthquake of 1906, but brick and stucco wings were demolished. The contents were severely damaged and the museum could not be reopened until 1909.

In the historical room is the museum showpiece, the "Governor Stanford," the first locomotive to be used in California. The engine was brought around the Horn and greeted on her trial run in November, 1862, with a 35-gun salute. Near the locomotive is the gold spike which for many years was in the custody of Wells Fargo Bank, San Francisco.

It is to be hoped that nuclear physics may become a weapon for health and peace, but Dr. David Starr Jordan's pacific spirit seems to hover over the steel-framed Hoover Tower on the Stanford campus, a cyclotron of paper and ink, to promote peace. Without Dr. Jordan's lifelong effort to abolish war, the tower might never have risen. It was projected by a favorite pupil, Herbert Hoover, one of the thirty-eight graduates of the first class, 1892. This tower (architect Arthur J. Brown) is 16 stories tall, rises 285 feet, and is inscribed:

> The purpose of this institution is to
> promote Peace. Its records stand as a
> challenge to those who promote war.
> They should attract those who search
> for Peace. I therefore dedicate this
> building to these purposes.
> HERBERT HOOVER
> June 20, 1941

At the top of the tower is a carillon of thirty-five bells, gift of the

Belgian-American Educational Foundation. The largest bell of the carillon bears this message:

> Because I am called Leopold the Royal
> for Peace alone do I ring
> Over the waves of the Atlantic.

The carillon symbolizes the purpose of the Hoover Institute and Library on War, Revolution and Peace, which is to collect, preserve, and publish material relating to war, revolution, and the efforts to obtain peace in the twentieth century. The building was erected at the cost of $775,000. Funds have come from individuals and organizations interested in preservation and use of such material, from close personal friends of Mr. Hoover, and from the university.

While crossing the North Sea in World War I, Hoover recalled that Andrew D. White said it was difficult to obtain contemporary documents and papers after the events had occurred. As chairman of the Commission for Relief in Belgium, Hoover collected documents on his trips to belligerent countries, assisted by friendly helpers. When he returned to Europe after the Armistice of 1918 as director general of relief, opportunities for collecting increased. President Wilbur of Stanford arranged to have Professor E. D. Adams of the History Department go to Europe to organize a group of collectors composed of youths released from military service. Much material relating to the revolutions of 1918–19 was secured. Many valuable documents from Finland, Turkey, and the states of Central and Western Europe were obtained. Tons of material on socialism in Germany, the Soviet, the Fascist Revolution in Italy, the League of Nations, plebiscites and mandates during the interwar period, were assembled.

Noteworthy are collections dealing with attempts to organize peace from the Alfred Fried Library, the papers of David Starr Jordan and also of Lou Henry Hoover. Dr. Fried was the Austrian winner of the Nobel Peace Prize, and his collection includes his war diary and parts of the library of the Baroness von Suttner, at one time secretary to Alfred Nobel. After Dr. Jordan's death, Mrs. Jordan continued to collect material on peace and gave the library his 1,000 books and pamphlets on peace, international relations, publications of peace societies. Mrs. Jordan's family and friends set up a foundation to support their collection and study materials in this field.

Later additions to the Hoover Library are the personal collection of a distinguished Nationalist Chinese general; books on World War I from the private library of Mary Roberts Rinehart; material relative to Vice-President Nixon's tour of Asia and the Pacific area in 1953; a research collection of photographs relating to wartime operations in North Africa during World War II, assembled by the 20th Century-Fox Film Corporation; 1,759 photographic reproductions of political posters from Germany used during the first half of the twentieth century; a rare collection of Hitler's speeches, from the beginning of his political career until 1939; manuscript material from concentration-camp files in Germany.

One floor of the Hoover Library contains the incomparable collection of the Paris Peace Conference, following World War I. A most important part of this collection is a file of the propaganda asking independence for the Poles, Czechs, and Finns. Mr. Hoover collected this material while he was in Paris, and these papers provide valuable information about the persons and ideas active in Paris when the Treaty of Versailles was being negotiated.

Most important is the two-year project begun in February, 1957, by the Hoover Library: the documentary series edited by Mr. Alexander Kerensky, last prime minister of Russia's only democratic government. The world's first victim of Communist subversion, Kerensky left Russia when the provisional government was overthrown in 1917, after having brought about the fall of Czar Nicholas. Assisting him is Dr. Robert E. Browder, associate professor of history at the University of Colorado, a graduate of Stanford in 1942.

Kerensky is working on secret papers which the Communists thought destroyed many years ago. They were shipped secretly from Paris to Stanford in 1926 by Basil Maklakoff, the last pre-Communist Russian ambassador to France. At that time he signed a statement that he had burned the entire lot. Maklakoff stipulated that the sixteen large packing cases were to remain sealed until his death and then not made public at least three months thereafter. In July, 1959, he died in Switzerland at the age of eighty-six, and now the secret papers will be made public and will doubtless be source material for many books. Some documents are so confidential that they will not be available for use for many years.

Kerensky, who has lived and made Russian history, could hardly believe that these official documents existed outside of Russia. They will reveal in detail for the first time how he strove to keep Russia in the war on the Allied side and how the Bolsheviks withdrew Russia, once they had assumed power. Reports of Cabinet meetings, memoirs of prominent leaders and high-ranking military officers, personal accounts of eyewitnesses and participants in important events will startle the world when Kerensky's three-volume work is published.

Annually 35,000 people visit the library and in recent times 1,000 came from abroad. Among them were Russian editors, young King Baudouin and Prince Albert of Belgium; Switzerland's minister to to United States, Henry de Torrence; Yugoslav ambassador to the United States, Leo Mates; U Win, Burmese ambassador to the United States; Vira Dharmawara, leader of the Buddhist Order of Cambodia; Hubert Pouter, president of the South Rhodesian Federation of Industries; and former ambassador George F. Kennan, who was writing a book on Russia and said that he was greatly aided by the papers in the library, that without them he could not have written his book.

So great was the admiration of Mr. and Mrs. John Kallsen of Seattle for Mr. Hoover that, although they had never met him, they gave their entire fortune of $280,000 to Stanford and the library. During 1948 President Tresidder announced the gift of $180,000 from the Carnegie Corporation to enable Stanford to begin a three-year study of "Present-Day Revolutions and Their Effects upon Relations among Nations." This program is carried on under the direction of Dr. Harold H. Fisher.

Development of the library's fields of specialization requires the services not only of librarians, archivists, and administrators, but of specialists who know the languages, histories, and institutions of the principal areas considered. Curators of Eastern and Western Europe, the Middle East, China, and Japan contribute their special knowledge to the development of the library. Increased use of the library raised the budget of $47,000 in 1940–41 to over $260,000 in 1960–61.

The eighty-five-year-old founder said, in 1959, that they have $200,000 fixed income now, but another $300,000 is needed. Rather than resort to solicitation, the library is seeking funds from friendly foundations. Several donations of $25,000 each have been promised. Mr. Hoover is proud of what he calls "the most complete library of the type in the world." The building must be expanded to hold its 24 million documents on war, revolution, and peace. Already ground has been reserved for the enlarged building that probably will be erected.

Mr. Hoover has renamed the library "The Hoover Institute on War, Revolution and Peace."

When nations are ruled by reason instead of violence, doubtless the founder's words on dedication day will be realized: "Out of these files the world can get warning of what not to do, and what to do when it next assembles around the peace table. True, there must be brought to that table a concept of new human relations, a concept that substitutes peace for war. But if the world is to have long peace, that concept must find its origin and its inspiration in human idealism."

The dream that began on Nob Hill has spread the light of education in faraway places. Stanford campuses in Beutelsbach, Germany, near Stuttgart, Florence, Italy, and at Tours, France, overlooking the Loire River proved so successful that a fourth was established in the spring of 1961 at Tokyo. It is estimated by President Wallace Sterling that when the four campuses are in operation "more than thirty per cent of our undergraduate students will be able to study overseas."

CHAPTER 8

Newspapers

PIONEER EDITORS carried pistols but today editors and publishers of San Francisco's three daily newspapers live in friendliness. James P. Casey of the *Weekly Sunday Times* shot James King of William, founder of the *Bulletin,* in 1856 and was hanged by the Vigilantes. William Walker, the filibustering editor, was executed in Honduras. J. F. Dunne of the *Police Gazette* was stabbed to death. J. F. La Fuente, one of the founders of the *Sud-Americano,* was sent to San Quentin for life. The *Alta's* E. C. Gilbert died in a duel and G. P. Johnston of the *Globe* killed State Senator W. I. Ferguson in a duel. Charles de Young, founder of the *Chronicle,* was the last San Francisco editor to be assassinated.

After the death of its editor, James King of William, the *Bulletin,* the city's oldest English daily newspaper, founded October 8, 1855, was taken over by Thomas King, brother of James, with C. O. Gerberding as part owner. At King's death James W. Siminton obtained a half interest. Gerberding sold his portion to George K. Fitch (Deacon Fitch). Fitch bought the holdings of his partners, James Nesbitt, F. Tuthill, and Leland Bartlett, but sold a portion to New Hampshire-born Loring Pickering. In 1869 Fitch, Pickering, and Siminton owned both *Call* and *Bulletin,* Pickering managing the *Call* and Fitch the *Bulletin.* Siminton went east to become president of the Associated Press and his partners ran the San Francisco paper. Pickering died in 1892, ten years after Siminton.

Fitch's *Bulletin* vigorously protested against municipal extravagance, bond issues, the stock exchange, and tried to hold the tax rate at $1. Pickering's *Call* developed news, publishing spicy scandals. The *Bulletin's* circulation fell below 10,000, the *Call* paying its losses. Finally, the *Bulletin* was sold for $65,000 to Rose Crothers

Pickering, widow of Loring, her minor son, Loring, and her brother, R. A. Crothers.

In 1897 Wisconsin-born Fremont Older, former city editor of the *Call,* became managing editor when the *Bulletin* was losing $3,000 a month. Older continued the Fitch policy of attacking corruption and monopoly, but he introduced novelties. Virginia Brastow was made city editor, the first woman to hold such a position on a metropolitan newspaper in the United States. Circulation was stimulated by factual serials. Donald Lowrie's *My Life in Prison, The Healing of Sam Leake,* and Alice Smith's *Voice from the Underworld,* skyrocketed sales.

The *Bulletin* became the testing ground for writers and artists who afterward achieved national fame: Sinclair Lewis; playwright Maxwell Anderson; Robert L. Duffus of the *New York Times;* radio speaker and author Bessie Beatty; playwright Sophie Treadwell; Rose Wilder Lane of the *Saturday Evening Post;* society editor Kathleen Thompson, later the popular and rich novelist Kathleen Norris. Among others on the paper were dramatist Bayard Veiller, Lemuel Parton, attorney John Francis Neylan, Congressman Franck Havenner, Judge Sylvester McAtee, attorney Eustace Cullinan, John Coghlan, later vice-president of the Pacific Gas and Electric Company, Edgar Gleeson, John D. Barry, Carl Hoffman, Pauline Jacobson, and Frances Jolliffe.

Sports editor Hiland Baggerly was first to employ Robert Ripley (Believe It or Not), a Santa Rosa boy, at $7 a week. Baggerly also selected cartoonist Thomas Aloysius Dorgan (Tad). Herb Roth's first work before the Fire was on the *Bulletin.* After leaving to study at Munich, he joined the New York *World.* Russ Westover, creator of "Tillie the Toiler," came to the *Bulletin* from the defunct *Globe.* Haig Patigian of the art staff became a successful sculptor. William McGeehan, special writer, married Sophie Treadwell, and they went to New York; he became managing editor of the *Herald Tribune.*

While on the *Bulletin,* Older was among those who brought about the candidacy of James D. Phelan for mayor and Hiram W. Johnson for governor. He organized the Graft Prosecution which resulted in the removal from office of Mayor Eugene E. Schmitz. After discovering the innocence of Thomas Mooney, who was in San Quentin for allegedly having thrown a bomb during a World War I parade,

Older crusaded for his release from prison. Mooney had been sentenced to death, but Woodrow Wilson had requested and obtained from the governor commutation of Mooney's sentence to life.

The owners of the paper disapproved of Older's efforts to free Mooney, and in 1918 he left the *Bulletin* to become president and editor of the *Call*. He continued to fight for Mooney's freedom, and after many years in San Quentin, Mooney was pardoned by Governor Culbert Olsen.

Older often aided ex-prisoners, employing them on his ranch near Saratoga. He published a serial by ex-highwayman Jack Black, *You Can't Win*, which became a national best seller. Al Jennings, a reformed highwayman, also related his life in prison with O. Henry. Among writers that Older discovered on the *Call* was Eleonore Meherin, author of *Ann, Chickie*, and other serials later filmed by Hollywood producers. Elsie Robinson who had a nationally syndicated column, "Listen World," was brought to the *Call* by Older and for the paper she did many articles.

Brown-eyed Evelyn Wells began her career at eighteen, writing serials on the Donner party, Sarah Althea Hill, and Lola Montez, under Older's direction. One of her popular books, *Champagne Days in San Francisco*, first appeared in the *Call-Bulletin*. After Older's death in 1935, she wrote his biography.

It was her first book. Since then she has authored books on such varying subjects as *A Treasury of Names* (*What to Name the Baby*), *The '49rs with Harry Peterson, Life Starts Today*, and the best-selling novels, *Jed Blaine's Woman* and *The Gentle Kingdom of Giacomo*. She has worked as collaborator and editorial consultant for General Carlos P. Romulo, and many other writers. She is now living in New York.

Among artists developed on the *Call-Bulletin* under Older was Jimmy Hatlo, creator of "They'll Do It Every Time."

The *Morning Call* merged with the *Bulletin*, in 1929, and, only a few months its junior, had a less stormy history. It was first published on December 1, 1856, by "An Associated Practical Printers" —James J. Ayers, David W. Higgins, Llewellin Zublin, Charles F. Jobson, and William L. Carpenter. George E. Barnes, later the paper's drama critic, who owned an interest, christened it *The Morning Call* for a popular play of that name. Barnes sold his interest to Loring Pickering, who soon bought out all partners. Among the *Call's* early writers were Mark Twain, Frank Soulé, and Gilbert Densmore, who dramatized Twain's *The Gilded Age*. Jack London's first published story appeared in the *Call*.

Best known of the *Call's* staff in later days was Harold Ross, founder of *The New Yorker*, easily identified by his bristling pompadour and hatless at a time when men were not seen without hats. Harrison Fisher, creator of the Harrison Fisher girl, first worked on the *Call*. W. W. Coulter, of the shipping page, developed into a serious painter, doing notable murals for the assembly rooms of the Merchants Exchange Building. Arthur H. Cahill, the portraitist of distinguished citizens, was a graduate of the *Call* art department.

The *Morning Call*, sold at auction in 1897, was purchased by Claus Spreckels for Charles Shortridge, who had made a success of the San Jose *Mercury*. Within a year his name was displaced by that of John D. Spreckels, who erected the present-day Spreckels Building. Several new managers failed to lift the *Call* from red ink, and it was purchased by William Randolph Hearst, who entered the evening field. F. W. Kellogg of the Scripps papers became publisher and merged it with the dying *Evening Post* for which an earlier San Franciscan, Henry George, had written his famous *Progress and Poverty*. He remained publisher until succeeded by John Francis Neylan with Fremont Older as president and editor. Rapidly losing circulation and prestige, the *Bulletin* was merged in 1929 with the *Call* as the *Call-Bulletin*.

Sports editor Jack McDowell was Pulitzer Prize winner of 1944. In 1946 Jim Chestnutt received the George Westinghouse Science Writing Award. Andrew R. Curtin, editorial writer, had the Propeller Club's award for writing in 1951, and received the American Legion Stephen Chadwick trophy for the best editorial in the United States. In 1952 he won the Freedom Foundation award for an editorial titled "Armistice Day: GIs Die on New Western Front." Jane Eshleman Conant, staff writer, and Alex B. Loomis, art director, on May 3, 1955, won the Public Interest Award of the National Safety Council for a series of stories that reduced traffic deaths. In 1952 Fred Storm received from the Press-Union Club the $200 award for the best news story of the year—on President Truman's reception for delegates to the Japanese Peace Conference. The sum of $500 came to Robert Z. Hall as the Pall Mall award for solution of a murder mystery re-created in *The Big Story*. George Rhodes in 1954 won one of five $300 "sweepstakes" awards for his coverage of the opening of the new San Francisco airport. William P. Walsh and Richard Hyer won several awards for their exposé of racketeers and general excellence of reporting, including $200 prize for their best city-wide news story from the Press-Union League Club in 1954. For tracking down and capturing a young murderer and obtaining his confession that he killed Hilda Rosa Pagan, a seventeen-year-old Mission High School student, Robert Z. Hall and John D. Keyes received the Press-Union League Club award for the best city-wide news story in 1952. Joining in the scoop were William P. Walsh and cameramen Bill Nichols and Howard Robbins. The $500 Pall Mall award in November, 1954, came to Bernard Averbuch who saved the lives of two persons and set them on their way to new starts in life by uncovering facts in what appeared to be a "suicide pact" in a Nob Hill chapel.

The outstanding success of the *Call-Bulletin* staff was made in 1953 by Leon Uris, a Marine whose book *Battle Cry* remained a best seller for thirteen months and became a big box-office movie. The editorial rooms first heard of him by the remark "There's a guy down in the circulation department writing a book."

Leon Uris was born in Baltimore in 1924. He said he couldn't spell and he didn't know grammar when he left high school to become a Marine at age seventeen. It took guts to survive Guadalcanal and Tarawa, where he developed asthma and malarial fever, but he was helped by his wife, Betty Beck, a sergeant Woman Marine. Uris says that if she hadn't been a sergeant she couldn't have endured his illnesses, caring for two children, cooking, and washing while he was working in the circulation department of the *Call-Bulletin*, sometimes driving a truck, to make a living for the family of four. Nights he worked and Saturdays and Sundays sixteen or seventeen hours a day, but, finally, the manuscript was ready for the publishers.

After receiving the first advance royalties, he gave Betty the keys to the car that they had always planned to buy. He was only 29, and they both thought that it was worth all that they had gone through when the reprint of 600,000 skyrocketed the book to more than a million sales. Warner Brothers bought it immediately for their stars, Mona Freeman and Tab Hunter. Uris wrote his own screen play and was receiving $1,500 a week in Hollywood, when he gave it all up and decided to write a big new novel—*Exodus*, the story of the Jewish people on their long road through the centuries to Israel. In order to do this he traveled 50,000 miles to Denmark, Iran, Cyprus, and last to Israel, where he covered 12,000 miles through that narrow little land. *Exodus* led best-seller lists and has become a great cinema success.

Third in age among San Francisco newspapers is the *Examiner*, born in 1863 as the weekly *Democratic Press*.

During the Civil War Captain William Moss so violently stressed the policy of States' Rights that the paper was suppressed by the government. When Captain Moss republished the *Press*, June 13, 1865, he named it the *Weekly Examiner*.

After President Lincoln was assassinated, mobs wrecked the plant, tossing the type out the window. Charles L. Weller, Philip A. Roach, and George Pen Johnston, who had killed Senator Ferguson in a duel, became associated with Moss in ownership. Another duelist, B. F. Washington, nephew of the first president, was made editor. The *Evening Daily Examiner* was born.

Fifteen years later B. T. Baggett and Company bought the *Examiner* for George Hearst, with Clarence R. Greathouse as publisher. Shortly after acquiring the *Examiner*, Hearst was elected United States senator.

Seventeen-year-old William Randolph Hearst had a burning desire to own a newspaper. His first opportunity came at Harvard when he found Eugene Lent, his friend from infancy, trying to rescue the *Lampoon* from the sea of red ink. Business manager Hearst asked his mother to solicit subscribers for the *Lampoon* in San Francisco. His success in paying the paper's debts and earning a profit of $650 in two years made him a confirmed newspaperman. To his parents he wrote: "Just wait till Gene and I get hold of the *Examiner*, and run her in the same way."

Two years before he left college he wrote his father a letter, quoted by M. Lincoln Schuster in *The World's One Hundred Great Letters:* "I'm possessed by the weakness which at one time or other besets most men—I am convinced I could run a paper successfully. Now, if you will let me take over the *Examiner*, with enough money to carry out my scheme . . ."

Senator Hearst thought it folly to invest in a newspaper and told his son to go into mining, ranching, anything but the newspaper business. Young Hearst would not abandon his plan. He cabled his mother in Paris, asking her to see the *World* editor, Ballard Smith, in London, and offer him editorship of the *Examiner* and an interest in the paper. In New York Will Hearst met Smith, who advised him not to engage a high-priced editor but to do the work himself.

When Will was twenty-three his father told him he might have the *Examiner*. On the same day that George Hearst was seated in the Senate after election, W. R. Hearst published the first edition of the 8-page *Examiner*, circulation 23,914. On the staff was a Harvard group in gay collegiate clothes: Eugene Lent, cartoonist Fred Briggs, and E. I. Thayer, later to author "Casey at the Bat."

In one month the *Examiner* had changed to twelve pages. The young editor wrote his mother: "I don't suppose I shall live more than three or four years if this strain keeps up."

Soon the *Chronicle* and the *Call* scooped the *Examiner* on the burning of the Hotel Del Monte. Hearst rushed California's first special news train to the scene. City editor Joe Ward got out a 16-page paper and three editions. Hearst went up in a balloon labeled "The Examiner," his first trip in the air. He sent a special train to Los Angeles with the balloon, advertising its arrival. Before he was twenty-four he published an edition of the *Examiner* at Washington, D.C., trying to bring the Democratic National Convention to San Francisco. He failed, but it was good advertising.

Gertrude Atherton then, beginning her career, wrote a series for the growing sheet, "Monterey, Then and Now." Among men employed were Edward H. Hamilton, nature writer Allen Kelly, Charles Michelson, later publicity director for the Democratic party, George Pancoast, inventor of the Pancoast presses, Edward W. Townsend, afterward congressman and creator of "Chimmy Fadden." S. S. Chamberlain, former editor of Bennett's *Paris Herald*, became managing editor. When Queen Liliuokalani was deposed, he took the first steamer to Honolulu and obtained the first interview she ever granted.

Arthur McEwen, a tall, fair-haired, caustic Scotsman, gave the editorial page idealism and wit. Ambrose Bierce produced his biting "Prattle." Thomas Nast, creator of the famed "Tammany Tiger," came from New York to cartoon local bosses. Oregonian Homer

Davenport drew political cartoons and became a national figure. Jimmy Swinnerton began drawing his cartoons. Now past eighty, "Jimmy" is still employed by the Hearst organization.

Annie Laurie (Winifred Sweet) organized funds for Children's Hospital wards, lived among lepers, went to Utah to get the story of Mormon wives, and was the first woman to report a prizefight. By ruse she boarded President Harrison's train in Nevada. Her articles were syndicated throughout the nation under the name of Winifred Black—Orlow Black of the *Examiner* being her first husband.

Drama critic Ashton Stevens gave Hearst banjo lessons. For more than fifty years he was drama critic of the Chicago *American*. No writer except Ambrose Bierce was so feared as Alice Rix who, educated in Paris, descended upon the *Examiner* office with the hairdo and authority of Sarah Bernhardt. After John D. Spreckels lured her away to the *Call*, she presented him with a reporter's then all-high expense account—$150 for a ball gown, worn to report the governor's ball at Sacramento. Imperiously she summoned taxis instead of messengers to carry her copy page by page to the office. One day the taxi failed to arrive at the *Call* with her story's ending. Her writing career in San Francisco then ended.

Hearst battled to overthrow "Blind Boss" Chris Buckley, who was driven into exile, but his most spectacular fight was against the Southern Pacific Railroad's funding bill. Bierce captained the Washington battle. "It is not expedient to give a man 100 years to pay a bill, the past consideration being that already for 50 years he has been engaged in beating you out of it." The funding bill was killed, but within a few years the railroad paid its debt.

Senator George Hearst died in 1891, leaving his fortune of $18 million to his widow, who gave more than half to the University of California. By this time the *Examiner* was highly profitable. In 1894 Hearst bought the lot at 3rd and Market Streets and there the Examiner Building stands today.

When Hearst purchased the New York *Journal* it became the second paper of his chain. He telegraphed S. S. Chamberlain, Arthur McEwen, Charles Dryden, Homer Davenport and Annie Laurie to come to New York.

Among the members of the *Examiner*'s staff to distinguish themselves was editor Bailey Millard who first published one of the world's great poems, "The Man with the Hoe," written by Edwin Markham, an Oakland schoolteacher. From the advertising department came Frances Marion, a popular Hollywood scenario writer. Leo Carillo, of the art department, convulsed his fellow workers with dialect impersonations and began his theatrical career at the Orpheum. Later he starred in *Lombardi, Ltd.* and in many motion pictures. Percy Gray went from the art department to painting attractive water color landscapes. Harry Raleigh developed into one of America's foremost illustrators of books and magazines. In 1951 Nevada-born Edward S. Montgomery received the Pulitzer Prize for exposing the link between the underworld and the Bureau of Internal Revenue offices. In 1955 he had a spectacular scoop when, aided by bloodhounds, he discovered the body of the murdered schoolgirl, Stephanie Bryan, who had been missing for several months. She had been buried in the area of the Trinity Alps. Clint Mosher has received several awards for his stories on alcoholism, maritime news, and the quiet grief of Memorial Day. His account of the care of drunks led to establishment of an outpatient clinic and earned him the first annual Edward V. McQuade Memorial award from the Association of Catholic Newsmen. Sports writers Curley Grieve, Prescott Sullivan, Jules P. Cuenin, Bob Brachman, and Eddie Muller have all received awards. Eve Jolly (Prudence Penny) so distinguished herself in helping homemakers that she has become an eastern magazine editor.

In his closing years Hearst was unfailing in his crusade against vivisection. Communism also was blasted daily. His son, William Randolph Hearst, Jr., who became head of the Hearst papers after his father's death, in 1955 achieved an unprecedented scoop when he, with Kingsbury Smith and Frank Conniff, was able to do what was thought impossible, enter Russia and interview Bulganin, Khrushchev, Zhukov, and Molotov. From January to August they flew 75,000 miles, interviewing prime ministers, government officials, and ambassadors. Hearst talked privately with President Eisenhower, Sir Winston Churchill, Sir Anthony Eden, Premiers Bulganin of Russia, Faure of France, Menderes of Turkey, Chancellor Adenauer of West Germany, Sharett of Israel, and Nasser of Egypt. He has given the Hearst papers what his father desired—"startling originality."

Under the brilliant direction of Lee Ettelson, former publisher of the *Call-Bulletin,* in 1961 the annual Newspaper Publishers' Association chose the *Examiner* as the paper of highest excellence in California.

Junior to the *Examiner* by two years, the *Chronicle* has belonged to one family, the de Youngs, longer than any other San Francisco newspaper. Founder Charles de Young told the story of its beginning as a neat little folio sheet, the *Daily Dramatic Chronicle,* which appeared January 16, 1865, and was distributed free in stores, hotels, and places of amusement.

I determined to start a gratuituous theatrical paper like the one I'd published in Sacramento, and call it The Dramatic Chronicle, but I hadn't a dollar in the world. I got credit at a job office for the use of room, type, press, and for paper by promising to pay at the end of the week.

Then came the struggle. In the daytime I solicited advertisements, and at night with the help of a young fellow, I set up the type. In this way, I worked five days to get the first edition ready for the press, and in the whole time slept not more than 13 hours, and that on the floor of the office, on papers. I was exhausted by the strain. I would often go to sleep at the case with the composing stick in my hand, and be awakened by the rattle of the "pied" type on the floor. I had borrowed $5 to live on during the first week, and with a portion of it, purchased a quantity of strong black coffee, and kept awake by drinking it.

The exhaustion nearly caused what would have been to me then a great disaster. The form was ready for printing and I was holding it up, while my only assistant was underlaying lines of display type. I grew so faint that I staggered, and the form was saved from falling into the "pi" by the boy. When the forms were ready for the press, I was hardly able to feed the sheets into the machine. But at the end of the week I began to feel encouraged. The payments of bills by advertisers enabled me to pay expenses, and I breathed a little freer.

In spite of difficulties, the *Chronicle*'s advertising the first year was more than $2,000 a month. The paper had a big scoop on a prizefight at Oakland by having a reporter on horseback race from the fight to the telegraph office and get control of the wires. Civil War news became the paper's specialty, using illustrations. Lincoln's assassination story was accompanied by a picture of John Wilkes Booth with a noose around his neck, which was followed by a scene at Ford's Theater, Washington. The pictures attracted so much attention that they were increased.

On September 1, 1868, the *Morning Chronicle* appeared: "We shall support no party, no clique, no faction. . . . Neither the Republican party nor the Democratic party, nor the Pacific Railroad, nor the Bank of California are great enough to frighten us or rich enough to buy us. We shall be independent in all things, neutral in nothing."

Nineteen-year-old Charles de Young managed the editorials and seventeen-year-old Michael Henry de Young had charge of the business. Charles, a fierce fighter, was either loved or hated. As circulation grew, he entered politics. At first he was friendly with Dennis Kearney's Working Man's party, but he opposed the nomination for mayor of Isaac C. Kalloch, who was ambitious to go to the United States Senate.

Blond, curly-headed Kalloch, a Kansan with fine eyes and a rich deep voice, looked more like a prosperous stock operator than a Baptist minister. His followers built for him the Metropolitan Temple, seating 5,000, and installed a fine organ. Sunday evenings he discussed events of the day, lauding Kearney and attacking the *Chronicle.* In his paper de Young advised Kalloch not to run for mayor, but his warning was disregarded. To establish Kalloch's unfitness, the *Chronicle* published an account of a previous unfrocking by an ecclesiastical body which had deprived him of his pulpit. Kalloch did not deny the charges, but from the platform of the Metropolitan Temple smeared the de Young family.

De Young drove to the temple and shot Kalloch in the thigh. He was held in jail until Kalloch recovered, and one month before election was released on $25 bail. Kalloch was elected mayor.

War was on between the two men, and the Rev. Isaac C. Kalloch, son of the mayor-elect, armed himself with a Colt revolver and about dark on April 27, 1880, entered the *Chronicle* office. His first three shots at de Young missed but the fourth brought instant death.

When tried, Kalloch pleaded self-defense. Attorney Henry E. Highton produced a witness for the defense who testified that looking through the plate-glass window, he saw de Young fire the first shot. Witness Clemshaw was sent to prison for perjury, but Kalloch was acquitted. M. H. de Young erected a life-size statue of his brother in the I.O.O.F. cemetery, and from that day until his own death directed the *Chronicle.*

Perhaps because of the tragic death of his older brother, M. H. de Young did not go out to battle. In forty-five years he established the paper's stability, giving it character and success. De Young never changed managing editors. John P. Young, legislative correspondent, engaged by Charles, remained on the paper forty-five years, until stricken at his desk in 1921, and was succeeded by Arthur L. Clarke.

One of the *Chronicle*'s ablest editorial writers, Edward F. Adams, founded the Commonwealth Club; he died in 1929 at the age of eighty-seven. Franklin K. Lane, future secretary of the interior, was a *Chronicle* reporter, and Will and Wallace Irwin were on the staff. Waldemar Young wrote for the *Chronicle*, but later went to Hollywood where he converted Peter B. Kyne's *Cappy Ricks* stories into film scenarios.

Reuben L. Goldberg began his cartoons on the *Chronicle* in 1899, at $9 a week, after being graduated from the University of California. Chicago-born Bud Fisher commenced creative work on the *Chronicle* when he did his first "A. Mutt" strip, November 3, 1907.

In 1890 M. H. de Young planned to have erected a 10-story steel-frame building at Kearny and Market Streets. "What will an earthquake like that of 1868 do to that?" asked the critics. Burnham and Root put up the Chronicle Building, San Francisco's first steel-frame structure. The Claus Spreckels, Mills, and Flood Buildings followed. All were gutted by the Fire, but they have been restored.

While filling the post of publisher Charles de Young, only son of M. H. de Young, died in 1913. After the father died in 1929 the *Chronicle* was left to a board of trustees in trust for the daughters, Helen M. Cameron, Kathleen Y. Thieriot, Constance M. Tobin, and Phyllis M. Tucker. Son-in-law George T. Cameron became president and publisher of the *Chronicle*, but died in 1955. Grandson Charles de Young Thieriot succeeded Mr. Cameron as publisher and president. Scott Newhall, of one of San Francisco's prominent pioneer families, is the capable editor.

In 1937 Seattle-born Paul Smith became the *Chronicle*'s editor and general manager. Leaving the Pescadero High School at fourteen, Smith became an investment banking house employee and the *Chronicle*'s financial reporter. At twenty-six he was the paper's executive editor. With Herbert Hoover, in 1938, he visited fifteen European countries and reported conversations with leaders.

In World War II he enlisted in the Marines as a private, and was voted "outstanding young man of the year" by the United States Chamber of Commerce. He was appointed one of the six editors of the Lilienthal Atomic Energy Committee to make available to Americans all possible information on the development of atomic energy.

After serving the *Chronicle* for many years, Paul Smith became president for a time of the Crowell-Collier Publishing Company in New York.

The *Chronicle*'s late distinguished literary editor, Joseph Henry Jackson, was New Jersey born and educated at Peddie School and Lafayette College. Coming to California in 1920, he became editor of *Sunset* magazine. As literary editor of the *Chronicle* he was an early enthusiast for John Steinbeck and William Saroyan. He held a notable position among critics, and his opinion was sought by eastern magazines and clubs in bestowing awards. His daily column, "Bookman's Notebook," also appeared in the Los Angeles *Times*. A prodigious worker, he not only found time for his daily column but wrote such successful books as *Mexican Interlude, Notes on a Drum, Anybody's Gold, Extra! Extra!, Continent's End, Viking Portable Murder Book, San Francisco Murders, Gold Rush Album, Bad Company, My San Francisco,* and *The Christmas Flower.*

Bad Company won the Edgar Allan Poe Award in the fact-crime field several years ago. At the time of his death in July, 1955, he was at work on a book, *The Girl in the Belfry,* based on the Durrant murders.

For eighteen years Jackson did an unsponsored weekly radio broadcast about books, and he collapsed while recording a book review in a National Broadcasting Company studio. William Hogan ably succeeded Mr. Jackson as literary editor.

The *Chronicle* received honorable mention by the Pulitzer Prize Committee for its part in settling the ship clerks and warehouse strikes. Royce Brier was given the Pulitzer award in 1934 for reporting the San Jose lynching. In 1946 he received the Commonwealth Club's Gold Medal for general literature by a California resident. Among books written by him are *Last Boat from Bayreuth, Crusade, Reach for the Moon,* and *Western World.*

In 1942 the Pulitzer award also came to Stanton Delaplane for reporting the planned secession of Oregon and California to form the 49th state of Jefferson. Seven years later he received the Head-

liners' Award for the "Ding Dong Daddy" bigamy story. In 1959
the Headliners' Award was given for his syndicated columns "Post-
cards from Delaplane" and "Around the World with Delaplane."

The Headliners' Medal of Merit came to Robert de Roos in 1946
for outstanding work by a reporter on a newspaper of more than
100,000 circulation. Headliners also honored Carolyn Anspacher for
her critique of *The Women,* Harry Lerner for an account of the
Samoan clipper disaster, and John U. Terrell for his interview with
Oklahoma's Jack Dawson.

Cloyd J. Sweigert, editorial cartoonist, won $200 and an Honor
Medal from Freedom Foundation for a cartoon entitled "Impreg-
nable Foundation." The *Chronicle* received an Edgar statuette from
the Mystery Writers of the United States for the best coverage of
mystery stories and writers of any newspaper in the United States.
A similar award was simultaneously given to Elenore Glen Offord,
the *Chronicle's* literary reviewer. George D. Carvalho not only
won the $1,000 Pultizer Prize for the best local reporting of the
year 1952, but also the National Headliners' Award as well as the
$500 Edward V. McQuade Memorial Award for a series of stories
on the Communist China ransom racket. In 1953 he was selected as
one of America's ten outstanding young men by the United States
Chamber of Commerce.

Esther Hall, food editor, was presented with the Vesta Award
from the American Meat Institute for outstanding presentation of
news about food in 1952. In the same year Polly Noyes, travel editor,
received from the Trans World Airlines $100 and a plaque for the
best travel feature, a story written on an around-the-world trip.
Pierre Salinger, today's press secretary for President Kennedy, won
the $500 Edward V. McQuade Memorial Award for his series of
articles on jail conditions in the state of California in 1953, and
Jack Morrison also received $500 in 1954 from the State Bar Associ-
ation of California for his articles on the pre-trial plan for California
courts.

Editorial writer Templeton Peck was presented an Award of
Merit by the Bar Association in 1954 for his editorial on pre-trial
procedure. The following year a citation came to him from the
English-speaking Union of the United States for his editorials to
improve British-American relations. Science editor Dr. Milton
Silverman in 1955 received the $1,000 Albert Lasker Medical Jour-

nalism Award for his article "The Drug That Fooled the Doctors," describing the first uses of Rauwolfia in hypertension and mental diseases which appeared in the *Saturday Evening Post*.

Photographer Joe Rosenthal made an international reputation when, during World War II, he took a picture of the flag raising at Suribachi. Reproduced many times, the picture has inspired magazine articles and been immortalized in a 10-ton bronze monument at Washington, D.C., by Felix de Weldon.

In 1957 Arthur Hoppe received the $200 Press-Union Club Award for the best feature story of the year, an account of the Elizabeth Arden cocktail parties held at the Mark Hopkins Hotel. For his photograph of a helicopter crashing into the water at the Ferry Building during civic ceremonies, Gordon Petters received the $200 Professional Newspaper Award by the Press-Union Club and also honorable mention in the fourteenth annual "News Pictures of the Year" competition and exhibition in Washington, D.C. In 1958 the California Newspaper Publishers' Association gave the *Chronicle*'s business and finance pages an award.

Herb Caen's brilliant daily column has a large following. His books *Baghdad by the Bay, Don't Call It Frisco,* and *Herb Caen's New Guide to San Francisco* are widely read.

Since November 15, 1959, the *Chronicle* has had the KRON-TV station with transmitter atop San Bruno Mountain. Its tower, reaching 1,480 feet above sea level, is on the highest point of any San Francisco television station. Beginning with a staff of eighteen, it has grown to seventy and is regularly on the air 120 hours every week.

The *News*, founded March 23, 1903, by E. W. Scripps, was one of a chain of more than twenty newspapers owned by Scripps-Howard. William D. Wasson became editor and the business manager was H. B. Clark. Scripps gave them $50,000 in credit and ordered them not to call for additional funds. Wasson owned a linotype in a downtown printing office, which he contributed, and a flat-bed press was purchased after being discarded by the *Chinese World*. Publication started in an abandoned frame saloon building at 408 Fourth Street.

Circulation was restricted to laboring people south of Market Street. Each evening about 500 papers were distributed free in the block nearest the office. Wasson covered City Hall by telephone, but at the end of the year a reporter was hired. Circulation increased and they rented a lot and erected a frame story-and-a-half building, installing a small rotary press and a stereotyping plant.

After the Earthquake of 1906, Wasson and Clark scrambled to the office over piles of brick and debris. The city was without water, electricity, or gas. Both editor and business manager realized that their new building, erected a few months previously on Ninth Street, was doomed by oncoming flames but with smoke in their nostrils decided to get out an "Extra."

Jack Smith's small printing office nearby had a hand-and-foot press, and when a reporter brought in the names of the dead and injured from Mechanics' Pavilion, where they lay, Wasson and foreman Al Hopkins set up the names in type. Six columns were filled with names, and Hopkins printed the papers which were given to the large crowd outside. Newsboys sold them as high as $1 a copy, and copies of San Francisco's first newspaper issued after the disaster are valued at ten times that sum. Soon the building was in ashes.

Wasson, a former Palo Alto realtor, recalls that among his brilliant assistants that day was Edgar T. Gleeson, who wrote stories faster than the linotype could set them. When Boss Ruef and Mayor Schmitz were indicted by the grand jury, "Scoop" Gleeson routed out a printer, a stereotyper, and the circulation manager, and got out an "Extra" almost singlehanded. The sale was so large that Wasson gave Gleeson his first bonus. Gleeson, a great reporter, was later managing editor of the *Call-Bulletin*.

With Gleeson on the waterfront was Karl von Wiegand, who later acquired fame as a war correspondent. Another newsman who became highly successful was Karl Bickel, afterward vice-president of the Scripps-Howard chain. Sophie Treadwell, who did features, later had plays produced in New York, among them *Machinal*.

Many of the *News* staff received awards: Dick Chase and Harry Press, in 1952, received the Edward V. McQuade Memorial Award, presented by the Association of Catholic Newsmen for an exposé of bilking elderly people in the Social Service section of the Health Department. The McQuade Award also went in 1953 to Harry Press for *These Are Our Children*, and in 1954 to George Murphy for a series *Good Kids*. In 1956 Murphy received five awards: $500 from *Big Story*, $500 from *Strike It Rich*, the McQuade Award, and

Press-Union Club Award for his stories on Robert Emzensperger, a schoolteacher unjustly accused of possessing narcotics; the Sigma Delta Chi and the State Bar Association gave him a prize for his editorials and for reporting and interpreting administration of justice in California. In 1957 Donald Canter had three honors: the McQuade Award of $500 for his columns resulting in finding homes and jobs for 101 Hungarian refugees, $200 from the Press-Union Club for the same articles; he also wrote so effectively about the Chinese refugees that he received the Sino-American Culture and Economic Associations News Award. Photographer Robert J. Warren won the United Press News Pictures April prize for the courtroom picture of Mrs. Lucas' son attacking Assistant District Attorney Jack Berman. In 1958 George Dusheck had the Press-Union Club's $200 prize for the best feature of the year, "Who is to Blame?" Alias Santa Claus, a series on twelve community benefactors, brought Joseph Sheridan the McQuade Award in 1958. Jack Rosenbaum in 1955 received the Press-Union Club prize for the best feature story, "The Governor." Mary Crawford and George Dusheck were given the Press-Union Club Award for the best local series, *The Truth about Skid Row*. Mary Ellen Leary in 1954 had the State Bar Association of California prize for her articles on the San Francisco public defender.

The *News*, that had started with a secondhand press, now became one of the most popular of the Scripps-Howard chain.

San Francisco and, especially, the newspaper world were startled on August 8, 1959, when it was announced that the *Call-Bulletin* and the *News* were to be consolidated—and known as the San Francisco *News-Call Bulletin*. The new paper was to be published by a new corporation equally owned by Scripps-Howard and Hearst Publishing Company, Inc. The editorial policy of the paper was to be that of Scripps-Howard, under direction of editor Charles H. Schneider, who had been editor of the *News*. World-wide news and picture services of United Press International and the Associated Press serve this newest San Francisco evening paper, which will occupy the Call-Bulletin Building on Mission Street. The *News-Call Bulletin* became the infant newspaper in San Francisco, but in reality its parents were the 56-year-old *News* and the more than a century-old *Call-Bulletin*.

CHAPTER 9

Graft

THE SPIRIT of the Vigilantes was not dead, but slumbering.

For months after the Fire, "earthquake goodness" reigned, but soon it was clear to San Francisco pioneers of 1906 that their government was as corrupt as during the two decades when "Blind Boss" Christopher Buckley, a saloonkeeper, made himself a millionaire with his Democratic machine that governed the city for the Southern Pacific Railroad.

Fremont Older, editor of the *Bulletin*, thought that something should be done. He believed the one man who could help was ex-Mayor James Duval Phelan.

Older and Phelan had been friendly since 1895, when the editor had called on Phelan to ask him to run for mayor, and to rid the city of the domination of bosses. "What put that idea into your head?" asked Phelan, who had held no office other than president of the San Francisco Art Association. Older told him that he was sure Phelan could win.

Phelan consented and the *Bulletin* published the first article supporting his candidacy. In January, 1896, Phelan took office, abandoning the life of a cultured millionaire to become San Francisco's most distinguished citizen.

Phelan gave San Francisco a high order of government. A new charter was drafted and streets were improved. He demanded that the gas company lower its rates. He projected bringing Hetch-Hetchy water to San Francisco. Planning city beautification, he gave sculptor Douglas Tilden a commission to make the Native Sons' monument at Market, Mason, and Turk Streets.

Phelan might have been mayor for many years, but during the

teamsters' strike in 1901 he used police to keep traffic moving. This made him so unpopular among the unions that he did not stand for re-election.

Profiting by labor's discontent, shrewd, politically minded Abraham Ruef, a lawyer, who had graduated from the University of California, organized the Labor party. His candidate was tall, black-haired Eugene E. Schmitz, member of the Musicians' Union and leader of the Columbia Theatre orchestra.

Older distrusted the oversmart, ambitious Ruef. Neither the boss nor the mayor-elect had ever worked manually, and yet they represented labor. He sent word to Schmitz that he would like to see him succeed as mayor. He might become governor, and perhaps United States senator, but he must not be dominated by Ruef.

Schmitz thanked Older for his message, but said that he and Ruef would stand together. Having long observed the machinations of bosses, Older soon said he could "smell graft" in Schmitz' administration. It was in Chinatown, in the underworld, everywhere. Older began attacking Schmitz and Ruef in the *Bulletin*.

Chinatown, Older thought, had flagrant graft. Certainly police were being bribed. With Ed Bowes (later Major Bowes of the radio) Older began an investigation. Formerly a member of the Grand Jury, Bowes was honest and daring. He joined Older eagerly in trying to prove that the Chinatown police were receiving money. If caught, they would probably give evidence against the city administration.

At Older's suggestion, Bowes kidnaped Chan Cheung, the Chinese gamblers' leader, and held him prisoner at the Occidental Hotel for two days. Older and Bowes took him before a group of friends, pretending that they were the Grand Jury, and tried to force him to confess to which of the police he had paid money. Opium was taken from the Chinese but he would not "squeal."

Failing in the Chinatown investigation, Older centered his fight on a brothel at 625 Jackson Street. Two of the inmates were on the verge of revealing to whom they had paid bribes; then, not daring to create political enemies, they were silent. Although unable to prove his suspicions, Older blared them daily in the *Bulletin* and fought Schmitz' second election by bringing about the nomination of attorney John Partridge on the Democratic ticket. Later he said that anyone not deaf, dumb, and blind should have known that Schmitz would be re-elected, but he had faith that decency would triumph. The Schmitz-Ruef machine was returned to power, and on election night the rejoicing rockets of their partisans parading the streets set on fire the Chronicle Building tower.

Older had a tip that French restaurants were paying Ruef for licenses but he could not establish it in court. He decided that people did not believe corruption existed in the city government and he must prove it. He recalled that Francis J. Heney in a pre-election speech at Mechanics' Pavilion had said, "If the people want me to come back to put Abe Ruef in the penitentiary, I'll come."

At that time Heney was working for the United States government, prosecuting Oregon land fraud cases. Although Older had never met Heney, he knew his reputation and believed that he would be the man for the job. He set out for Washington to see Heney. The prosecutor agreed to come to San Francisco if he could bring with him William J. Burns and his corps of detectives. On the following day Older saw President Theodore Roosevelt, who promised to do all in his power to help after Heney and Burns completed their Oregon work. Burns said that about $100,000 would be required for the investigation. Brashly, Older promised to raise it.

Back in San Francisco he told his plan to Phelan, who was enthusiastic and said, "I will contribute." Older did not know Rudolph Spreckels at the time, but Mrs. Spreckels' sister, Frances Jolliffe, was the *Bulletin's* drama editor. She told him that Rudolph was indignant about local conditions and she thought he would help. Rudolph Spreckels was a blue-eyed, thirty-five-year-old millionaire with the bearing of a Prussian officer. When Older revealed the plan, Spreckels said, "I'll back this to the limit, but the investigation must lead to the railroad which has corrupted California politics."

Three weeks before the great Fire, Heney came from Washington and lunched with Phelan, Spreckels, and Older at the University Club. The graft prosecution was under way when downtown San Francisco was destroyed by fire. The half-billion dollar blaze could not stop the four determined men.

Heney was back in San Francisco within a month. In Rudolph

Spreckels's board office on the ruins of his bank, surrounded by acres of burned and tangled girders, the organizers went on with their plan. After collecting about $12,000, Spreckels asked Heney what his fee would be. "Nothing. I was born and raised in San Francisco. I have a little money. I'll put my services against your money."

The graft prosecution forces established themselves in a red house on Franklin Street. With Heney were two excellent lawyers, Joseph J. Dwyer and Charles W. Cobb, employed by Spreckels. Burns had several detectives.

At the time of Schmitz's second election Ruef made the error of naming as district attorney the former educator William Langdon, who appointed Heney deputy district attorney. Brazenly Ruef removed Langdon and seized the office himself. The city was stunned. It was for Judge Graham to decide which should be recognized, Langdon or Ruef.

Ironically, after the fire Graham held court in the synagogue at the corner of California and Webster Streets. Outside the courtroom a wrathful, threatening crowd assembled and the judge recognized Langdon. "PUT RUEF AND SCHMITZ IN JAIL!" thundered the *Bulletin*, in its largest type. "Go ahead, investigate!" taunted Ruef.

For six years Older had been investigating, and within several months three supervisors were trapped into admitting they had received bribes for their votes. Their confessions led to those of fourteen others, involving Ruef and Schmitz, as well as leaders of the bar and of San Francisco financial and industrial life. Bonds were fixed for each defendant at $2,000.

After being brought a prisoner to the Little St. Francis in Union Square, Ruef went into hiding at the Trocadero roadhouse. He was placed under guard, and refused to confess. Rabbis urged him to unseal his lips, but he was obdurate. Under heavy guard, the fallen boss was taken to see his dying mother, who implored, "Oh, Abraham—" The boss wept: "I'll do whatever you want me to."

Ruef confessed to receiving $200,000. He gave $50,000 to Schmitz, $50,000 to Supervisor James G. Gallagher, "Big Jim," for the supervisors, retaining the remainder for himself. Gallagher also received $160,000 corporation money to be distributed among members of the board. Other sums were paid directly to supervisors by corporation representatives, most important being Patrick Calhoun, president of the United Railways, who had broken the strike on his street railway line shortly after the Fire.

On the witness stand, French restaurateurs and dance-hall proprietors told of tribute levied. Pressmen came from New York and London. San Francisco had a sensation almost as great as the recent Earthquake and Fire. Mayor Schmitz, who had gone to Europe, hurriedly returned. Ruef went to meet him in Nevada. Police accompanied him with warrants for the mayor's arrest.

After Ruef's confession Mayor Schmitz was charged with and found guilty of having received a bribe from a French restaurateur and was sentenced to serve five years in the penitentiary. On the night of June 13, 1907, San Francisco's mayor ate dinner from a tin can in the county jail. "I will run again."

This he never did, but he escaped prison only because of a technical error—the indictment failed to specify that he was mayor of San Francisco when he accepted the bribe. San Francisco was without a mayor. Lawyer-poet Dr. Edward Robeson Taylor, author of the "City Charter," dean of Hastings Law College and acting president of Cooper Medical College, was selected.

At Ruef's first trial the jury disagreed. Word came to District Attorney Langdon that members of the jury panel had been bribed. An ex-convict named Haas boasted to his mistress that he was to have several thousand dollars for voting "not guilty." Heney exposed Haas's prison past and was shot down by him in the courtroom. "This is terrible," said Ruef, "the worst thing that could have happened to me." Haas committed suicide. Hiram W. Johnson was engaged to take Heney's place.

Heney was apparently dying. In Greenland Rink that night a mass meeting was presided over by Mayor Taylor. Ex-Mayor Phelan, Rudolph Spreckels and District Attorney Langdon spoke. Later a lynch mob stretched from corner to corner on Market Street before the *Bulletin* office. Pale and trembling, Hiram W. Johnson said, "I'm ready for anything that is right. If it's the rope, I'm ready for that." Johnson and Matt I. Sullivan were employed to take Heney's place. Closing his argument in his organlike voice, Johnson called each juror by name. "You dare not acquit this man!" He knew that the jury was "fixed."

Day and night the jury was out. About six o'clock of the second day Heney, who had recovered from two operations, telephoned that he was coming into the courtroom to pay his respects to Judge William P. Lawlor. Dark, menacing, six-foot-two Older entered with limping Assistant District Attorney Heney. The jury heard the shout of hundreds of voices, and when they filed in they voted "Guilty!"

Emotion always governed Older's conduct and when he heard Ruef sentenced by Judge Lawlor to serve fourteen years in the penitentiary, and saw Ruef shed tears, his triumph lost its sweetness. Later he aroused much criticism among his friends by advocating Ruef's parole.

At first substantial citizens applauded the graft prosecution, but Patrick Calhoun, an attractive man with high intelligence and distinction, had made himself a hero after the Fire by breaking the strike and keeping streetcars running. The trial of Calhoun and his friends aroused hostility in the upper strata of society. Spreckels, Phelan, Heney, Older, and Burns were sustained by the spirit of James King of William, founder of the *Bulletin*, who had been shot down in 1856 while trying to keep law and order in San Francisco.

Older was warned that men were being hired to kill him at his streetcar bathhouse at the ocean beach where he and I went daily to dine. Letters inked in red told him to keep away from the beach, and so when he went to the ocean he took with him a special policeman. Later he learned that the officer saved their lives because a dynamite fuse was found under the streetcar cabana. The man who placed it there confessed. The house of Supervisor Gallagher, chief prosecution witness, was blown up. Two Greek agents of the dynamiters were sent to San Quentin, but the chief culprit became a fugitive.

The graft prosecution group was determined to convict the "higher-ups" represented by Calhoun. "Bad for business," said the critics. "Calhoun saved the city by breaking the strike." President Theodore Roosevelt, however, wrote: "It is a dreadful thing to see men high in state politics, high in finance, high in social life of the rich and fashionable, united to stifle prosecution of offenders against civic integrity, if these offenders happen to be their friends and associates."

Threats poured in upon Older by telephone and letter, and while conferring with Heney's partner, Charles W. Cobb, in their office, the telephone rang, calling for the editor. "If you'll come down to the Savoy Hotel, I'll give you important information about Calhoun," said a strange voice. "Why not come here?" "I'm being watched. I don't dare." "I'll be right over." At the door Older turned back, "This may be a trap. If I'm not back in twenty minutes, let Spreckels know."

On his way to the Savoy Hotel, a car swung to the curb beside Older. Two men leaped out. "Warrant for your arrest." "On what ground?" "Libel in Los Angeles." After studying the warrant, Older said, "Take me to Judge Cook's chambers." As he entered the car, the man seated at his side searched him. Older always went unarmed. "This is not the way to Judge Cook's chamber." "You're not going there." A gun was pressed against his side. "Don't try to escape." Older recognized Calhoun's attorney and a detective in the car following him. His inevitable cigar lighted, Older said, "This isn't very sporting of Calhoun. He's dealing cards from under the table."

Down the Peninsula went the car, and at Redwood City Older was thrust aboard a southbound train. The gunmen and Calhoun's attorney went with him. In the compartment Older said to the gunmen, "My wife will think I'm dead. If only I could get word to her." "Write the telegram. I'll send it." Older wrote a telegram but it was never sent.

Chance placed on the train a young attorney who recognized Older and heard one gunman whisper to his companion, "We'd better take him off the train and run him through the mountains." The attorney had never met Older, but he felt certain that the editor would be killed unless he gave the alarm. At Salinas he got off the train and put through a message to the *Morning Call*. "OLDER KIDNAPED!" was the next morning's headline.

By coincidence Older's friend, Franklin K. Lane, later secretary of the interior, was at Santa Barbara. Lane and editor Thomas Storke, later United States senator and University of California regent, formed a rescue party at the station by obtaining a writ of habeas corpus for Older and placing the entire train crew under arrest. Older was admitted to bail on the trumped-up libel charge.

The deputies who kidnaped him turned state's evidence, but the instigators of the crime were acquitted.

San Francisco was dragging itself up from the rubble of the Earthquake and Fire, and people were tired of the graft prosecution. Heney was defeated by Charles Fickert in the election of 1909. The new district attorney dismissed charges against Schmitz and Calhoun, although Ruef was in prison for taking Calhoun's bribe. The prosecution cost $213,391,050, given largely by Spreckels, some being raised by subscription.

Burns went east to become America's leading detective. Heney received nothing for his services but impaired hearing from Haas's bullet. When he ran for the United States Senate he was defeated, and while holding a judgeship in the Los Angeles Superior Court he died. Charles W. Cobb, Heney's partner, became assistant attorney general under President Taft. Langdon became a justice of the Supreme Court of California, and died in office. Rudolph Spreckels, who financed the graft prosecution, was offered the ambassadorship to Germany by Woodrow Wilson, but he had no interest in a political career and declined. In trying to aid his older brother, C. A. Spreckels, he crippled his finances and lived a quiet secluded life in his final years at Burlingame. In 1958 he was the last of the graft prosecution group to be taken by death.

Hiram W. Johnson rose to power when the Lincoln-Roosevelt League organized at Los Angeles by Chester A. Rowell, of the Fresno *Republican*, and Edward A. Dixon, of the Los Angeles *Express*, urged him to run for governor. In the *Bulletin* Older declared for his candidacy. "No," replied Johnson, "I'd get two votes, yours and the Boss's [Mrs. Johnson]."

Friends climbed three flights of stairs to Johnson's hillside dwelling on Green Street to beg him to run. "No," said he, "as a candidate for governor, people will hurl at me the one thing from which I can't defend myself, my paternal ancestor, Grove L. Johnson." Johnson's father, a brilliant lawyer and congressman, was subservient to the Southern Pacific Railroad. Father and son each abominated the other's political affiliations. After many pilgrimages of persuasion by Rowell, Dixon, Older and others, Johnson became a candidate.

Driven by his son, Hiram Johnson, Jr., 20,000 miles, Johnson

spoke from the car or in halls: "I'm going to kick the Southern
Pacific out of the Republican party, and out of the state government
of California." Elected by a margin of more than 20,000, he obtained
many reforms as California's greatest governor.

Johnson ran for vice-president on the Bull Moose ticket in 1912
with Theodore Roosevelt, four years later entering the United
States Senate.

By strange destiny he was turned back twice from the office of
president. Senator Philander Knox during the Republican Convention of 1920 said to Johnson, "I've been offered the Presidency on
condition that you run with me as vice-president." Johnson, a
liberal, could not see himself as the running mate of Knox, the
reactionary, and he declined. Had the ticket been Knox and Johnson, the Californian would have been president—Knox died before
the four years had expired. Harding was nominated in place of
Knox. He also urged Johnson to be his running mate. Harding was
not Johnson's kind of Republican. On Harding's death Calvin
Coolidge became president. Twice Johnson had turned his back on
high office.

As an isolationalist, Johnson led insurgent senators. When he
died in 1945 his body was brought back to San Francisco, where
his political career had begun as a fighter for the graft prosecution.
His body lay in state in the rotunda of the City Hall, covered by
the Stars and Stripes.

CHAPTER 10

Characters

ONE OF the pioneer San Francisco's unique individuals was the fighting filibuster, William Walker, called by Joaquin Miller the "gray-eyed man of destiny." Five feet tall and weighing 125 pounds, in ill-fitting clothes, with white eyebrows and lashes, tow hair and freckled face, he looked little like a military chieftain as he stalked Montgomery Street. His sharp newspaper pen attacked Judge Levi Parson of the District Court. The judge fined him, but Walker refused to pay and was sent to jail for contempt. His release on a writ of habeas corpus was cheered by the entire city.

Editing a newspaper was too tame for Walker. Inspired by Sam Houston of Texas, he planned to conquer part of Mexico. After many difficulties he and his band set out on the *Carolina*, October 28, 1853, for La Paz. They seized Lower California, captured the government, and proclaimed it a republic. Walker called an election, established himself as governor, and made officials of ten followers.

With less than a hundred men, Walker annexed the state of Sonora by proclamation. The Mexicans rose and drove out the filibusters.

Nicaraguan revolutionists, hearing about Walker's adventures, summoned him to their country. Quickly he assembled a small army, each man armed with two large Colt revolvers and a bowie knife. This company stole away from San Francisco to travel 2,700 miles to a hostile port.

"The Savior from the North" was placed in command of a large force of Nicaraguan troops. His army increased, Walker ordered an election and was chosen president of Nicaragua. He adopted the religion of the country. Dictator Walker seized $20,000 worth of nuggets being shipped through the country from San Francisco.

87

His power was lost, however, when he established a degrading slavery in his adopted country. A new government displaced his and Walker surrendered to the United States navy, May 1, 1857.

Once more the fighting Tennessean dreamed of conquering an empire. Three years later he sailed from New Orleans for Honduras on the steamer *Clifton*. There he was shot on September 12, 1860. His troubled life is marked by a simple marble slab at Trujillo, Honduras.

Several of San Francisco's unique individuals were philanthropists. In the M. H. de Young Memorial Museum is the portrait of Lily Hitchcock Coit in a red gown, white-plumed black hat, on her breast the figure 5, standing for the old fire company, Knickerbocker No. 5, to which she belonged. As a child she lived with her parents, Dr. and Mrs. Charles M. Hitchcock, at the Oriental Hotel near the fire station and made a practice of running to every fire with the engine. She was made an honorary member of the company. Once, in a bridesmaid's gown, she rushed away from a wedding at the clang of the gong. She always appeared at the company's birthday banquets wearing a red fire shirt, black silk skirt, and black helmet. On parade days she was either atop the beflowered engine or waving a red handkerchief to the marching laddies from her window.

After being engaged many times, suddenly, at twenty-five, she married Benjamin Howard Coit, chairman of the Stock Exchange. She shocked the neighbors in Napa County where the Coits had a country home, by wearing short skirts on horseback. She rode like a cowboy, smoked, and played poker like a man. Dr. Hitchcock sent his daughter to Europe for aiding a Confederate to escape arrest. There she was presented to Empress Eugénie. In spite of Lily's eccentricities that led to divorce, Coit left his wife his fortune at his death. When the new City Hall was built in 1872, two of her photographs were placed in the cornerstone. After her death in July, 1929, her death notice read: "Elizabeth Wyche Coit, aged 87, wife of the late Howard Coit, cousin of the Nathaniel Wyche Hunter family of Palestine, Texas, and honorary member of Veteran Volunteer Fire Department No. 5." Day and night, No. 5 stood guard in the San Francisco funeral parlor where her body lay. Three of the four living volunteer firemen preceded the pallbearers to her grave.

AERIAL VIEW OF SAN FRANCISCO
San Francisco's famed Ferry Building is in the foreground.

CABLE CAR ON POWELL STREET

FISHERMAN'S WHARF

TETRAZZINI SINGING IN THE OPEN AIR, CHRISTMAS EVE, 1910

PALACE OF FINE ARTS

CHINATOWN—GRANT AVENUE

SCENE IN JAPANESE TEA GARDEN, GOLDEN GATE PARK

GOLDEN GATE BRIDGE

TRANSPORTATION DISPLAY AS SEEN FROM MUNI PIER

LOOKING EAST FROM RUSSIAN HILL
The San Francisco-Oakland Bay Bridge is in the background.

COIT TOWER AND TELEGRAPH HILL

FAIRMONT HOTEL ON NOB HILL

CITY HALL AND CIVIC CENTER

SAN FRANCISCO AND THE GREAT BAY BRIDGE

CANDLESTICK PARK

MRS. GEORGE HEARST

MRS. LELAND STANFORD

MRS. LILY HITCHCOCK COIT

MRS. ADOLPH B. SPRECKELS
Portrait by Sir John Lavery

California Palace of the Legion of Honor

LAND'S END

One-third of Mrs. Coit's estate was left to San Francisco's Board of Supervisors "for the purpose of adding to the beauty of said city, which I have always loved."

Because Mrs. Coit had wished to buy the top of Telegraph Hill, Arthur M. Brown was commissioned to build Coit Tower on the summit, 500 feet above sea level. There is an elevator, but pedestrians walk up the 245 winding steps, to enjoy not only the murals but the view of the bridges and the bay. At the dedication of Coit Tower, October 8, 1933, old engine No. 5 was brought from the de Young Museum, dragged up the hill, and placed in the parkway. On the engine lay Lily Hitchock Coit's black belt and helmet.

James Lick was another eccentric philanthropist. Legend said that he had loved a miller's daughter at his birthplace, Fredericksburg, Pennsylvania. Denied her hand by her father, the suitor replied that he would build a better mill, and left for South America. There as a cabinetmaker he accumulated the nucleus of a fortune amassed in San Francisco. Fulfilling his boyhood vow, he erected a handsome mahogany mill that still stands on Guadalupe Creek, near San Jose. His workmen lived in a spacious house nearby, dining on chicken and turkey, but he occupied a shack and ate meager fare. Lick had his own way of employing workers. He told several to plant trees upside down. All but one man disobeyed and placed the roots in the ground. One man, however, placed the roots in the air and the top in the ground. He was the one Lick employed—he obeyed orders.

In 1862 Lick built San Francisco's Lick House, but lived in the poorest room, wearing frayed garments. He would not permit his windows to be washed. With an income of $250,000 a year, he drove an old horse about the streets. Its harness was repaired with string.

When Lick's illegitimate son, John, appeared from the East, his father adopted him but quarreled with him, as he did with other associates. He planned erecting a giant statue of himself in Golden Gate Park but was dissuaded. Then he considered a mammoth observatory at Fourth and Market Streets. Scientists tactfully induced him to select a mountaintop. After changing his mind several times, he decided to rear the observatory on Mount Hamilton (4,209 feet), Santa Clara County, and have the most powerful telescope in the world. Under its dome he lies entombed.

Lick Observatory is a part of the University of California. Its astronomers made the first successful pictures of the Milky Way and comets. Here also were discovered the fifth, sixth, seventh and ninth moons of Jupiter. Lick astronomers also pioneered in spectroscope analysis and wave length of light. At the Observatory there is a priceless astronomical library and the second most powerful telescope in existence, which was begun in 1949 and has been in operation since 1959. It peers a billion light years into space. The Mount Hamilton telescope cost between two and three million dollars. (The world's most powerful telescope is at Palomar, Southern California.)

In Golden Gate Park stands a monument erected by Lick to Francis Scott Key, author of "The Star-Spangled Banner." His other benefactions were a $600,000 building to the Academy of Sciences; $500,000 to establish a School for Mechanical Arts, and many thousands for public baths, the Old Ladies' Home, and other institutions. His monument stands in front of San Francisco's old City Hall.

Dr. Henry D. Cogswell was almost as eccentric as Lick. Born in a Connecticut poorhouse, he worked in a cotton mill at 50 cents a week and taught himself dentistry. He came to California in 1849 and became a millionaire in real estate speculation. Cogswell Polytechnic School, founded by him, is a manual training school for boys. A teetotaler, the doctor distributed twenty drinking fountains to keep people from consuming liquor. Each fountain was topped by a life-size bust of Dr. Cogswell, or some celebrated nondrinker like Benjamin Franklin. Many fountains were never set up, and all have been removed. San Francisco still retains, in Washington Square, an interesting monument which was placed there by the California Historical Society and donated by Dr. Cogswell. It contains documents of the California Historical Society which were placed in the sealed crypt, not to be opened until 1975.

On New Year's Eve, 1894, young Bostonian Gelett Burgess, an instructor of mechanical drawing at the University of California, toppled a cast-iron statue of Dr. Cogswell onto the Market Street cobblestones. His career at the university ended, but his little house on Hyde Street, the "Peanut Shell," continued to be filled with artists and writers. It was the headquarters of *The Lark* which Burgess edited with Bruce Porter, a native San Franciscan who was a gifted landscape architect. Fame came to *The Lark* with Burgess's verse:

> I never saw a Purple Cow,
> I never hope to see one;
> But I can tell you anyhow
> I'd rather see than be one!

Ernest Peixotto, just back from Paris, did the cover. *The Lark*, 5 by 7 inches, sold for 5 cents. *Fin de siècle*, it was called. London and New York thought it the most unusual journal that had appeared since *The Chap Book*. As *The Lark* continued its song, the price was increased to 10 cents. Additions to the staff were made: Yoni Noguchi, Porter Garnett, Florence Lundborg, Morgan Shepherd, Herbert Van Black, Reginald Rix, Willis Polk, and Juliet Wilbur Tompkins. "Faddists," these artists and writers were called, but others said, "They appeal to the Greek within us." Burgess coined the expressions "goop" and "bromide." The blithe *Lark* sang two years, but before its second birthday its delightful nonsense was silenced. Its last song was called "The Epi-Lark" shortly before the *Lark* expired. Gelett Burgess wrote as sequel to his famous quatrain:

> Ah, Yes! I Wrote the "Purple Cow"—
> I'm Sorry now, I Wrote it!
> But I can Tell you Anyhow,
> I'll Kill you if you Quote it!

Burgess continued to write brilliantly through a long lifetime until his death at Carmel in 1951.

San Francisco's best-known fountain was given by the lovely eccentric Lotta Crabtree because the city was the first metropolis to acclaim her. Charlotte Mignon Crabtree was discovered and trained at Grass Valley by Lola Montez in the early fifties. Her clogs, jigs, banjo playing, and songs bewitched San Francisco. California's first child prodigy long played Little Nell and the Marchioness in Dickens's *Old Curiosity Shop*, and also *Under Two Flags*. After acquiring $4 million, she lived like a hermit in a Boston hotel, hoarding her fortune.

Traffic was blocked one hour at Third and Market Streets on September 9, 1875, when Lotta's gift of the iron-carved fountain,

24 feet tall, was presented to the city, and received by Mayor James Otis. Lotta's aunt, Mrs. Vernon, took the first drink from one of the cups. At her death, Lotta bequeathed $2 million to a Fund for Veterans of World War I. She also left money to finance the battle against vivisection. The remainder was devoted to relief funds for active students and discharged prisoners.

Lotta would have been pleased to behold the great crowd on Christmas Eve, 1910, listening to peerless Luisa Tetrazzini, who sang before the fountain in appreciation of the first American city to welcome her after being discovered by William H. ("Doc") Leahy, of the Tivoli, in Mexico City, where she was with a stranded opera company.

This scene was re-created Christmas Eve, 1960, when Olga Chronis, proclaimed by critics as a "new great voice," sang "Auld Lang Syne" and "The Last Rose of Summer" and other songs with which Tetrazzini charmed a quarter of a million listeners fifty years previously. Accompanying Miss Chronis at this memorial concert was the San Francisco Boys' Chorus in white robes with red bows. All stood on a platform decked with flags just as the original platform was in 1910. Miss Chronis wore a costume-dress with hat and feather boa such as Tetrazzini wore. Mayor George Christopher presented her with flowers as Mayor P. H. McCarthy gave them to Tetrazzini in 1910.

Joseph A. Norton was born in Scotland and made a fortune in grain speculation, trying to corner rice. He bought a large cargo from Macondray and Company but could not meet his contract. His mania became manifest when he offered to compromise by marrying Mr. Macondray's daughter and investing her with the title of empress. He declared himself Norton I, Emperor of California and Protector of Mexico, *Dei gratia*. Possessed of imaginary millions, Norton became San Francisco's only royal philanthropist.

The city adopted him with his royal regalia of an army uniform, military cap, or hat, from which extended waving cock plumes, a sword dangling from his belt. He always carried a cane or an umbrella. When the Emperor's uniform was overshabby, he ordered the supervisors to supply him with another. They obeyed their emperor and he bestowed upon each a patent of nobility. The Emperor sent telegrams to his "dear cousins," Queen Victoria, the Czar of Russia, and the Emperor of China. To Adelaide Neilson, the world's most beautiful woman, he telegraphed: "I love you. I will make you Empress, Norton I. Please let me hear from you." He "brought about" the peace at the close of the Franco-Prussian War. During the Civil War messages from him were received by Lincoln, Davis, Grant, and Lee. The Emperor abolished both Democratic and Republican parties in the interests of peace. "They engender dissension." "Bridge the bay by way of Yerba Buena Island," he commanded. "Fill in Yerba Buena shoals!" Both orders have since been carried out despite long protests from engineers that the bay could not be bridged.

Always with the Emperor were his two dogs, Bummer and Lazarus, who, unleashed and unmuzzled, were allowed the freedom of the city. Lazarus, a humble nondescript, was run over by a fire engine, and Bummer, with a big Newfoundland head, died after being kicked by a drunken hoodlum. The man was arrested and fined. Lazarus had a public funeral, with Norton I leading the procession. For many years both dogs, stuffed and preserved, were at the de Young Museum. On January 8, 1880, His Royal Highness sank to the sidewalk, in front of Old St. Mary's Church, and died in a Sacramento Street room, leaving an estate of a $2.50 gold piece, a one-franc piece, and 93,300 shares of worthless mining stock.

Thousands attended his funeral at Lockhart and Porter's, 16 O'Farrell Street. Before his interment at Masonic Cemetery, an autopsy showed that the Emperor's brain was heavier than average.

Fifty-four years later the Emperor Norton Memorial Association was formed, with Ernest Wiltsee, president, and Frederick S. Moody, treasurer. They raised money to buy a granite monument engraved: "Emperor Norton I, Emperor of the United States and Protector of Mexico."

Then the Emperor was removed to Woodlawn, where in 1934 burial rites were performed for the second time. John McLaren, representing Mayor Rossi, and civic leaders laid wreaths on the Emperor's last grave. The Rev. John Collins said the final prayer. A salute was fired by an honor guard from the Presidio.

During the seventies and eighties, Mrs. Robert Johnson lived in a large house at O'Farrell and Jones Streets, where she kept 350 cats, the city's largest pet collection. Forty-two of her cats are memorialized in Carl Kahler's portrait, "My Wife's Lovers," the world's most notable cat painting. After her husband's death, Mrs.

Johnson moved to Sonoma, built a "castle" and lived there with her adopted daughter, Rosalind, and the cats. At Sonoma she reduced their number to 300. The third floor of the castle belonged to her pets. Some were housed in cages, but they also roamed the grounds and became a mixed breed. Before her death about fifty years ago, she is said to have disposed of some of her cats, but she left $5,000 to care for the survivors, and most of her fortune went to the Archbishop of San Francisco.

Mammy Pleasant was long a woman of mystery. A black woman from New Orleans, wearing a broad hat tied under her chin, a long shapeless dress, and a white kerchief around her neck, she looked like a voodoo priestess, but was known to be a procurer of women for rich men. San Franciscans were not surprised to learn that she supposedly financed Sarah Althea Hill's suit against Senator William Sharon, alleging that she was his contract wife. "Blackmail," Sharon termed it, but the public feasted on the story revealed in the courts. "Sharon's Rose," Sarah was called by many, but others thought she was his wife. "The damndest lie," said Sharon. Sarah Althea Hill had been his mistress at $500 a month—nothing more.

Avidly the public read of the wooing of blonde young Sarah by the sixty-two-year-old financier who recited Shakespeare to her and sang "Auld Lang Syne." She said he installed her at the Grand Hotel, took her to the Belmont mansion, inviting her to the wedding of his daughter, Flora, and Sir Thomas Hesketh, finally making with her a secret marriage contract.

Mammy Pleasant was always at Sarah Althea's side during the trial. Before the trial was over ex-Justice Terry of Vigilante fame joined her legal force. Judge J. M. Sullivan decided Sarah Althea was Sharon's wife. "I'll sink every cent in the bay before I'll give it to that woman." Sharon declared she forged the alleged marriage contract over his signature. Meanwhile Mrs. Terry died at Stockton and Terry, sixty-two, married Sarah Althea.

Before the case was decided Sharon died. His executor and son-in-law, Senator Francis Newlands, transferred his residence to Nevada, where the case was tried in the Circuit Court, with Justice Stephen J. Field presiding.

"Judge Field, we hear you're being bought," shouted Sarah Althea in court. "How much are you being paid by the Sharon people?" "Marshal, put that woman out," commanded Field. "Don't touch her," shouted Terry, "she is my wife." It was said that Terry drew a dirk. When ordered out of the courtroom Sarah Althea screamed wildly. Both she and Terry were sentenced to the Alameda County jail. "When I get out of jail I'll horsewhip you," Terry told Field. A friend warned, "If you do, he'll resent it." "If he does, I'll kill him!"

When Judge Field returned to California six months later he was accompanied by a guard. Field and Terry met in the hotel dining room at Lathrop. Terry was unarmed, but he rose from the table, and bent over Field, slapping his face on both right and left cheeks. In a flash, Field's bodyguard, Deputy United States Marshal David Nagle, fired twice at Terry, who sank to the floor, shot through the heart. Nagle was tried for murder, but the court said he only did his duty.

Sarah Althea was shortly found wandering in San Francisco streets, in evening dress, asking plaintively, "Where is Mammy Pleasant?" A strange mad light was in her eyes and for fifty years she was in the Stockton Mental Hospital, calling herself the "Queen of Hawaii" or the wife of General Grant. She distributed $25,000 checks among the attendants. San Francisco forgot that she was alive until she was discovered still babbling of her "wonderful husbands," by Evelyn Wells of the *Call-Bulletin*. She is buried in the Stockton cemetery beside David S. Terry and his devoted first wife, Cornelia.

Mammy Pleasant's most admirable effort was her attempt to abolish slavery. She lived to be ninety-two, but in spite of all her schemes she died penniless, asking that her tombstone carry this epitaph: "She was a friend of John Brown."

San Francisco's most sensational woman of the upper class was Amy Crocker-Ashe-Gillig-Gouraud-Miskinoff-Galatzine, called by her contemporary, the late J. Downey Harvey, "California's most beautiful woman." Even in the mid-Victorian eighties she tossed husbands away like cast-off slippers. Born the pampered daughter of the conservative E. B. Crockers of Sacramento, she wept when her parents would not buy her Barnum's elephant, Jumbo. At age ninety-four Mrs. Reginald Knight Smith recalled that when she was a little flower girl at her uncle Henry T. Scott's wedding at Sacramento, Amy shocked the wedding party with a cigarette, in days when only harlots smoked.

Amy floated between Sacramento and San Francisco, where she

visited her cousins, the Charles Crocker children. She became "Aimée," At seventeen she was proposed to by two men, Porter Ashe and Harry Gillig. "I like you both. Fight for me."

Being friends, the men didn't fight. Some said that they shook dice, others that they played cards—Ashe, a nephew of Admiral Farragut, won. The marriage lasted less than a year, and a daughter was born. Harry Gillig, taking his place as husband number two, lasted longer. Third husband, song writer Jackson Gouraud, died. Between husbands, admirers came and went, so that Sunday supplement editors never found news dull. Aimée could always supply a headline.

One of her spectacular exploits was setting out alone on a 70-foot schooner, *Tropic Star,* with a crew of ten men and a Chinese cook, to visit King Kalakaua, who had admired her in London. With five royal guards, the King received her as if she were a queen. Kalakaua called her "Bliss of Heaven," and gave her an island with 300 subjects. Occasionally, she dropped in among her subjects to dance the hula. In her book, *And I'd Do It Again,* written shortly before her death, she told how she scandalized missionaries by dressing like a dancing girl. Unable to convert natives so long as Aimée was present, they commanded her to leave the islands. Kalakaua had his revenge. When he gave a farewell ball for Aimée he ordered the missionaries to attend. She danced the hula for them, to royal applause.

After leaving Hawaii Aimée cruised through the South Seas and was captured by Borneo savages. A rajah died of apoplexy while wooing her. She said that men and her passion for the East controlled her life. The meaning of existence was found by her in the "sunshine of that agonizing, pulsating, suffering, beautiful country, India," where she would have liked to end her days.

Her life, however, was spent between New York and Europe. She became Princess Miskinoff, but the prince was cast off, like the other husbands. Twenty-five-year-old Prince Alexandre Galatzine of Lithuania married the aging Aimée, and fared no better than his predecessors. In her farewell to life, *And I'd Do It Again,* she said that for three years she had only one thought, one heartbeat, and that was for novelist Edgar Saltus.

Aimée loved not only men but snakes. A Hindu woman, Princess Mara, she said, taught her to love snakes. Her most famous party was given for H. H. Kaa, Maharajah of Amber, with fifty guests. Aimée received them wearing a green evening gown, with jade and emerald ornaments and "the Maharajah of Amber, "a boa constrictor, wrapped around her—another Sunday supplement sensation.

In *And I'd Do It Again,* she said she was glad she had lived and would enjoy even making her mistakes again. Death, her last lover, took Aimée Crocker on February 7, 1941, at the Savoy-Plaza Hotel, in New York City.

CHAPTER 11

Stage-Struck San Francisco

SAN FRANCISCO was stage-struck from pioneer days. Thomas Maguire, "Napoleon of theatrical managers," supplied forty-niners with entertainment when under his management there appeared the great Booth, Edwin Forrest, John McCullough, Ellen Tree, Lotta Crabtree, Madame Ristori, and Mrs. John Wood. The last was a charmer, like her great-granddaughters, Constance and Joan Bennett, of screen, radio, and television. Adah Isaacs Menken, the glamour girl of Civil War days, so dazzled the critics that they flung their hearts at her with flamboyant adjectives. La Menken's alluring face and voluptuous curves caused one to write, "Let a pure youth witness Mazeppa, and he is no longer pure." (She was less naked, however, than thousands of women today in shopping centers.) Her admirers tried to leap upon the stage when her beautiful body, strapped to a trained circus horse, was carried away from their gaze, as it dashed up the runway. Adah smoked cigarettes and cigars, rode astride, visited saloons, and gambled, declaring that a clever woman was rarely good. After a wild love affair with poet Joaquin Miller she married prizefighter Heenan—briefly. She lay on a tawny rug before her fireplace, swathed in golden silk, recounting to admirers her disappointments in love. She assured Bret Harte and Joaquin Miller that she wished to leave the theater and write verse. Instead, the alluring pagan acquired a fourth husband, Captain James Paul Bartlett. During the last ten years of her thirty-three years of life she continued to attract men like Swinburne, who wrote of her, "Lo, This Is She, Who Was The World's Delight." When she died in Paris, Alexandre Dumas, one of her lovers, commented sadly, "Poor girl, why was she not her own friend?"

Maguire not only brought out La Menken, but he dared produce

East Lynne and *Camille,* both considered "shocking." Tights were first seen on the San Francisco stage when Maguire introduced a meaty blonde chorus in *The Black Crook.* Until then tights had been worn only by performers from the Barbary Coast.

Maguire and E. J. Baldwin, the millionaire mining man and horse-trader whose fortune later produced the Santa Anita race track, were partners in the Baldwin Hotel Theatre. Maguire owned the land and Baldwin the building. Both were proud of the $6,000 drop curtain, the $1,600 crystal chandelier, and the frescoed walls. When the partners quarreled, stage manager David Belasco was ambassador for peace.

Spectacular Maguire's San Francisco career was shortened after he produced the *Passion Play* by Salmi Morse, who had spent twenty years writing it, even going to the Holy Land for research. Maguire wept when Morse read the play aloud. He billed it for production at the Grand Opera House, with Belasco as stage manager. James O'Neill, father of Eugene O'Neill, played the Christus. During rehearsals he forswore tobacco and liquor, while Belasco, Bible in hand, murmured that he might enter a monastery. After this Belasco wore the clerical collar until his death. Lewis Morrison of the cast (grandfather of Constance and Joan Bennett) strove to be as devout as O'Neill and Belasco. Belasco assembled 100 nursing mothers for the "Massacre of the Innocents" scene and also engaged a flock of sheep. Actors who used a coarse word during rehearsal were dismissed. The super-production night came with 200 singers, 400 men, women, and infants.

The curtain rose. On walked Mary and Joseph, followed by the sheep. When Jesus appeared wearing a halo, some of the audience knelt, and when he was dragged before Pontius Pilate, others wept or fainted. The producers gloated over their "smash hit"—until the papers appeared. "Fearful impiety," Bishop Kip called it. Dr. Smith of the Tabernacle invoked the thunders of Sinai to destroy the Grand Opera House. Jews and Christians were equally horrified. The *Argonaut* jeered:

> Men's wrath at James they level,
> Because while looking like the Lord
> He's acting like the Devil.

Only Archbishop Alemany held his peace.

San Franciscans had tolerated the *Black Crook* girls in tights, wicked *East Lynne* and *Camille*, but the *Passion Play*, although reverently produced, they called irreligious. The supervisors passed an ordinance against "impersonation of any scriptural character upon any stage or any theater." Maguire closed the Grand Opera House—and reopened it eight days later.

Police descended upon the *Passion Play*, and dragged O'Neill into court still in the costume of the Christus. O'Neill pleaded "Not Guilty," paid $50 for violating the new impersonation ordinance and $5 for each of his fellow defendants. This ordinance was not repealed until 1938.

Back to his bread-winning Monte Cristo went James O'Neill, who as Edmund Dantes continued to thrill audiences by splashing up out of the sea, crying "The World is Mine!" Six thousand times he shouted the words before he ended up in vaudeville.

The *Passion Play* was Maguire's last great gesture in San Francisco. Later he tried to produce plays, but his funds were so limited that he was reduced to paying actors "six-bits for breakfast." Back in New York, he was cared for by other actors. After the New York failure of the spectacular *Passion Play*, author Salmi Morse was found drowned in the Harlem River.

David Belasco, schooled by Maguire, was San Francisco's first theatrical genius. He was born in 1853 in a basement at Third and Howard Streets, his parents, the Humphrey Belascos, being English Jews. At thirteen he wrote his first play, *Jim Black, or, The Regulator's Revenge*. Pawning a medal won at Lincoln Grammar School to obtain food for the family, washing windows, sweeping floors, reciting for a few coins "The Maniac" and "Curfew Must Not Ring Tonight" in saloons—from this he developed into America's greatest showman. For Maguire he doctored Boucicault's *The Octoroon*, also William DeMille's *A Woman of the People*. In order to brighten *Not Guilty* he introduced a battle scene, with chorus from *Carmen*. Belasco used realistic stage effects, and James O'Neill was supposed to fall nine feet from a ladder, but only a dummy fell. Rose Coghlan, however, was actually drenched during a water fight with buckets of suds.

In 1879 San Francisco gave Belasco a benefit netting $3,000. He and James Herne went east, taking with them *Chums* which later appeared on the stage as *Hearts of Oak*. In New York Belasco collaborated with William DeMille, father of Cecil and William Jr., and produced many successful plays.

Belasco never forgot his California background, and one of his perennial successes was *The Girl of the Golden West*, starring Blanche Bates, a San Francisco schoolteacher, who made her debut with the Frawley Stock Company. She retired briefly to marry Lieutenant Milton Davis, later General Davis, in charge at West Point. Army life was not for Blanche; she returned to the stage and played with great success in *Under Two Flags, Madame Butterfly, Hedda Gabler,* and *The Darling of the Gods.* On one of her trips to California, at Denver, Mrs. Bonfils (Annie Laurie) introduced George Creel, the writer, to the actress. Soon they were married and Mrs. Creel, retiring from the stage, spent the last years of her life in her native city.

Belasco also made a New York success for Nance O'Neil, another San Francisco girl. Born Gertrude Lamson, tall, slender, with reddish-blonde hair and an organlike voice, at seventeen she made her debut with the McKee Rankin Stock Company at the Alcazar Theatre. Nance's father, an auctioneer, was so puritanical that after his daughter appeared on the stage he rose in church asking the congregation to pray for her.

After starring with the Rankin Company for ten years in Australia, San Francisco beheld her for the first time, a star when she returned in *Leah, the Forsaken,* fleeing from the mob. "Another Ristori," cried the critics, and indeed she wore the stage jewels of Madame Ristori. She filled the California Theatre with *Camille,* and *Ingomar, Oliver Twist, Lady Macbeth,* but the demoded technique of Rankin limited her career. She came into her own after she left him and appeared under Belasco in New York as the old maid in *The Lily.* After becoming the wife of Alfred Hickman, she won great success in *The Passion Flower.*

Belasco also presented San Francisco's David Warfield to New York in his first starring vehicle, *The Auctioneer.* Later *The Music Master* repeated Warfield's success. Fay Bainter, also a Californian, became a Belasco star.

Belasco was responsible for presenting the plays of Richard Walton Tully, of the University of California, in 1901. A few years after Tully left college he offered to a small San Francisco audience a Spanish-Californian romance, *Juanita of San Juan.* Belasco read it in New York and acquired a half-interest, renaming it *The Rose of the Rancho*. *A Bird of Paradise*, with a Hawaiian background, followed *The Rose*, with San Francisco's Oliver Morosco. *A Bird of Paradise* outlived *The Rose of the Rancho*, not only on the stage but in the movies. He staged *Poor Little Rich Girl* by Eleanor Gates, then the wife of Tully. This play not only had a long run but the title became part of the language. Mary Pickford played the heroine in the movies.

Another native San Franciscan who was greatly helped by Belasco was Frank Mandel. After being educated at the University of California and Hastings Law School, Mandel went east, became a reporter, and tried to write plays, placing them in the hands of an agent. When he received a wire signed "David Belasco," and expressing an interest in one of his plays, he thought it a hoax and tore up the telegram. He later collaborated with Belasco in *Bosom Friends*.

During the 1920's Mandel wrote the books for such musical comedy hits as *The New Moon, The Desert Song,* and *No, No, Nanette*. Among the composers with whom he collaborated were Sigmund Romberg and Victor Herbert. He was also one of the producing team of Laurence Schwab and Mandel. Their first show, *Sweet Little Devil*, was followed by *The Firebrand, Captain Jinks,* and *Queen High*.

San Francisco's classical theatrical period was while Ralston, the magnificent, met the losses of the old California Theatre. After the body of the tycoon was found in the bay at North Beach, John McCullough canceled *La Tentacion* for that night. Subsequently he found that Ralston had forgotten to credit him with $75,000, but the actor had canceled checks as proof, and the executors adjusted the matter.

Adelaide Neilson, not yet twenty, came in 1874 and the audiences shouted "Divine!" "Incomparable!" Incomparable was her salary, $500 a night! When her season was extended, her manager demanded half the gross. San Francisco was "Neilsonized"—Neilson hats, bracelets, scarves, were shown. Local Romeos strove to embrace like her leading man, Lewis Morrison. When she returned six years later, her beauty faded, she canceled her first night because of illness, but *As You Like It* and *Romeo and Juliet* had standing room only. San Franciscans shed tears when her jewels were sold in Paris after her death in the following August. Neilson became the city's greatest theatrical legend.

After Ralston there was no one to cover the losses of the California Theatre. In 1888 Booth returned to the city where he first played Hamlet, and his three weeks of Shakespeare paid the debts of the theater marked for destruction. San Francisco never saw Booth again. Mrs. Kate McDonough, sister and heir of William O'Brien, of Comstock's Big Four, built the new California Theatre and Hotel on the old site. Lawrence Barrett as Othello and Booth as Iago opened the house, and first-night receipts were $10,000.

In the early seventies Clay M. Greene, another native San Franciscan, began his career as playwright. His *Struck Oil* was played several years, and *M'liss*, a dramatization of Bret Harte's story, was many times presented by Katie Mayhew and Annie Pixley, and has recently been produced. Before his death in San Francisco, Greene had twenty-five plays presented.

So eager were San Franciscans for entertainment that even during the panic of 1873, dentist Thomas Wade, with an $8,000 shoestring, began building the $200,000 Grand Opera House on Mission Street, third largest in the United States, with a seating capacity of 4,000. "The doctor can't pull enough teeth to finish that building," said his friends. Capitalists J. C. Flood, William O'Brien, and Jasper McDonald, however, took a mortgage of $197,878 on the property.

Bejeweled and bespangled, first nighters appeared for the opening with Annie Pixley in *Snowflake*. They "ohed" and "ahed" over the Romanesque and Italian front, the grand vestibule, with a crystal fountain showering cologne water from a myriad needle jets. In the 80-by-40-foot gallery above the entrance hall were paintings by local artists, as well as European masters. On the stage stood Thomas Newcomb, president of the Bohemian Club, reciting:

> Welcome, thrice welcome, all who are now here,
> In box, parquet, dress circle, upper tier.
> Welcome, fair dames and damsels, welcome too,
> Ye gods, who from the topmost gallery lean.
> . . . .
> Welcome to all, on this opening night,
> And may the "Snowflake" fill you with delight.

Newcomb retired to permit the Fabbri Opera troupe to group around the American flag and sing "The Star-Spangled Banner."

After *Snowflake* the Grand Opera House was always half empty. Not even James O'Neill could fill it. Nor could Clara Morris, nor the Californian, Eleanor Calhoun, who made her debut as Juliet. Only a wrestling match between William Muldoon and Donald Vinie showed a profit.

World-famous Adelina Patti changed everything when she arrived with Her Majesty's Opera Company, managed by Colonel J. H. Mapleson. People stood in line all night waiting for the box office to open. Fifty-dollar bonuses were given for choice seats, but San Franciscans felt rewarded when Patti sang *Lucia*.

This idyl over, nothing could lift the opera house from the red until a benefit was given on May 23, 1884, for James W. Marshall, discoverer of California's gold. Bohemian Club's George T. Bromley introduced Marshall, and Nellie Holbrook, mother of actor Holbrook Blinn, recited. The venerable Marshall, who had uncovered the gold that built the city, stood on the stage as a suppliant. Later the legislature granted him a pension and he returned to his cabin at Coloma, where he died in the following year. On a high hill over the Coloma Valley stands an impressive monument, a figure of Marshall, looking down on another figure of himself at the point of discovery.

Only 50-cent thrillers filled the opera house until Patti returned with Emma Nevada (Wixom). The new singer, California's first prima donna, was born Alpha and was a Mills College graduate. Reared in Nevada, she took the name of that state. When Emma Nevada appeared in *La Sonnambula*, she was showered with roses. Six times she was recalled, but when she attempted to sing "Home, Sweet Home," her voice failed and she fled from the stage in tears.

Patti came to San Francisco again and again. She demanded $5,000 in gold for each performance before stepping on the stage, and San Franciscans willingly paid $2–$7 a seat. There was only one Patti! They crowded her "farewells" for thirty years, but she was so greedy that managers lost on her engagements. The last time she tripped lightly onto the Grand Opera House stage was in 1894, to sing "Home, Sweet Home" and "The Last Rose of Summer." Forty years she had reigned as the world's greatest prima

donna, and to the last she had charm that none other has ever
equaled.

Frank Mayo in *Davy Crockett* drew almost as well as Patti and
was far less expensive. When Sarah Bernhardt came in 1891, the
great building could hardly hold the audience. Nine-tenths of those
who fought to enter knew no French, but they fell under the spell of
the tall, svelte Sarah with honey-colored hair, as La Tosca, Jeanne
d'Arc, and Cleopatra.

San Francisco's own William A. Brady, a graduate of the Mission's 10–20–30–cent theaters, repeated his New York success,
thrilling the audience with Boucicault's *After Dark.* Throngs also
attended the supercolossal *Uncle Tom's Cabin* with two Topsies,
two Marks, two educated donkeys, and eight ferocious bloodhounds.

When Henry Irving and Ellen Terry came in 1894, in *The Bells,
The Merchant of Venice, The Vicar of Wakefield,* and *Becket,*
they drew almost as great a crowd as the Topsies. Praise for Irving
was sometimes qualified, but Ellen Terry's arch humor and woman-
liness bewitched audiences. At San Francisco they had the largest
box-office returns they ever received.

Morosco, a former circus man, showed theatrical genius when
he remodeled the opera house, to produce ten 50-cent melodramas.
The great building was often so crowded that he was arrested for
seating people in the aisles. He went in for realism—an express
train running sixty miles an hour, a real steamship in a wreck, real
flames, real horses dashing across the stage. Theodore Roberts, a
tall, striking San Franciscan, afterward popular on the screen, was
one of his actors.

Society went to see what amused thousands in *Ten Nights in a
Bar-room, The Great Diamond Robbery,* and *The Dark Street.* They
remained to enjoy spectacles employing spark-sputtering railroad
trains, buzz saws and planes. Supervirtues and supervillainies were
more fun than Patti. Lucille LaVerne, Landers Stevens, William A.
Brady, and Fred Butler suffered fire, flood, and shipwreck to make
Morosco's large fortune.

Culture then attracted the manager, and he imported Melba,
Gadski, and Zelie de Lussan. Torrid Zelie crowded the aisles with
her Carmen, which had as great success as Melba's Marguerite.

Morosco was unerring in his sense of popular taste. He produced comic opera in English at from 15 cents to 75 cents—*The Beggar Student, Erminie, The Pirates of Penzance. Trilby* also filled the house when brought by the Frawley Company, with Wilton Lackaye as the unforgettable Zvengali.

At fifty-seven, and old enough to know better, Sarah Bernhardt returned to play the part of Napoleon's eighteen-year-old son, L'Aiglon, but her San Francisco public was still faithful. Coquelin had a real triumph in *Cyrano de Bergerac*, but the season belonged to author Rostand.

Walter Morosco retired suddenly, and died a few months later, at age fifty-five. His adopted son, Oliver, carried on, later establishing himself in Los Angeles and New York. With the sure theatrical sense of his foster father, he made successes of plays rejected by eastern managers: *Peg o' My Heart, Abie's Irish Rose, The Bird of Paradise,* and *Linger Longer, Letty.* Among his many discoveries were Carlotta Monterey, Eugene O'Neill's widow, Lenore Ulric, and Leo Carillo. Morosco's name is still emblazoned on a New York theater.

After Walter Morosco's passing, his opera house had many musical seasons. One unforgettable season was when the Metropolitan Opera Company opened in 1901, with Emma Calvé, Schumann-Heink, Edouard de Reszke, Emma Eames, Antonio Scotti, Sybil Sanderson, Louise Homer, Marcella Sembrich, David Bispham, and Ernest Van Dyck.

San Franciscans thronged the house to see Sybil Sanderson, who had left the city ten years previously. She had appeared in Paris in operas written for her by Jules Massenet: *Esclarmonde, Thais,* and, readapted for her unique voice, *Manon.* She had sung for the crowned heads and been painted by great European artists.

The social Sanderson family had opposed her operatic career, but the prima donna-to-be swept her mother and sisters across continent and ocean to Paris. There she studied at the Conservatory of Music and with Madame Marchesi. The exquisitely beautiful young San Franciscan made her debut at The Hague. "Wages," she called her first $400. Worshipful Massenet said that "la belle Sybille's" voice was miraculous.

Paris agreed with him. Women copied her walk, voice, and manner. A German nobleman shot himself, gossip said, for love of her. Even the czarina was said to be jealous of the czar. Antonio Terry, a Cuban millionaire, as soon as he could disentangle himself from his wife, married Sybil in 1897. Sybil announced that she would retire from the operatic stage, to live happily as his wife. He died after a year of marriage, and Sybil, heartbroken, was stricken with paralysis at thirty-three.

Sybil recovered from the paralysis and went on with her career. An American tour returned her at last to her home city.

All San Francisco turned out to greet its prima donna. Sybil was only thirty-six, but disappointment filled the opera house at the sight of a tired woman so nervous that she had to be prompted. Her glowing health and beauty were gone. Her voice was as weary as her face, and applause was faint. Critics strove to be kind, but the *Examiner's* Ashton Stevens called her Juliet "a pretty little success." Sybil was entertained by old friends for several weeks in California. Her tragic attempt at a resumed career had failed. She retired to her villa at Cannes and died two years later.

Ned Harrigan of San Francisco's historic Bella Union was always cherished by the city. When he came to the opera house as a lovable drunkard in *Old Lavender,* theatergoers gave him their hearts. For the last time he sang songs of his own composition, "Dennis O'Grady's Hat," "Baxter Avenue," "Put on Your Bridal Veil," and "The March of the Mulligan Guards." The city never again saw their favorite after this.

Richard Mansfield, the perfectionist actor, filled the Grand Opera House with *Dr. Jekyll and Mr. Hyde, The Scarlet Letter,* and *Beau Brummell.*

Utterly different from Mansfield was Death Valley Scotty who packed the house in *Scotty, King of the Diamond Mines,* "one of the worst melodramas that ever insulted the stage." Scotty's engagement in 1906 closed only three weeks before old San Francisco ended.

The Grand Opera House, blacked out for a time, then opened its doors for Caruso, Fremstad, Bessie Abbott, Madame Jacoby, Messrs. Joubet, Dufriche, Reiss, and Caroli. Goldmark's *Queen of Sheba* was presented the first night, but the true opening came on April 17, 1906—*Carmen.*

It was good to be alive that warm spring evening as people in formal dress drove to the opera house. Fremstad was somewhat heavy as Carmen, but Bessie Abbott as Micaela was much applauded. It was Caruso who made the audience forget diamonds and dressmakers and brought shouted "Bravos!" It was not opera but life as he dashed through open arena doors, daring Carmen to enter. He sang as no one else in the world could sing, and his voice echoed through the dreams of those who heard him.

Next morning Caruso was jostled from his bed by the Earthquake. He roamed the streets of the burning city. " 'Ell of a place—'ell of a place—I'll never come back!" He never did, but his voice gave Wade's old Grand Opera House and San Francisco's pioneers of 1906 one final, unforgettable night of glory.

CHAPTER 12

Famous San Franciscans

"I SPRANG full-fledged from the head of Zeus," said Isadora Duncan, who was born in 1878 at 507 Geary Street, near today's Curran Theatre. She inherited her love of beauty from her auctioneer-art collector-banker father, Joseph C. Duncan, but she never saw him until she was several years old. Two weeks before she was born, he was arraigned in the municipal criminal court, charged with raising certificates of capital stock of the Pioneer Bank by changing the numbers. When Duncan tried to escape, his luggage was taken from the steamer bound for Central America, and he was lodged in the city prison. Forgery, felony, and larceny of 17,000 shares of safe-deposit company stock worth $1 million, were charged against him. Bail being fixed at $120,000, he remained in jail two and a half years. He was released after four mistrials and went to Los Angeles, where he remarried and reared a new family.

Valiant Dora Gray Duncan struggled to support her older daughter, Elizabeth, sons Augustine and Raymond, and the infant Isadora. Dora Duncan knit garments to be sold in shops. When her mother could not sell the garments, little Isadora peddled them from house to house. Fifteen times in two years landlords evicted the family for nonpayment of rent. The children wore leaky shoes and were often hungry, but the mother read Shakespeare and poetry to them.

"You have only yourself," she pointed out to the little girl.

One day a tall handsome stranger appeared at the door, saying to Isadora, "I'm your father." Her mother hid, crying, "Don't let him come in!"

Duncan took his daughter for a stroll, purchasing ice cream and cake. Having made another fortune, he bought the family a large house with a barn—Augustine Duncan's first theater. On its stage Isadora made her theatrical debut. At four she danced in public. At ten she put up her hair and said she was sixteen. She refused to continue school, and helped Elizabeth teach dancing. When she was twelve the Duncan family gave shows in small towns.

Isadora, the youngest, always the leader of the family, insisted that they must leave San Francisco to retrieve their fortune. Augustin Daly engaged her to dance in *Midsummer Night's Dream* in New York. The Duncans sailed on a cattle boat for London and fame.

At the British Museum Isadora studied movements and figures on Grecian urns and began creating her classical dances. Edward VII called her a "Gainsborough beauty." In Paris she met Rodin and was introduced to the world of art. Her California intensity carried her and the family to Greece. Soul uplifted, she stood before the Parthenon: "This is my own country." Adopting Greek draperies, she danced barefoot across Europe. "Godlike and holy," the Germans called her. She became more than art, she was religion. With her sister, Elizabeth, she opened a school near Berlin, and there met Ellen Terry's son, Gordon Craig, a great stage designer. Isadora described him as "flesh of my flesh, blood of my blood, we were two halves of the same soul." Craig wrote of her as "springing from the great race . . . to maintain the world and make it move, the guardian of beauty."

Realizing her mother's bitter experience, Isadora vowed never to marry. Craig became the father of her child, Deirdre. Their love was rapturous but stormy; they soon separated.

Back in the United States, Isadora found New York's art world at her feet. In Italy, d'Annunzio tried to add her to his other conquests. "Oh, Isadora, it is only possible to be alone with you and nature. All other women destroy the landscape. You are part of the trees, the sky. . . . I've conquered all women but you."

Her devotion to Duse caused her to reply, "I'm going to be the only woman in the world to resist d'Annunzio."

When Isadora met the Lohengrin of her memoirs, six-foot-six Paris Singer of New York, for the first time she had jewels and life on a yacht. Picturesque Singer became the father of her second child, Patrick. But even their son could not hold her to Lohengrin. She flung his gift of a diamond necklace at him and went her way.

After both children had been killed in an automobile accident, Isadora said that for twelve years tears streamed from her eyes. It was thought that she would never dance again, but she went to South America, and then back in New York she thrilled the audience at the Metropolitan Opera House by improvising "La Marseillaise."

Twenty-two years later she returned to her birthplace, San Francisco, where her dancing was described as being like "moving antique marble." But she could remain nowhere long. She went to Moscow and opened a school, with hundreds of pupils. At last she married—a mad young poet, Sergei Essenine, many years her junior. The marriage ended brutally. Sergei hanged himself. Those who saw her at her last Paris concert on July 8, 1927, declared that never had she appeared so completely a dancing Greek goddess.

Two months later while at Nice with her closest friend, Mary Gesti, an Italian automobile salesman asked Isadora to permit him to demonstrate a car he wished to sell. Gaily she entered the automobile, turning to Mary on the sidewalk, "He is not a chauffeur—he is a Greek God." Waving farewell, she called, "Adieu, mes amis, je vais à la gloire!" When her red scarf became entangled in the wheel, her life ended like a Greek drama—her neck was broken. The chauffeur sobbed in Italian, "I have killed the Madonna!"

All Paris wept when she was carried through the street to Père-Lachaise, to be reduced to ashes.

Isadora's father also met a tragic end. Having made and lost two fortunes, he was on his way to England when his ship was wrecked off Falmouth's rocky coast. He died cheering his companions, "Courage, the lifeboats will come to rescue us!" Raymond Duncan devotes his life to teaching "the eternal dancing of my sister, Isadora." When he returned to San Francisco in 1958, clad in toga and sandals, he said to the press, "I am not eccentric, the world is."

Like Isadora Duncan, Maud Allen suffered tragedy. She was the sister of Theodore Durrant, who was executed at San Quentin for a double murder. Born in Toronto, she came to San Francisco as a child. She graduated from Cogswell Polytechnic School. Adolph Sutro sent her to Berlin to study with Busoni, and she won high honors at the World Academy of Music. Inspired by her townswoman, Isadora Duncan, she studied painting and sculpture in Italy, in order to acquire rhythm in the classical dance. After her debut in Vienna in 1903 she proceeded to Moscow, New York, the Orient, South America, Egypt, making her home in London, where she was warmly received. There she founded a school for teaching underprivileged children.

For years she avoided San Francisco because of her brother's crime, the most shocking ever perpetrated in San Francisco. On April 13, 1895, the nude corpse of young Minnie Williams was found gagged, stabbed, outraged in the library of Emmanuel Baptist Church. On the succeeding Easter morning the decomposed body of Blanche Lamont, another Sunday-school girl, was discovered in the belfry. Both girls had disappeared from sight after having been seen in Sunday-school teacher Durrant's company. Circumstantial evidence was complete, and he was hanged January 7, 1898.

Twelve years later Maud Allen came to San Francisco. Her townspeople pitied the exile and thronged the theater for her recital, shouting and stamping approval of the Peer Gynt suite. Some shuddered at the Salome dance, in which she fondled the decapitated head and passionately kissed the dead lips of John the Baptist. At the close of the program she came to the footlights, spoke of her happy San Francisco childhood and of the tragic dark days. She said she had determined never to return until she could come as a success. Above all else she yearned for the appreciation of this, her native city. "Take me to your hearts. I know you have, but, oh, keep me there . . ." Tears were in her listeners' eyes and in her own on this her first and last visit. In 1956, unnoticed, she died in Southern California.

"Eddie" Bowes, friends called him before the Fire, little realizing that he would become radio's beloved Major Bowes, with the friendly "Wheel of Fortune" ever turning for some gifted youth.

Son of a weigher for the Southern Pacific Railroad, at his father's death Eddie left grammar school to become the mainstay of his mother and two sisters. From being an office boy at $3 a week, he became a real estate salesman, acquiring a small interest in the firm of John R. Spring. He was interested in boxing and yachting, but the theater held his heart. Before the Fire he enlisted Herbert Fleishhacker in the project of building a theater, but the enterprise ended with the conflagration.

When Margaret Illington came to San Francisco in *The Thief*, a sudden attachment sprang up between her and Bowes. After she divorced Manager Daniel Frohman, they were married at Reno. Bowes and his bride honeymooned at the Fruitvale estate of the John R. Springs. "I want to darn socks," said Mrs. Bowes, turning her back on the theater.

Nonetheless, Margaret Illington appeared several times under her husband's management before she retired. *Kindling,* by a San Franciscan, Charles Kendall, was acclaimed by New York critics.

The turning point in Bowes's career was when he acquired an interest in New York's Capitol Theatre. One of the Vanderbilt mansions was being razed, and Bowes bought most of the costly interior for a song, giving the Capitol a palatial new look. Bowes took charge of the theater's radio program, making it the most popular hour on the air. Several of his road companies toured the United States. Mr. and Mrs. Bowes developed a beautiful estate, Laurel Hill, at Ossining, overlooking the Hudson, where they had paintings by Whistler, Sargent, and Duveneck. Mrs. Bowes preceded her husband in death. The Major left several bequests to Californians, willing $10,000 to the California Pioneers. Although his grandfather was a north-of-Ireland Methodist minister, Bowes's fortune of several millions went largely to the Roman Catholic Church in New York City.

"San Francisco is my home town," says Elsa Maxwell. "I am proud of it, and I always will be." She was, however, born in Keokuk, Iowa. She describes herself as without beauty, background, or money, and she had to make her own way. She cuts her hair short, wears anything that is comfortable, but finds open doors to fashionable circles throughout the world. She even taught royalty how to be happy. "Don't bore others, and don't let others bore you. Let's have fun." Elsa has laughed all her life. "I began as a prize baby in the old Mechanics' Building, San Francisco, in 1883, and I've been laughing ever since. I'm fat and funny and fifty-six," she said in 1939.

A musical prodigy at four, after seeing the opera *Lohengrin* she changed her name to Elsa. She could play anything on the piano after hearing it once, improvise in any key, transposing music by ear. As a teen-ager in Berkeley she directed a light opera of her composition. Her first professional appearance on the stage was with Constance Crawley in an open-air Shakespearean production at Fruitvale. She left California with the Crawley-Ben Greet Company and later toured South Africa in vaudeville as a pianist.

During the Treasure Island Exposition she gave a barnyard party at the St. Francis Hotel. Farmer Elsa entered wearing overalls, hip boots, and hickory pants, had flaming whiskers, smoked a pipe, and pulled a cart on which stood a donkey. "Society is too sophisticated, occasionally they should go back to nature."

Elsa neither drinks nor smokes. She doesn't need stimulants— she describes herself as "born drunk." She does not frequent café society—"people with no homes, no friends. I adore people." In 1955 she chartered a yacht and took a group of rich and celebrated people on a tour of Greece, visiting the King and Queen who are among Elsa's royal friends. She has done dramatic criticism, had a radio program, and at seventy-seven writes a newspaper column.

San Francisco's only heavyweight champion was James J. Corbett, conqueror of John L. Sullivan, Charles Mitchell, Tom Sharkey, and Bob Fitzsimmons. Son of Patrick Corbett, a Hayes Street livery stable owner, Jim was expelled from St. Ignatius College in 1885— for fighting. At sixteen he graduated from Sacred Heart College and became a bank clerk.

His boxing career began when he fought Choynski on a barge in Suisun Bay at seven in the morning, June 6, 1889, and won in twenty-eight rounds. He became San Francisco's hero in 1892, when he defeated John L. Sullivan at New Orleans. Sullivan said he was glad he was "licked by an American." Corbett's homecoming was a great event in San Francisco. He became a friend of Theodore Roosevelt and was starred by William A. Brady in *After Dark*. For a short time he appeared in Bernard Shaw's *Cashel Byron's Profession*. He was the highest paid vaudeville performer of his time, and he also wrote a syndicated column. Errol Flynn played Corbett in *Gentleman Jim*. In the film Harry Crocker appeared in the role of his kinsman, Charles Crocker.

After five years of glory, Corbett was knocked out in 1903 in San Francisco by Jim Jeffries in ten rounds, the only time the San Franciscan fought for the heavyweight championship in this area.

In his sixties Corbett developed a heart ailment and was advised to live quietly, but at a football game he became so thrilled rooting for Old St. Mary's playing Fordham in 1930, a football classic, that the condition worsened. Three years later he fell ill at his Long Island home near Riverside, where he collapsed in his wife's arms.

The most gentlemanly of champions had earned large sums, but his estate was only $2,769.

No woman held the world tennis championship as long as Helen Wills (Little Miss Poker-Face). From 1923 to 1929 she reigned over the tennis world. Before she played in Golden Gate Park she had made her tennis debut at seventeen at Berkeley with two long braids hanging down her back. Daughter of Dr. and Mrs. C. O. Wills, she was developed by "Pop" Fuller on the Berkeley tennis courts. Early she acquired a mannish stroke that gained her eight Wimbledon championships and seven in United States tournaments. She became the best-known young woman in the world, and when she was presented at the Court of St. James's, it was said that she looked like a beautiful Athenian statue.

She married Frederick S. Moody, of the pioneer San Francisco family, taking her marriage so seriously that she wished to be addressed as Mrs. Moody. She refused to wear shorts, to become a professional, or sign a movie contract, although she received many large offers. She said she played for fun.

Miss Wills's portrait by Louise Janin was shown in the Salon de Tuileries at Paris. She, herself, took up painting, and also did etchings. At an exhibition of her water colors in New York one of Helen Wills's fans bought twenty of her canvases.

The first marriage proved unsatisfactory and her second husband was the handsome polo player, Alden Roark, who authored Hollywood scenarios. After she retired she wrote a mystery story, studied dress designing, and took lessons in piloting a plane. She swam, rode, skated, and hunted quail with her husband. During a political campaign she spoke for Wendell Willkie and made radio addresses.

Her hand was bitten while she was trying to stop a fight between her German police dog and another dog. Several bones were removed, and now she plays only exhibition matches for charity, or relief, or teaches young players in Southern California, where she lives. At the Treasure Island Exposition she was a guest as one of San Francisco's thirteen most distinguished women born in California. Again in 1959 she made headlines when she was elected to the National Lawn Tennis Hall of Fame for having eight times won the world championship at Wimbledon, England. The ceremony took place in the Casino at Newport, Rhode Island. Many rank her as the greatest tennis player among women.

Born in Martinez, baseball hero Joseph Paul ("Joe") DiMaggio spent most of his boyhood in San Francisco. The lad was a disappointment to his fisherman father because he preferred playing baseball to going out with him in his boat. "It's a bum's game," said the practical Italian. He was also disappointed when his other sons, Vince and Dominic, acquired the baseball habit. Later, Papa DiMaggio not only became reconciled to his son's occupation but rooted for baseball. He was especially proud of Joe, who was a hero to millions.

Joe early said good-by to high school and began selling the *Call-Bulletin* on the street. Dismissed for not making enough sales, he turned to baseball, and at seventeen was a rookie for the Seals at $7,500 a year. After a knee injury, he was bought by the New York Yankees for $25,000, becoming their outfielder. Joe's ambition was to be a better player than his hero Babe Ruth.

With the Yankees his outstanding feat was hitting in 56 consecutive games, which made baseball history. During his twenty years of baseball he had several accidents, causing him to realize that a champion should quit while still champion. Although earning $100,000 a year, more than even Babe Ruth, Joe, at the age of thirty-seven, said good-by to his life on the diamond. Later, however, he acquired additional fame by becoming, for a few months, one of Marilyn Monroe's husbands.

Sport lovers say Joe is not only a great athlete but a great gentleman. Rules were suspended in 1955 when he was elected to the Baseball Hall of Fame at Cooperstown, New York. The sports writers of the United States thought that he should be honored. His uniform, his favorite glove, and the bat which he hit his last home run were placed with those of Ty Cobb, Walter Johnson, Babe Ruth, Lou Gehrig, and other heroes of Joe's boyhood.

Asked "How does it feel to be an immortal?" he said it was a strange feeling to become a museum piece at the age of forty. "But to the fellow who has made baseball his lifework, Cooperstown is more than a collection of relics and fancy-word plaques. It is the final touch every major leaguer would like to add to his career.

There is no greater honor." He likes to feel that a part of him will be at Cooperstown forever.

In 1959 Joe was vice-president of the V. H. Monisette Company, Smithfield, Virginia, which deals in everything from hams to baseball gloves. Joe spends his time traveling for them, selling especially to the commissaries of the armed forces.

At the Western States Trail Riders' banquet in the auditorium, Auburn, California, in August, 1959, the winner was presented with a 26-inch high silver cup by William S. Tevis, Jr., better known as "Will." He, himself, has been acclaimed "the greatest living rider in America." The cup was given by Tevis in memory of his grandfather, Lloyd Tevis, a forty-niner who served as president not only of the Central Pacific Railroad but also of Wells Fargo and Company.

From childhood Will Tevis lived in the saddle on his father's vast Kern County Stockdale Ranch. In September, 1923, when he was thirty-two, he competed on horseback with nine of the fastest cavalry riders in the United States army. They went from the Nevada state line to San Francisco and stopped at the Tanforan race track. Tevis rode 257.5 miles on relay horses in 11½ hours.

When Tevis was forty-one, Hal Roach, Hollywood's producer of westerns, wagered $5,000 with him that he could not repeat his record speed. "I can better it by fifty miles," replied Tevis. Some weeks later the Horse-A-Thon was arranged at Dreamland Auditorium, San Francisco. Great was the excitement and many bets were made. In 10 hours 2 minutes, Tevis rode 200 miles, changing mounts every 20 miles, and he won the $5,000 wager from Roach.

After twenty-seven years, it was fit that Tevis should donate the silver cup to the winner of the Western Trail Riders' race at Auburn. One of those competing was his own daughter, Sandra, student at Finch College, New York City.

Will Tevis, California's "Iron Man" rider, advocates that the grueling ride over the Sierra Nevada on old pioneer and gold-rush trails from Tahoe City to Auburn be made an event for the Olympic Games, and "if we made it an international event, we could even invite Russian Cossacks." The horseman who can ride the same horse 100 miles over the rough Sierra trails in 24 hours "has to be a real rider with a real horse—not a plug."

It has been said that Tevis rides like a caballero, and such is his inheritance. His mother was Mabel Pacheco, daughter of the first Spanish Californian to be governor of the state after the American conquest, Romualdo Pacheco. In 1874 he became governor and later served as United States senator.

Swim "Queen" Ann Curtis is descended from San Francisco pioneers. Her great-grandfather, James Curtis, was a prominent Vigilante. The blonde mermaid, 5 feet 10½ inches tall, while reigning, weighed 156 pounds. Although born in San Francisco, she learned to swim at the age of eight while at the Ursuline Covent in Santa Rosa. At the Fleischhacker Pool she swam her way to glory. When she was seventeen her coach, Charlie Sava, called her the "greatest swimmer that ever lived." After leaving Roosevelt Junior High School, she was a popular Kappa Alpha Theta at the University of California. Her zenith of fame was reached in 1948 at the London Olympics when she established a 400-yard water Olympic record and held 31 world records. She still holds two world records—for 440 yards and 880 yards.

"Queen" Ann said she thought they were kidding when she was told that she was to meet England's King and Queen at Buckingham Palace. "I suppose I must put on my gold slippers." In reality, she wore her team uniform and oxfords. She didn't know whether she was expected to curtsy to royalty, but when the King thrust out his hand, she shook it. He asked her if California really was "Paradise."

From London she flew to Paris and shopped so wildly that when she arrived in New York she had only two dollars, and that was borrowed. Back in San Francisco, her admirers gave her a new Chevrolet convertible, and she was honored with a parade. Mayor Robinson made her "Miss San Francisco" and tendered her a reception at the City Hall.

Although "Queen" Ann had glory, she always needed money, and when she was offered $750 a week in 1949, she turned professional, traveling with sports shows in the Midwest and the East. In Chicago she raced with the seal, Jumbo, who delights in outswimming human beings. After she had won many national titles and traveled 100,000 miles to swim, in 1949 she married Gordon B. Cuneo, basketball star at the University of California. They honeymooned at Honolulu. Then she folded up her bathing suit and became a housewife, cooking and making her own clothes. Now the mother of several children, she never expects to enter a contest again, but she teaches swimming in her own pool.

When Charles Stewart Howard bought three-year-old Seabiscuit for $7,500, no one expected much of the smallish animal, but Howard, Georgia born and a wholesale automobile dealer, believed in the son of Hard Tack-Swing, owned by Ogden Mills. Under Howard's red and white colors, racing fans were soon placing their money on the Biscuit. Race after race was won by him, and Howard was $100,000 richer for the great horse's victory the last time he ran at Santa Anita.

Howard, however, had raced 250 horses and did not intend to see his favorite begin going downhill. He sent the animal, while still triumphant, to his 17,000-acre ranch, Northridge, near Willetts, where he lived luxuriously in a red and white stable with brick floors. Fifty thousand visitors came to visit the retired Seabiscuit. There he sired more than a hundred colts and became a movie star with Shirley Temple in the Warner Brothers film, *The Story of Seabiscuit*.

At fourteen he developed a heart ailment and died. Howard said it was like losing a relative. Seabiscuit was buried in front of the ranch house on May 1, 1947. His life-size statue at Santa Anita commemorates the greatest moneymaker in turf history.

Grace Ethel Cecile Rosalie ("Gracie") Allen is the only San Francisco woman to make a campaign for president—on radio. A born entertainer, her mother was Irish and her Scotch father, George Allen, Gracie proudly says, "was the best clog and minstrel man in San Francisco." When Gracie was three she sang an Irish song at a benefit. In a man's full-dress suit, long tails dragging on the floor, with top hat and red whiskers, she went on the stage. She was such a hit that she became stage-struck. Gracie's sisters, Bessie, Pearl and Hazel, also wanted to be actresses, and they were encouraged by their next-door neighbor, Alice Neilsen, the popular light opera singer. Every time Gracie had 10 cents she went to the Orpheum or the Alcazar.

George Allen died when Gracie was a child, and she went to live with her grandmother in the Richmond District, attending the "Star of the Sea" School and dancing at May Day celebrations in Golden Gate Park. First of the Allens to go into vaudeville was

Bessie, the tap dancer, who organized an act that included Gracie and Hazel. It was not a hit on Broadway, however, and Bessie and Hazel gave up and returned to San Francisco. Gracie kept on trying without success in New York until she met George Burns, and teamed up with him in a skit, 60–40.

At first Gracie couldn't think of marrying George because she was an Irish Catholic and he was an orthodox Jew, born Nat Birnbaum. Finally, George told her she'd have to marry him or they'd split the act. She still continued to say no, but finally, at 4 o'clock in the morning she called him to say she had changed her mind. They never had religious problems. They were married by a justice of the peace and their children, Sandra and Ronnie, were brought up Catholics. Gracie says she is sure their marriage is right because it has lasted more than thirty years and that George is not only a good husband but a good friend.

After Gracie tossed her hat into the ring for president in 1940 she was a guest at "First Lady's Night" at the Washington Press Club. Mrs. Roosevelt told her that she hoped that if she won the election, Gracie would ask her to attend the next banquet. Although Harvard endorsed Gracie for president she received only two votes.

She has a handsome home in Beverly Hills and often flies north to see her sisters and her birthplace. "My favorite city is San Francisco." She is loved by millions.

Poet Joseph T. Goodman was one of the editors of the Golden Era but his fame is not due to that. When the Comstock stampede of the early 1860's took him to Virginia City, he became owner and publisher of the *Territorial Enterprise* and also the discoverer of Mark Twain. While in Nevada Goodman developed a new interest, ancient Mayan hieroglyphics found on the Gieger Grade near Virginia City and Star Mountain. This discovery determined his life work—deciphering the story of the ruins in the Yucatan peninsula in Mexico which at that time was thought to be the oldest civilization on this continent. Goodman offered his manuscripts to San Francisco Academy of Sciences, but their value was not appreciated. After becoming the property of English scholars they appeared in *Biologia Centrali,* and in 1917 when the poet-editor died in his Alameda home he had found fame as an archaeologist of world renown.

San Francisco schools have produced three Nobel Laureates, two of them native born. The first was Albert A. Michelson, a graduate of Lincoln High School. President Theodore Roosevelt won the Nobel Prize in 1906, one year before Michelson, who was the first private citizen to be so honored. Michelson was born in Strelno, Germany, on December 19, 1852. His parents moved to San Francisco, where his father was a merchant. When young Michelson hitchhiked to Washington to ask President Grant for an appointment to the United States Naval Academy, the President so admired his pluck that Michelson graduated from Annapolis in 1873.

He preferred teaching physics to service in the navy, and after studying at several universities occupied the chair of physics at the University of Chicago. His invention of the interferometer for measuring light brought him the Nobel award. The late Albert Einstein, who suggested the atomic bomb to President Roosevelt, stated that his theory of relativity was based upon Michelson's work. In one of the large murals in Coit Tower, Michelson is pictured with the interferometer in his hand. His last work which measured the velocity of light with error not exceeding 1/1000 of 1 per cent, was at Santa Ana, California. His sister was Miriam Michelson, the San Francisco novelist, and his brother Charlie Michelson was the Democratic publicity head under Roosevelt.

San Francisco's first native son to be a Nobel laureate was Joseph Erlanger, born in 1874, son of Herman Erlanger, a merchant, who came with the gold rush. Young Joseph spent two years at the Boys' High School, which later became Lowell High. Then he entered the University of California by special examination and was graduated in 1895 with a degree of Bachelor of Science. His Nobel Prize in physiology arrived in 1944. Dr. Erlanger is a resident of St. Louis, Missouri.

San Francisco's second native son to win the Nobel award is Owen Chamberlain, who was born in 1920 and lived in the city until he was ten. His father, Dr. William Edward Chamberlain, was assistant professor of medicine at Stanford University Hospital, and later moved to Philadelphia. Dr. Chamberlain was educated at Dartmouth but received his advanced degrees at the University of California. In 1959 he shared with Italian-born Dr. Emilio Segre, the Nobel Prize for their creation of a long-sought fundamental particle of the atomic world, the antiproton, a proton carrying a negative charge instead of the normal positive charge. Dr. Segre was a coworker of the late Dr. Enrico Fermi before he and Chamberlain became two of the principal builders of the atomic bomb. During the 1960–1961 academic year, Dr. Chamberlain has been teaching on the Berkeley campus. Both Nobel Laureates are married and live near the University of California.

San Francisco was first to hear the controversial music of Henry Cowell, "the most publicized composer in the world. Born in Menlo Park, the son of two California poets, Harry and Clarissa Dixon Cowell, Henry began his march to world fame in San Francisco when at the age of four he played in public as a child prodigy and the pupil of Louis Persinger. Since then his compositions have been played by orchestras everywhere in the world and on many recordings and he has been honored by many countries. He has authored several books on music and musicians, in collaboration with his wife, Sidney Cowell. In 1956–57 the Cowells toured the Far East on a Rockefeller grant, returning with a notable collection of Far Eastern recordings.

CHAPTER 13

San Francisco Authors

SAN FRANCISCO has always been a writing city. Perhaps the voluminous letters mailed "home" by the forty-niners, letters that told of gold and high hopes, of failure and loneliness, and which now crowd archives in America and England, gave impetus to the great school of writing that was to spring up beside the Golden Gate.

Even during the Civil War world literary reputations were made in San Francisco. Apparently Bret Harte's "The Luck of Roaring Camp" and "The Outcasts of Poker Flat," first published in San Francisco in the 1860's, were inspired by incidents recorded by that authoress of gold-rush days, Mrs. Laura A. K. Clappe, whose "Shirley Letters" appeared in the *Pioneer Magazine* in 1851 and 1852.

Harte, a shy, slender youth, scion of cultured Jewish and English families, came from New York in 1854 to join his mother who had married Mayor Andrew Williams of Oakland. He worked as a druggist's clerk, tutor, expressman, schoolmaster, and printer's devil, venturing into verse that was published by the *Golden Era* and for which he was paid nothing. His talent was first recognized by Jessie Benton Frémont, who introduced him to the world of society and power. To provide him with security and time to write she secured a minor post for him in the office of General Edward Beale, head of the Coast Survey. In 1863 he became head of the San Francisco Mint, at a comfortable salary.

He found time to act as editor of the *Californian*, the city's first cosmopolitan magazine, founded by New Yorker C. W. Webb. One of his first moves was to engage a new contributor, a new-

123

comer to the city, one Samuel L. Clemens from Hannibal, Missouri. Clemens had acquired some fame in Nevada under the pen name Mark Twain. Drifting down to San Francisco from the mines, he worked first on the lively, chatty *Call* as a reporter at $25 a week, and lost the job, he boasted, because he was too lazy to accept reportorial drudgery.

Both Harte and Twain were twenty-five years old when they joined forces on the *Californian.* Twain acknowledged his debt to Harte's editing of his flamboyant prose, pruning his articles, giving them shape and form. Both were to leave the West to find world acclaim. When Twain later returned to San Francisco he was famed as the world's foremost humorist and San Franciscans flocked to hear him give his farewell lecture in 1868.

Harte remained until success came to him as editor of Anton Roman's *Overland Monthly.* It was Roman who suggested that the gold rush would take an important place in romantic literature. Harte accepted his suggestion and his "Luck of Roaring Camp," which appeared in the second edition of the *Overland,* brought tears to readers' eyes. Harte admitted, "I wept when I wrote it."

The short story made him famous. "The Outcasts of Poker Flat" and "Tennessee's Partner" followed as world sensations. "Idyll of Red Gulch," "Brown of Calaveras," "Iliad of Sandy Bar," continued the steady line of successes for which the new magazine paid the young author $100 apiece. The glowing reception given to his poem, "The Heathen Chinee," annoyed Harte, who called it "the worst poem anyone ever wrote."

The sale of the *Overland* sent Harte from San Francisco. The University of California made a gallant effort to keep him in the West, offering him the posts of professor of recent literature and curator of the library and museum, but he was lured away. It was a serious mistake. Scant success came to Harte after leaving San Francisco, as either novelist or lecturer. He left the East for England, and success continued to evade him. He never again wrote with the genius that had marked his work on the *Overland.* He never returned to the San Francisco that had provided the impetus for his early writing.

Friends finally obtained a minor consular post for Harte in Germany. California was so far forgotten by him that when writing of her poppies he did not know their color, causing a versifier to protest:

> But what kills me plumb dead
> Is to see where he's writ
> That our poppies is red—
> Which they aint red a bit,
> But the flamingest orange and yellow—
> O Bret, how could you forget?

Both Mark Twain and Bret Harte were said to have been in love with Ina Donna Coolbrith, the auburn-haired, gray-eyed Sappho of her day. Ina was the only San Franciscan to receive a message from Harte. To a friend visiting England he said, "Tell Ina that I still remember."

Ina Coolbrith's was a tragic story. She was Katherine D. Smith, niece of Joseph Smith, founder of Mormonism, and of his brother Hyrum, both killed by a mob near Carthage, Illinois. Don Carlos Smith, Ina's father, married Ina Coolbrith. After her husband's death, Mrs. Smith left the Mormons and became the wife of William Pickett, a printer on the St. Louis *Republican*. Early in the fifties, the family moved to Los Angeles. At the age of eleven Ina began writing verse signed Ina.

At seventeen, Ina became the wife of Robert B. Carsley, but within three years her husband's jealousy drove her from him. Seeking to forget both Carthage and Los Angeles, she moved with her parents to San Francisco, where she taught in a school of languages. She became one of the *Overland* trinity and on June 30, 1915, during the Panama-Pacific Exposition, she was named California's first poet laureate, which honor she held until her death in 1928. San Francisco's Coolbrith Square commemorates the poet.

Mark Twain and Bret Barte were transients, but Joaquin Miller was rooted in the West. It is said that no one knows precisely where Miller was born, but doubtless somewhere on the Wabash in Indiana. In the Far West in 1861 he was a pony express rider. Miller was carrying express in Oregon when he read the burning verses of Minnie Dyer, a fisherman's daughter at Port Orford, who wrote under the name Minnie Myrtle. Both Miller and Minnie had been inspired by Byron. After writing her a letter of praise, he rode over the hills to visit her. He arrived on a Tuesday and married her on Sunday, despite paternal protests. Later he described their meeting:

> He came to fall like a king in the forest,
> Caught in the strong arms of the wrestler;
> Forgetting his song, his crags and his mountains,
> And nearly his God, in his wild, deep passion.

After arriving in 1862 with his poet wife he was a part of San Francisco. These honeymooners were a striking pair—he with blue eyes and long curling yellow hair, and she with dark eyes and unruly dusky locks. At their little house on Folsom Street, San Francisco, they wrote verse, receiving no remuneration. At that time Minnie Myrtle's poetry gave more promise than Miller's. He sent her back to her parents at Port Orford: "A man never becomes famous till he leaves his wife, or does something atrocious, to bring himself into notice. Besides, literary men never get along with their wives. Lord Byron separated from his wife, and some of my friends think I'm a second Byron."

He had a wild love affair with Adah Isaacs Menken, but he later rejoined his wife and fathered their three children. He described their final separation:

> I clutched my hands, I turned my head,
> In my endeavor, and was dumb.
> And when I should have said "farewell"
> I only murmured "This is Hell!"

Joaquin Murietta, the Mexican-Californian bandit, inspired a poem that Miller had printed at his own expense. At Ina Coolbrith's suggestion, Cincinnatus Heine Miller became Joaquin Miller.

In 1873, without wife or children, he decided to go to England to visit the shrines of his favorite poets. He went to Sausalito with Ina Coolbrith, to gather a wreath of California laurel for Byron's tomb. Mrs. Frank Leslie bought some of his poems, but his traveling expenses were paid by the San Francisco *Bulletin,* for which he wrote letters.

At Ayrshire, Scotland, he knelt at Burns's grave and at Melrose Abbey he was so entranced by thoughts of Scott that he was locked in for the night. At Newstead Abbey, he visited Boatswain's tomb and slept in the guest room. He hung the laurel wreath over Byron's

resting place in Hucknall Church. London's ancient buildings and
thronged streets made him feel lonelier than he had been among
Mount Shasta's Indians.

London publishers declined Miller's verse. He pawned his watch
and at his own expense printed a hundred copies of *Pacific Poems*.
After Miller distributed them among critics, Jean Ingelow invited
him to dinner and Tom Hood took him under his wing. London
felt that the California gold rush had arrived when he appeared
in a sealskin coat, with only a shirt underneath. His later costume
was a red shirt, high boots, and sombrero. "It helped sell the poems,
and tickled the Duchesses."

Swinburne, William Morris, the Rossettis and their circle listened
eagerly to his exploits and sympathized with his devotion to animals. Longmans published his *Songs of the Sierras*. Critics outdid
each other in praise, but Joaquin said that he always saw the snowy
peaks of the great emerald land, Oregon, where plants were trees
and trees were towers.

Minnie Myrtle told the press that she and her children were half
starved while he was London's literary hero. Accused by Oregonians
of once having "borrowed" a horse, he protested, "It was a mule."

Back in San Francisco, he turned Cali-Shasta, his daughter by a
Pitt River Indian girl, over to Ina Coolbrith to rear and returned
to London. There he became engaged to Isa Hardy. He kissed girls'
hands, told them they were pretty enough to set in a ring, crawled
across drawing-room floors on his knees and bit women's ankles.
He showered his sombrero full of rose petals upon Lily Langtry.
One evening at Lord Houghton's he disappeared, but returned with
a poem that he read to the famous beauty from a torn piece of
paper:

TO THE JERSEY LILY:
If all God's world a garden were
    And women were but flowers,
If men were bees that busied
        there
    Through endless summer
        hours,
O! I would hum God's garden
        through
    For honey till I came to you.

In 1886 Miller came back to California and bought 69 acres near Oakland, "The Hights." Here, with the aid of friends and visitors, he planted 70,000 eucalyptus, pine, cypress, and acacia trees.

Separated from his second wife, who was of the New York Leland Hotel family, he longed for his daughter, Juanita, and sent her this plea:

> You will come, my bird, Bonita?
> Come! For I, by steep and stone
> Have built such a nest for you, Juanita,
> As not eagle bird hath known.

In 1913, when Miller died at age seventy-five, his ashes were scattered according to his wishes from his funeral pyre on the Hights overlooking San Francisco and the bay. His daughter Juanita keeps his memory alive in the Hights.

Another picturesque San Francisco writer of the Golden Era was Prentice Mulford, a Harvard graduate and a believer in spiritualism. "A wildcat religion," Mark Twain called it, but to Mulford spirits were as real as mountains. Mulford lived like a hermit on a sailboat in the bay, eating only fruit and vegetables. After leaving San Francisco, he withdrew to a New Jersey swamp and became a devotee to occult science. His White Cross Library, issued in 5-cent tracts, set forth his doctrine of spiritualism and mental healing. He died mysteriously on a boat in which he had set out from New York for Sag Harbor. His friends found him wrapped in blankets, his spirit lamp and banjo at his side. They believed that hieroglyphics found on his writing pad were his message from the spirit world. Mulford's tracts still have a large audience in Germany.

Most notable of all books produced in San Francisco was Henry George's *Progress and Poverty*, setting forth his theory of a single tax on land. England named the author the "California prophet." His subsequent work, *Protection or Free Trade*, brought him three million readers. "Single tax" became a religion to multitudes, selling two million copies.

Short, blue-eyed Henry George, was from boyhood a rebel. Three months in a Philadelphia high school finished his formal education. Going from job to job, often quarreling with employers, at nineteen he came through the Golden Gate as steward on the *Shubrick*. After prospecting futilely in the Fraser River gold rush of 1858, George returned to the city and set type on the *Home Journal*. At the What Cheer House he read Adam Smith's *Wealth of Nations*. The twenty-one-year-old youth, while earning $30 a week as foreman, in 1860 eloped with Annie Fox, who was a stabilizing influence. Striving to increase his income, he wrote on spiritualism, gambled disastrously in Comstock mining stock, sold clothes wringers, invented a wooden brake, differed with so many employers that once he desperately stopped a stranger in the street and asked for $5. Had the stranger not assisted him, he said he would have used a gun.

In the *Overland* George prophesied that hard times would follow the completion of the railroad, and they did, because of drought, land speculation, and Comstock gambling. Great stretches of unoccupied land made George resentful that men should be hungry while land could produce wealth. In a pamphlet *Our Land and Land Policy*, he wrote that a remedy for depression and poverty would be tax equal to rental value on any land not worked by the owner himself. Rejoicing that he was not a "learned fool," he attacked John Stuart Mill, David Ricardo, and Thomas Malthus. When he finished he had written a 500-page book that no publisher would accept.

His printer friends on the San Francisco *Evening Post*, of which he was editor, helped him set up type, make plates, and run off an edition of 500 copies. Then D. Appleton and Company ventured. The *Edinburgh Review* hailed *Progress and Poverty* as America's most original work on economics. George's tour of Great Britain was a triumph. His tract on land tax had repercussions in England and on the Continent, and in proposed legislation for division of great estates. From the time George wrote *Progress and Poverty* until his death in 1897 while campaigning for office of mayor of New York, he lived only to spread his gospel, declaring that he had "humanized the dismal science of Political Economy."

There is a monument to Robert Louis Stevenson in Portsmouth Square. He was far from happy when in the 1870's he journeyed here from Scotland seeking Fanny van de Grift Osbourne, who

two years previously had separated from her husband, Sam
Osbourne. Stevenson had met her in France where she was traveling with her two children, Lloyd and Isobel. His austere Scotch
parents disapproved of their son's love for a married woman. Cut
off from parental allowance, the young writer traveled steerage
from Europe and crossed the continent on a cattle train. He was
so impecunious that he lived in a Bush Street workingmen's lodg-
ing house on 45 cents a day, dining on a 10-cent roll and a cup of
coffee. He was so weak that it took him six hours to write a page
of *Prince Otto:* "God only knows how much courage and suffering
is buried in that manuscript."

"Cold wet sweats" brought Fanny from Monterey to nurse him,
and he said that he owed his life to her. Recovering, he went to the
Oakland cottage where Mrs. Osbourne's sister, Nellie Sanchez,
lived, there dictating to her portions of *Prince Otto.* When little
Lloyd Osbourne, Fanny's son, pleaded with Stevenson for a sea
tale, the group invented continued stories. This was the start of
Treasure Island. Fanny became Stevenson's wife on March 19,
1880, at Oakland. For the benefit of his health, they all went
with their cats and dogs to a cottage near St. Helena, where he
found inspiration for *The Silverado Squatters.*

After many wanderings they left San Francisco for Samoa,
where he died in 1894. Of Fanny, Stevenson wrote: "She is everything to me: my wife, mother, sister, daughter and dear companion,
and I would not change her to get a goddess or a saint."

One of San Francisco's landmarks is a large house on Hyde
Street, now converted into apartments and owned by Frederick
Murphy. There Mrs. Stevenson lived for several years. She died in
Montecito, Santa Barbara, at the home of her daughter, Isobel
Strong.

While Stevenson was struggling in San Francisco, Gertrude
Atherton, then twenty-two, was one of the beauties of the Authors'
Carnival. Drama was in the air when she was born in 1857 at
Second and Harrison Streets. The Vigilantes had just disbanded.
Her grandfather, Stephen Franklin, a nephew of Benjamin Frank-
lin, was an official in Ralston's bank. She especially lamented
Ralston's death. Had he not promised her a ball at Belmont for
her debut into society?

After divorcing Thomas Horn, Gertrude's mother, a famous beauty, became Mrs. John Uhlhorn. Soon she was loved by George Atherton, fourteen years her junior. When eighteen-year-old Gertrude appeared from Sayre's Institute, Kentucky, George, South American born and half Spanish, transferred his love to the daughter. Because it was romantic and Ouida-ish, Gertrude became his bride secretly at St. Joseph's Church in San Jose. The unexpected marriage startled the conservative Menlo Park circle of which George was a member.

Gertrude Atherton became the mother of two children, but her life was in books. Reading incessantly, she was determined to become an author; but how? Her first work, "The Randolphs of Redwood," the story of an alcoholic mother and daughter, was offered to *Argonaut*. Editor Jerome A. Hart, recognizing her gift, agreed to publish the story as a serial. He suggested that for her sake it should appear anonymously.

With a check of $150 the young author bought a new dress at The White House, spending the remainder on books by Emerson, Taine, Herbert Spencer, and Daudet.

"The Randolphs of Redwood" stupefied San Francisco and Menlo Park. Who was the author? Men were accused, but no one suspected golden-haired Mrs. Atherton with the perfect profile and shoulders. When she was revealed as the writer, some of her best friends ceased to speak to her. The serial, rewritten, later became a best seller, *A Daughter of the Vine*.

Gertrude Atherton chafed in the fetters of marriage, and while still in her twenties she was set free. Her husband was invited by his cousin, a Chilean naval officer, to go on a battleship to South America. Aboard ship, George Atherton suddenly died. Embalming was impossible, and the young widow experienced the shock of having her husband's body arrive unexpectedly in a barrel of rum. She never remarried.

Now her determination to become an author was firmer than ever. Her home became a literary salon. One of her genius visitors was Joaquin Miller, who exclaimed, "What a pity we are both blond! O-oh, I'd like to go up and take God by the beard!"

San Francisco, far away from New York and London, seemed a prison to the struggling author. Gertrude Atherton decided to leave, as did her friend, Sybil Sanderson, who wished to be an opera singer. Sybil was engaged to young William Randolph Hearst, but she brushed off romance and set out for Europe. Mrs. Atherton went first to New York. Metropolitan publishers were inhospitable. *What Dreams May Come* made the rounds of editorial offices, but for four years was unpublished. *Hermia Suydam*, the story of a plain girl transforming herself into a beauty, appeared but met derision.

Gertrude Atherton sailed for Paris, where her brother-in-law, Lawrence Rathbone, was consul general. Already her friend Sybil Sanderson had made her debut in opera and had Paris at her feet. Mrs. Atherton was not so favored.

Inspiration, however, came in London when she read an article by Kate Field asking why California writers neglected their state's romantic Spanish history. Soon she was back exploring Spanish California—reliving the glamourous dead days of Monterey and Santa Barbara. London editors acclaimed her work and *Harper's Weekly* published "Pearls of Loreto." She wrote *The Doomswoman* at Fort Ross. San Francisco remained cold. She went back to London determined to return to the United States only after she had been acclaimed in her own country.

When *Patience Sparhawk and Her Times* appeared, London critics hailed Gertrude Atherton as the greatest living fiction writer, but American critics were still unconvinced.

In her mid-forties Gertrude Atherton conquered the United States with *The Conqueror*, Alexander Hamilton's biography, written with fiction technique. She had sought out Hamilton's birthplace, and re-created the childhood of the illegitimate boy who became the illustrious secretary of the treasury, to be killed in a duel by Aaron Burr. *The Conqueror* made Mrs. Atherton's return to the United States a tour of triumph. More than a million copies were sold.

After Cora Urquhart Potter told her she was the reincarnation of Aspasia, Mrs. Atherton went to Greece to write *The Immortal Marriage*, with Aspasia as the heroine. In later years her most successful novel was *Black Oxen*, the heroine of which took the Steinach treatment and recovered youth and beauty. When Mrs. Atherton was about sixty, fearing that her mind was becoming sterile, she underwent the treatment and found herself writing like a whirlwind. The motion picture *Black Oxen* brought her letters from thousands of women eager to regain youth and beauty.

Not only did she write many books, but she participated in the Woodrow Wilson campaign as speaker. During World War I she raised so much money for the French wounded in New York that she was decorated by the French government, with the Medaille d'Honneur and the Medaille de la République.

In the closing two decades of her life Mrs. Atherton and her daughter, Muriel Atherton Russell, several times each winter received the San Francisco branch of P.E.N.—the city's only salon. On her ninetieth birthday a large group assembled when Mayor Roger Lapham awarded her a decoration from the city of San Francisco. With her mind alert and her distinguished appearance, Mrs. Atherton seemed younger than women twenty years her junior. She died shortly after this, just as she was about to begin to write a history of California.

Ambrose Bierce was the man who revered no one but himself. Even his parents were "unwashed savages." He was born at a religious camp ground on Horse Creek, Meigs County, Ohio, the youngest of twelve. The boy worked in a saloon, made bricks, saw revolting sights in the Civil War, and in 1866 was night watchman in the San Francisco Mint. There he began writing.

As Town Crier in the weekly *News Letter*, Bierce shocked the public: "Successful abortion—woman died." "Priest has abandoned the errors of the Roman Church for those of the Protestant Church." "Young ruffians insult schoolgirls. Schoolgirls like it." "The fact that boys are allowed to exist at all is evidence of remarkable Christian forbearance among men. Were it not for mawkish humanitarians, coupled with imperfect digestive power, we should devour our young as nature intended." "One day last week a woman at the Brooklyn Hotel attempted to refute some implications against her character by passing through an ordeal of arsenic. She was speedily pumped dry by a meddling medico, and her chastity is still a bone of contention."

Arsenic was suggested by Bierce for suicide. (One of Bierce's sons later committed suicide.) Bierce called Yosemite an "infernal valley that should be blown up with giant powder." He published his first Poe-esque horror story, "The Haunted Valley," of an insane man frightening a miner to death. While honeymooning in England with his wife, Molly Day, he produced a collection of macabre tales, one about a girl who killed her mother so that her lover might have a skull to play with. *The Fiend's Delight* and *Cobwebs from an Empty Skull* were published in England.

Young William Randolph Hearst supplied Bierce with his first wide audience; his "Prattle" column appearing Sundays in the *Examiner*. "Prattle" often contradicted the *Examiner's* editorial page, but Hearst never interfered, although Bierce's verse, widely quoted as causing the assassination of President McKinley, brought nationwide attacks upon the publisher. Bierce's biographer, Carey McWilliams, said that in his neurotic moods, intensified by asthma, Bierce frequently resigned, but he was "pampered, mollified and befriended by Hearst." While in his employ, Bierce produced *Tales of Soldiers and Civilians,* considered by many equal to the work of Poe.

In *Adventures of a Novelist* Gertrude Atherton said that when she went with friends to call on Bierce at Sunol, where he lived because of asthma, they quarreled all day. As she was leaving, they passed a pigsty on the ranch and Bierce tried to kiss her. She escaped laughing. "The great Bierce, master of style, tried to kiss a woman by a pigsty!" He almost flung her onto the train: "You're the most detestable vixen I ever met. I've had a horrible day!"

Bierce quarreled frequently with his friends. Edwin Markham was attacked for "The Man with the Hoe." Bierce parted from George Sterling and Jack London after the two became Socialists. Bierce's preachment of suicide was absorbed by Sterling, London, and two poet friends, Herman Scheffauer and Dr. Doyle of Santa Cruz—all followed Bierce's teaching and killed themselves.

Bierce's most effective work was at Washington while assisting Hearst's campaign to defeat the Central Pacific funding bill which would have liquidated the railroad debt of $60 million. Although only fifty-four, he did little important work after that. Ill, embittered, he disappeared seventeen years later across the Mexican border, like one of his own Poe-esque characters.

Archibald Clavering Gunter is almost forgotten, but he was the first man educated in San Francisco's public schools and graduated from the University of California, to write a world best seller, *Mr. Barnes of New York*. At the age of six Gunter came with his parents from his birthplace, Liverpool, England, and after leaving the university became a civil engineer, chemist, mine superintendent, and broker. In 1879 he moved to New York and married. *Mr. Barnes of New York* was first written as a comedy, in which a persistent New Yorker woos an English girl on a train, prevents her from obtaining food in her compartment, and starves her into submission.

Producers disdained the play, but Gunter transformed it into a novel, and again it was rejected. The enterprising author organized a company and published *Mr. Barnes of New York* with gaudy, yellow covers. Within a year sales passed a million. Gunter's dramatization of his book ran eighteen years, with ten companies touring England. *Mr. Potter of Texas* and *Miss Nobody of Nowhere* attained almost equal popularity, making the author America's most widely read and prosperous novelist.

Frank Norris died in his early thirties, after giving promise of becoming America's greatest novelist. He is still mourned by critics and public. Chicago born, Frank was eager to become an artist when his family moved to San Francisco. During two years at Julien's Paris atelier, he devoured Zola. He wrote a medieval serial, *Gaston Le Fox*, which he sent chapter by chapter to his brother, Charles. When practical businessman Norris Sr. found that his son was not giving all his time to art, he summoned him home to enter the University of California.

At twenty Frank became a special student in the class of '94. Mustache, sideburns, and a sallow skin made him seem like a foreigner, older than the others. He abhorred science and mathematics, but history and French appealed to him.

Norris grew to have a contempt for poets, but in his freshman year he published in a university paper the verse: "At Damietta A.D." signed "Norrys '94." His talent for acting was inherited from his handsome mother, Mrs. B. B. Norris, who had been on the stage in Shakespearean roles and often gave readings. Also from her came his height and good looks. She sent his poem "Yvernelle," a tale of medieval France, to Lippincott's with his own illustrations. The publisher bought the poem, but rejected the drawings.

Norris left college with hair prematurely gray and without

having graduated. At the age of twenty-four, he went to Harvard
for a special course. His *McTeague* was dedicated to Harvard's
L. E. Gates. No "teacup tragedies" for Norris. He would write
"low-life stuff like Zola." He wrote stories for the *Argonaut* and the
Overland, but especially for J. O'Hara Cosgrave, co-owner of the
Wave, and later editor of *Everybody's.* Norris joined Dr. Jameson's
filibustering raid into the Transvaal Republic as a war correspondent.
Back in California, his *Moran of the Lady Letty* was soon published. *Blix* was inspired by the pretty dark-eyed San Francisco
girl, Janet Black, who became his wife.

Norris was reading proof for Doubleday, Page when he wrote
The Octopus, picturing California in the tentacles of the railroad.
"This is life," pronounced William Dean Howells. The railroad
owner was suggested by C. P. Huntington and the highwayman by
Chris Evans, who was said to have turned to crime after being
evicted from his Mussels Slough property. Norris wrote *The Pit,*
which pictured a speculator cornering Chicago wheat. He planned
a trilogy showing the story of wheat from the time of sowing
until it relieved famine in Europe. A third novel was to be called
The Wolf. The Pit, dedicated to Norris's wife, had an even larger
sale than *The Octopus,* but was less acclaimed. The public was
eagerly awaiting *The Wolf* when Norris died on a surgeon's operating table in San Francisco.

No writer's boyhood could have been more different from
Norris's than that of his contemporary, Jack London. Norris had
everything, London nothing. His unfortunate mother, Flora Well-
man, daughter of a prosperous canal builder of Massillon, Ohio,
ran away from home at sixteen. Her life for a decade was obscure.
At thirty she appeared in San Francisco giving piano lessons and
attending séances. She allied herself with the free lover-writer-
attorney-astrologer-spiritualist William Henry Chaney, from Maine,
who lived precariously, sometimes being in jail. Chaney left her
when he found that she was with child, and she tried to kill herself
in San Francisco (1875). Jack London's mother gained security
by marrying widower John London, a laboring man and unsuccessful vineyardist. London did the best he could for his odd
little stepson. The boy sold newspapers, lived on the waterfront,
got drunk, and went to sea, but always pored over books.

Eager to find his father, London wrote Chaney at Chicago, who denied him. Depressed, the boy grew closer to his stepfather, but away from his mother, with her scarred forehead, resulting from attempted suicide. Jack loved boats and always had one. Fascinated by hobo life, he saw the United States from brake beams. After a few months at the University of California adventure called him to the Alaska gold rush of 1897.

The Far North gave him a setting for his *Call of the Wild,* written at Oakland. He never again equaled his masterpiece, the story of Buck, the dog that escapes human control, returning to the wild to lead a wolf pack. Later came *The Sea Wolf,* portraying a brutal sea captain, which was widely read and filmed many times. *The Iron Heel* and *The Revolution* made preachments against poverty. *Martin Eden* and *John Barleycorn* revealed his own experiences with drink.

Early in life London ran for mayor of Oakland on the Socialist ticket. He lived with Charmian, his second wife, on 1,400 acres of land purchased in the Valley of the Moon, Sonoma County. He easily earned large sums by producing a thousand words a day. He was openhanded, and many in need settled at his ranch. Jack and Charmian sailed the meandering waterways of Sonoma County in his little boat, the *Roamer.* They erected "Wolf House," a three-story stone dwelling, quarried from red rock. Fortunately the Londons had not moved their splendid library to the house before a mysterious fire broke out, leaving only gaunt chimneys and denuded walls in the blackened redwood grove. The house was not rebuilt.

London and his wife set out for the South Seas in the *Snark,* a boat built at his order, but they abandoned the trip as the *Snark* was unseaworthy. Hair tousled, driving his bell-decked team about Sonoma County, Jack was a well-beloved figure, and the community was shocked when he was found dying in 1916, with bottles of morphine sulphate and atropine sulphate at his side. Irving Stone, Jack's biographer, asserts that the writer committed suicide. Joan London, Jack's daughter by his first wife, in her biography of her father stated that his last words written to her were: "I leave the ranch next Friday. I leave California, Wednesday following. Daddy."

Jack London's ashes rest by a boulder on his ranch which has a historical marker. Charmian died in 1954 on the Sonoma property. The Glen Ellen Women's Club established the Jack London Memorial Library and Community Center. Oakland, where he lived for many years, has a Jack London Square, dedicated to his memory and ornamented with his bust. Nearby is a restaurant named "Sea Wolf." A Little Theater group call themselves the "London Circle Players." A saloon built of timber from an old sailing vessel, at 50 Webster Street near the Oakland estuary, is famed for having cradled London's genius. The owner, John Heinhold, assisted him financially as a beginner, and London's picture hangs on the wall, also a letter from him inviting Heinhold to visit him at Glen Ellen.

San Francisco's most prolific native-born novelist is Kathleen Norris. When her father, Joseph Thompson, a bank employee, died leaving a large family without means, valiant Kathleen worked in shops, libraries, also becoming a reporter on the *Bulletin, Examiner,* and *Call.* After she married Charles Norris, brother of Frank, *Mother,* her first long story, appeared. Theodore Roosevelt praised it, and the public liked it so much that the young author's future was assured. No San Francisco writer has earned so large a fortune as Kathleen Norris, usually reproducing the Cinderella story in attractive form. At times she has brought forth novels of pioneer life, like *Barberry Bush.* Mrs. Norris's stories have frequently been filmed. She has always found time for political and social activities, taking part in campaigns against capital punishment and war. She has also made addresses for the Republican party. She is much in demand as an after-dinner speaker.

In 1955 Kathleen Norris published *Miss Harriet Townsend,* a story of mid-Victorian San Francisco and in 1959 she jetted to New York to confer with her publishers about her autobiography.

As business manager for his wife, Charles Norris, Kathleen's late husband, related how he succeeded in placing some of her stories after many rejections by publishers. Charles Norris was the author of several notable novels, among them *Salt* and *Brass.*

"Is she crazy or is she joking?" asked Sinclair Lewis, about Gertrude Stein, who, like her friend, Alice B. Toklas, was a San Francisco product. Before Gertrude Stein's wealthy parents died, and she went east to Radcliffe, she had read everything, even the Congressional Record. Philosopher William James became her friend when, instead of sending in a paper on psychology, she wrote him, "I don't feel like having an examination today." "I understand perfectly how you feel," replied James. "I often feel that way myself."

Gertrude Stein spent four years studying medicine at Johns Hopkins University, but scorned a degree. Ten years after leaving San Francisco, she was in Paris with Alice Toklas. Modern poet and dramatist, Gertrude became a patron of Picasso and Matisse, who influenced her greatly and who in turn were influenced by her. "My poodle always recognizes paintings. He knows a Renoir when he sees one."

She was the inspiration of a generation of young writers in Paris, including Ernest Hemingway.

Clad in rough-spun clothes and no-nonsense shoes, in 1935 Miss Stein came to San Francisco for the last time on a lecture tour. Although she had passed her mature life in Europe, she insisted that she was never expatriated, giving wholehearted hospitality to American soldiers.

In *920 O'Farrell Street* eighty-year-old Harriet Levy wrote the story of her childhood neighbors, Gertrude Stein and orphan Alice Toklas, who lived with opulent relations. She described Alice B. Toklas's monastic beauty, her flights from her grandparents' home to Monterey, where in a red mandarin coat she dined at Hotel Del Monte, damning her rich relations. Vacation over, she returned to "escape" in Henry James's novels. Miss Levy's book, her first and last, became a best seller.

Talent appeared often in the Levy family. One cousin, Dr. Albert Michelson, was a distinguished Nobel Prize winner and his sister, Miriam Michelson, who spent most of her life in San Francisco, made her literary debut, with the sprightly and humorous national best seller, *In the Bishop's Carriage*. Channing Pollock dramatized it for the stage, and later for the films. President Theodore Roosevelt congratulated her on *The Madigans*, portraying family life in Virginia City. Miss Michelson and her coworkers were said by the late O. K. Cushing, chairman of the Democratic State Central Committee, to have been responsible for the election of Woodrow Wilson. She organized the women's section of the

Democratic party, which made an effective campaign, their few hundred votes probably carrying the crucial state of California after Hughes had been prematurely congratulated on his announced election.

Stewart Edward White, who died in 1947, came to California from Michigan, and for more than thirty years lived in the San Francisco suburb of Burlingame. In his youth he wrote adventure novels, but in later years his books dealt with pioneer California which his father had visited in his youth. During their last decade together, White and his wife, Elizabeth Grant, were interested in occultism and spiritualism. Many of his last books dealt with subjects expressed by the title *The Unobstructed Universe*. White's widely read "Betty" books he believed were communications from his wife after death.

San Francisco-born Peter B. Kyne wrote many popular stories for the *Saturday Evening Post*, which later appeared in book form. *Cappy Ricks*, of whom Captain Robert Dollar was the original, delighted a large public. *Cappy Ricks* was filmed, as *The Pride of Palomar*. At the time of his death he was at work on another book.

Another San Franciscan, Ruth Comfort Mitchell, lived at Los Gatos for many years with her husband, Sanborn Young. One of her most widely acclaimed San Francisco novels was *The Wishing Carpet. The Night Court*, a dramatic poem of great strength, has many times been published, with other verse. Mrs. Young frequently took part in Republican political life, especially in helping President Hoover.

During the past two decades John Steinbeck's books and films gave him a world reputation and earned more than a million dollars. After being graduated from the Salinas High School, before becoming California's most celebrated novelist among men, he worked as a fruit picker, hod carrier, surveyor, caretaker of a Tahoe estate, and on a WPA literary project. *Tortilla Flat*, a story of Monterey ne'er-do-wells, found a large public. His success increased with *Of Mice and Men*, both in book form and on the stage—a protest against the sordid living conditions of ranch laborers. Most widely read is the Pulitzer Prize winner, *The Grapes of Wrath*, the story of refugees from Oklahoma. A quarter of a million strong they descended upon California and found the state unprepared to receive so many impoverished guests. California was arraigned for the resultant confusion and suffering. Its name ironically altered to "Paradise America," the book has been widely shown in Communist countries as an accurate picture of working conditions in the United States.

Steinbeck lives in New York and in 1954 had published *East of Eden* which as a film received the first award at the Cannes International Film Festival in 1955. His *The Short Reign of Pippin IV* was the Book-of-the-Month selection for May, 1957.

Almost at the same time that *The Grapes of Wrath* was published, William Saroyan, an Armenian-American of Fresno living in San Francisco, swung into fame with *The Daring Young Man on a Flying Trapeze*. Steinbeck and Saroyan are as opposite as the gloom of a German forest and California sunshine. Saroyan's play, *The Time of Your Life*, expressed only happiness, but his early youth was shadowed. At two he lost his father, a preacher and Fresno fruit grower. For a time he was in an Alameda orphanage, but he became a telegraph messenger, fruitgrower, reporter, and manager of a local Postal Telegraph office in San Francisco. His first story, published in an Armenian magazine when he was twenty-five, was listed by O'Brien in 1934.

When the Pulitzer Prize was awarded Saroyan for *The Time of Your Life*, he refused to accept it on the ground that commerce should not patronize art. *The Beautiful People* and *My Heart's in the Highlands* are two later plays radiating Saroyan's gay, humorous sympathy. After leaving the army he published *The Human Comedy*, which delighted many. In 1951 all America seemed to sing his "Come on-a My House."

A literary fairy tale was lived by a San Franciscan, Katherine Forbes, wife of Robert McLean, a Burlingame contractor. Her father's family founded Forbestown, but her mother was of Norwegian descent, delightfully portrayed in "Mama's Bank Account" and in the play and film *I Remember Mama*.

The mother of two half-grown sons, Mrs. McLean joined the short-story class at the adult night school of San Mateo Junior College. "Mama's Bank Account," a short story, was brought into the classroom as an exercise. Teacher Mrs. Lewellyn Peck advised her to send it to a magazine, but New York agents replied that it was unmarketable. Mrs. McLean persisted, and the *Reader's Digest* recognized its value, asking a Canadian magazine to publish it first, at that time it being contrary to their custom to purchase original material. "Mama's Bank Account" was followed by more stories, also read aloud in the classroom. Afterward they appeared in book form and were translated into many languages.

Before a Hollywood producer filmed the story, John Van Druten arranged it in play form. All actresses appearing as Mama in either play or film have had national success—Mady Christians, Charlotte Greenwood, and Irene Dunne. "Mama" has also had TV popularity.

Another adult night school literary success in 1950 was *Little Britches* written by Ralph Moody, San Francisco manager of a chain of sandwich shops. Although obliged to leave grammar school in Colorado to aid his widowed mother and his brothers and sisters, he studied nights in both high school and college courses. At fifty he produced *Little Britches*, the Moody family story. So movingly was it related that in condensed form it appeared in the *Reader's Digest*. *Little Britches* was followed by *Man of the Family*, *The Home Ranch*, and *The Fields of Home*, a popular saga of brave young America.

Song of America, another best seller, was written by a restaurateur, George Mardikian, owner of Omar Khayyam, San Francisco's famed, exotic eating place, called by Mrs. Roosevelt one of the two best restaurants in the United States.

Mardikian's birthday is November 7, but he celebrates July 24, because on that date in his eighteenth year he first saw the Statue of Liberty. Armenian George arrived in this country in 1922, but he had already been in the army since he was thirteen. When the Communists came into power, George's father was killed in the massacre. Remembering gratefully the American Relief Program of 1917, he decided that America was to be his country. At Ellis Island, the man in uniform smiled at him—the smile of America.

Beginning as a $12-a-week dishwasher at Coffee Dan's in San Francisco, after three or four years he became manager of an Oakland cafeteria. The culmination of his dream was his Omar Khayyam restaurant.

George was on every front in World War II supervising the

food for the army, for which he was given the Medal of Freedom by President Truman. He also dined with President Eisenhower. In his moving *Song of America,* George expresses his gratitude to America for giving him fame and fortune. He has aided many of his countrymen in finding homes in the United States; his scholarships have helped Armenian boys to attend American universities.

Completion of George Mardikian's dream would be to have the prison removed from the rock of Alcatraz and placed thereon a huge Statue of Liberty, like the one that greeted him when he came into New York. Cost of this would be millions, to be paid for by pennies of American school children.

Among widely read nonfiction writers is Oscar Lewis, who after six years of research produced *The Big Four,* vividly relating the building of the Central Pacific Railroad over the Sierras, as thrilling as fiction. In collaboration with Carol D. Hall Lewis wrote *Bonanza Inn,* the story of the Palace Hotel and its guests. It had as many readers as *The Big Four.* His other books, *High Sierra Country* and *Bay Window Bohemia,* also had a large public.

Dr. George Lyman was a writer by avocation. His biography of Pioneer John Marsh was written with the realism of a surgeon and the skill of an artist. In *The Saga of the Comstock Lode* and *The Ralston Ring,* Dr. Lyman portrayed phases of Nevada where his father had been a well-known mining engineer.

Few have written so long and so prolifically of San Francisco as Robert O'Brien. *This is San Francisco* and *California Called Them* both made best-seller lists.

When the late Will Irwin returned to San Francisco in 1947 with the play *Lute Song,* he had come back to the city where he did his first writing fifty years ago. *Lute Song,* a translation from the Chinese, resulted from Irwin's collaboration with another Californian, Sidney Howard, author of *They Knew What They Wanted, The Silver Cord,* and the film of *Gone with the Wind.*

After graduating from Stanford, Will Irwin wrote many books, including the biography of his friend and classmate, Herbert Hoover. With Bayard Veiller he collaborated in a highly successful play, *The Thirteenth Chair.* Will Irwin is fondly remembered in San Francisco by his moving *The City That Was,* written in the office of the New York *Sun* in 1906, while the city was burning.

San Francisco's twentieth-century Byron was George Sterling, Bohemia's king. Charmed by his verse and his Dantesque profile, women fell into his arms. Few could resist his phrase-making and romantic gestures, such as wading in a Golden Gate Park pool by moonlight to gather water lilies for a lady-love. In 1907 the beautiful but doomed Nora May French swallowed poison at the Sterlings' Carmel house. Her ashes were strewn over Point Lobos, and the poet is said to have visited the spot frequently.

When *The Wine of Wizardry* was published Sterling lived in New York. Finding it too difficult to be married to a genius his Junoesque wife, Caroline Rand, departed and was later found dead by poison in her Piedmont home. From that time Sterling carried a vial of poison. Such a character attracted Ambrose Bierce, who after *The Testimony of the Sons* was published in 1903 wrote, "You shall be a poet of the skies, and a prophet of the sun."

Sterling was schooled to be a priest at Sag Harbor, Long Island, where he was born. Celibacy, however, was not for him, nor was employment in his uncle's Oakland real estate office. Sterling moved to San Francisco, "the cool gray city":

> At the end of our streets is sunrise;
> At the end of our streets are spars;
> At the end of our streets is sunset;
> At the end of our streets are stars.

Often till midnight Sterling sat at Coppa's or Bigin's drinking whisky and soda, surrounded by admirers, giving away poems. His verse brought slight monetary return. He tried writing jazz, scenarios, and stories. He sold a plot to Jack London, who in his last years bought plots.

Friends paid the troubadour's bills at the Bohemian Club, where he lived. London and Sterling discussed death, agreeing that when their life was spent they would bow themselves out.

Sterling began to realize that he was no longer a force. Eating caused him pain, drinking ended in sickness, and the lovely young avoided his rendezvous. His last effort was collecting wine to entertain his friend, H. L. Mencken, the Baltimore columnist and critic, lingering in Hollywood. After consuming the liquor, Sterling became melancholy because he had no money to buy more. He called on editor Fremont Older of the *Call-Bulletin,* gave him a book, and warmly shook hands. He visited Austin Lewis and left a manuscript with Ethel Turner. None realized that it was farewell.

When Mencken finally arrived, Sterling was unable to preside at the Bohemian Club dinner. Mencken tapped on his door—no answer. The next morning the club valet found the poet sleeping. At noon the manager opened the door, and in a litter of poems and letters, George Sterling was found dead of poison. Today's critics call the poet's unrestrained verse flamboyant, but his tribute to beauty lingers:

> We know we shall seek her till we die,
> And find her not at all, the Fair and Far.

Russian Hill has a bench with a plaque in memory of the poet, placed there by the late William B. Bourn, president of the Spring Valley Water Company. To many Sterling is not dead. He seems eternally to be seeking the "Fair and Far."

One of the most prolific and applauded native-born San Franciscans writing today is Irving Stone, whose *Lust for Life* in cinema form was big box office at the same time that his *Men to Match My Mountains* was high on best-seller lists. As a child of three, Stone, born Tennenbaum, and his mother were made homeless by the Fire of 1906. The mother began selling in a department store and became manager of her section, thus supporting her two children. So valiantly did Pauline Stone Tennenbaum battle adversity for her two small children that Irving changed his name to Stone and dedicated his first successful book, *Lust for Life,* to his mother.

While a student in the San Francisco schools, Stone flunked Latin, geometry, and chemistry. Briefly living in Los Angeles, he returned north with $245 earned by him, to enter the University of California. By playing the saxophone at dances, running an elevator, and working summers in fruit, he graduated in 1923 in political science. His Master's Degree came later.

His first literary attempts were stories and plays, but success came in 1934 when he married Jean Proctor and wrote *Lust for Life.* He calls her his editor. *Lust for Life* resulted from following the footsteps of Vincent van Gogh, even sleeping in his bed, but the story was rejected by many publishers. Van Gogh's popular biography was followed by *Clarence Darrow for the Defense, A Sailor on Horseback,* revealing Jack London, and *Immortal Wife,* inspired by Jessie Benton Frémont. Stone's *Men to Match My Mountains* portrays the pioneers who made the West, and it has received wide acclaim.

Modestly Stone says that he might not have tried to write the biographical novel of van Gogh had he not been inspired by Gertrude Atherton's *The Conqueror,* the biography in novel form of Alexander Hamilton, and also by Dmitri Merezhkovski's *The Romance of Leonardo da Vinci.* Mr. and Mrs. Stone spent some time in Florence, where he finished his recent noteworthy biographical novel of Michelangelo.

Most recent native-born San Francisco novelist is Barnaby Conrad. Educated at the University of North Carolina and the University of Mexico, he received his Bachelor of Arts degree from Yale. He began writing while he was secretary to Sinclair Lewis. His books *Matador* and *Death of Manolete* were both best sellers. His latest book was *San Francisco: A Profile with Pictures.*

Doubtless 1630 Sacramento Street, San Francisco, will one day have a historical marker, for this was the birthplace of the celebrated poet Robert Frost. Here he was born on March 26, 1875. His father, William P. Frost, Jr., worked for ten years in the editorial department of the *Call.* After the father died in 1885, Robert, together with his mother and sister, left San Francisco for Lawrence, Massachusetts. Much of his youth was passed in New England, but he returned to his native state in 1958 and made an address at the Greek Theatre at the University of California.

A curious literary phase bubbled up in San Francisco's North Beach bistros in the mid-1950's. Leaders of the new school were Jack Kerouac, whose novel *Subterraneans* had a North Beach background, and Allen Ginsberg, who authored the poem "Howl." A wave of sensational publicity swept from coast to coast in the wake of this pair and their bearded followers, but at present writing the beatnik phase seems to be passing and with no promise of leaving a lasting impression upon George Sterling's "cool gray city of love."

CHAPTER 14

The Arts Develop

EVEN BEFORE Yerba Buena became San Francisco there were some excellent paintings at Mission Dolores. Itinerant Mexican artists portrayed the families of the great rancheros. These canvases have disappeared. San Francisco's first museums were auction rooms, like those of J. C. Duncan, father of Isadora. Duncan also served as president of the Art Association which was founded in 1871. Proprietor Woodward of the What Cheer House had an early collection of art. After developing Woodward's Gardens, he sent Virgil Williams to Europe to copy old masterpieces for his museum.

Toby Rosenthal was the first San Francisco artist to win European fame. He arrived in the city in 1857 from New Haven, Connecticut, and was given drawing lessons by Lewis Bacon. Fortunato Arriola taught him free for fourteen months, then persuaded Toby's German-born parents to send him to Munich for instruction. After studying at the Royal Academy, Rosenthal's first painting, "Affection's Last Offer," was acclaimed in Europe and the United States. Leipsic's city museum purchased his "Morning Services in the Home of Sebastian Bach."

When young Rosenthal returned to San Francisco in 1881, Tiburcio Parrott commissioned him to paint "Elaine, the Lily Maid of Astolat," suggested by Tennyson's *Idylls of the King*. From Munich Toby wrote Mr. Parrott that, since the canvas was more ambitious than he thought, he was forced to ask a larger fee. Receiving no reply, when Mrs. Robert C. Johnson ("the cat lady") admired the picture in Munich, he sold it. Was the artist guilty of breach of contract? Controversy raged in the press. When "Elaine" was exhibited at the galleries of Snow and May, thousands viewed the

147

painting. The third day the canvas vanished—cut from its frame! Two days later it was recovered unharmed. Thieves had made off with the painting only to collect a reward.

At the Philadelphia Centennial Exposition of 1876, "Elaine" won a gold medal. Senator Fair purchased the picture from Mrs. Johnson for $5,000, then sold it for $6,000 to the Art Institute of Chicago, where it hangs today.

Excitement over "Elaine" had hardly subsided when thirty-year-old Rosenthal brought forth "The Seminary Alarm." Hailed as another masterpiece, it was exhibited in Germany and San Francisco. The painting is owned by the de Young Museum. Irving M. Scott bought Rosenthal's "The Punishment of Constance de Beverly." During the Fire of 1906 his daughter, Mrs. Reginald Knight Smith, with quick thinking and execution, cut the canvas from its frame, rolled it up and buried it. The painting was later retrieved virtually undamaged. It is in the Memorial Art Gallery of Stanford University, a loan from Mrs. Smith and her brother, Lawrence I. Scott.

Two of Rosenthal's most notable paintings, "The Cardinal's Portrait" and "The Seine Madonna," belong to the Jacob Stern collection which is on long-term loan at the California Palace of the Legion of Honor.

Contemporaneous with Toby Rosenthal was William Keith, whose entire life as an artist was passed in San Francisco, painting California and Californians. Born in Scotland, Keith came by steerage to San Francisco in 1859 and worked as a wood engraver, but he is the only California painter whose brush made him a millionaire. For William P. Harrison, his first employer, he made letterheads and wine labels, largest orders coming from Irving M. Scott, president of the Union Iron Works. He engraved the Bear insignia of the *Overland* for Bret Harte, and also made the frontispiece for *The Lost Galleon*.

At that time there were already thirty professional artists in San Francisco, but an art teacher, rosy-cheeked Elizabeth Emerson, distant cousin of Ralph Waldo, urged Keith to become an artist. Following her advice, he had lessons with Samuel Brooks, a still-life painter. Keith and Elizabeth were married on February 5, 1864. For a wedding trip they went down to the waterfront, and, legs dangling over the edge of the wharf, breakfasted gazing at the bay.

At first Keith used wood-engraving technique in painting Mount Tamalpais and San Mateo scenes, but he did not abandon his trade. Irving M. Scott, a man of enthusiasms, saw Keith's paintings and ordered four canvases of the four seasons, now the property of his family. Through Scott the Oregon Railway and Navigation Company commissioned Keith to do five oil paintings and five water colors. The artist had an orgy of scenic grandeur, sketching Mounts Hood, Rainier, and Shasta. "On that trip I was suddenly revealed to myself."

Back in San Francisco, he opened his first studio in the new Mercantile Library Building on Bush Street, painting with freedom and breadth. J. C. Duncan bought some of his pictures, and Newhall and Company auctioned his canvases, making him richer by $10,000.

At that time the sensation of the art world was Thomas Hill, who also sold his "Yosemite" for $10,000. Art-loving San Franciscans debated—was Keith or Hill the greater painter? Critic Benjamin T. Avery, later minister to China, praised Keith's work in the *Overland*. Art collectors considered his opinion final.

Elizabeth said they must go to Europe. Leaving their two young children with relatives in Maine, they ventured. At last he was feasting his eyes on Rubens, Murillo, and Rembrandt. "I'm going to be a good artist or die."

Keith was soon homesick for San Francisco, however, and the European trip was cut short. In New York he exhibited paintings of "Tamalpais" and "Shasta." Bostonians bought his scenes of Maine and California. The Keiths spent a formal evening with Elizabeth's cousin, Ralph Waldo Emerson. The Concord philosopher liked "Man," but with men was aloof. Keith was glad to be once more among his uninhibited San Francisco friends, naturalist "Johnnie" Muir and the Scotts.

At the suggestion of Keith and Hill, the San Francisco Art Association was born in 1871, with rooms on Pine Street over the California Market. So many came to the semiannual exhibition that it was difficult to see the pictures. Muir called Keith a "poet-painter," and John H. Hittell insisted that his work was better than that of Turner or Claude Lorraine. Ina Coolbrith wrote, "You drink of Art's immortal spring."

Keith's popularity increased and Hill's lessened when Senator Stanford repudiated his contract with Hill to paint the driving of

"The Last Spike." The canvas was widely exhibited, but not sold until after Hill's death. His "Donner Lake," shown at the Philadelphia Centennial, brought him the first medal for landscape. Hill took up his residence at Wawona near the Yosemite Valley and continued to sell his paintings until he died in 1908.

Artists in the seventies and eighties strove to reproduce the Yosemite. When he began, Keith said sunsets couldn't be too gorgeous and mountains couldn't be too high for him to attempt. Finally, however, he concluded that the Yosemite was unpaintable. and contented himself with putting a wooded hillside on canvas.

America's premier landscape artist, George Inness, was determined to conquer the Yosemite, and in 1881 he arrived from New York. Handing Inness his watch and purse, Keith said, "My studio is yours." After a long struggle to paint the Yosemite, Inness also gave up. A canvas on which both Inness and Keith worked is owned by the Gump family.

Elizabeth Emerson Keith lived to see her husband surpass even her ambitions for him, and when she died in 1882 Keith was desolate. "Eighteen years married, and never a cross word from her, but so many from me!" Despairingly he went to Laurel Hill Cemetery and painted weird pictures. Among consoling friends was Mary McHenry, an art student, who had become a lawyer. Sympathy for Keith's loneliness drew them together, and she became his wife two years after Elizabeth's death.

Again fortunate in marriage, Keith took his bride on a tour of the missions, painting seventeen of the twenty-one. When women gushed over him, Keith said, "Thank God, I can go home to Mary, who doesn't know or care anything about my pictures." "Oh, yes, I do, Willie, but there's so many of them!"

Keith did not like visitors at his studio watching him paint, and one day a strange lady entered. "May I look around?" Keith went on painting. "How much is this picture?" "$5,000." "And this?" "$5,000." "I'll take the two. I'm Mrs. Armour of Chicago. My husband will send you a check." At this time he could paint seven large pictures in a week, all different. If buyers tried to haggle, he said, "The picture is not for sale."

C. P. Huntington posed for three different portraits by Keith. "I'd give all my wealth if I could paint as you do." A tireless worker himself, Keith's industry appealed to Huntington. "You're always working in your studio. Other artists are anywhere else."

Governor Stanford, Fred Crocker, and Mark Hopkins bought many Keiths. Gordon Blanding acquired eleven. He paid the highest known Keith price, $11,000, for "The Glory of the Heavens." Henriette Blanding, now Mrs. B. H. Lehman of Saratoga, wrote excellent verse to her father's Keiths. Architect McKim of New York expended $35,000 for Keith pictures for the Metropolitan Museum, of which he was trustee. Again Keith went to Europe, but after five weeks in the galleries he returned to San Francisco. "Lord, it's a great country. I've been a native son ever since I came in 1859."

Keith's rich patrons advised him how to invest his rapidly increasing fortune. Mary was active in the suffrage movement. Although never enthusiastic about suffrage, he gave thousands to Mary's cause and to a society for the protection of animals. Mary Keith made crusading suffrage speeches, and he teased, "Remember, if you go to jail, I won't get you out." His greatest happiness was walking with Mary, the children, and their dogs in the Berkeley Hills.

When from their heights Keith saw San Francisco burning, he experienced the suffering portrayed by him in what his biographer, Brother Cornelius, calls his greatest painting, "Gethsemane." Hastening across the bay, when he was turned back by soldiers he realized that his paintings and studio were insured for only $4,000. "My forty years' work lost!" On learning that his studio had been dynamited, he said, "I will paint better pictures. I have much to be thankful for. I'm in perfect health, and I will work harder than ever. I could be happy in San Quentin, if I had paints and brushes."

Keith had forgotten that his closest friend, the Rev. Joseph Worcester, had a key to his studio. The clergyman had taken twenty-five of the best canvases to his own residence on Russian Hill.

The half-billion-dollar fire did not discourage Keith. At sixty-seven he could not paint fast enough. He produced Rembrandtesque canvases, also his superb "Burning City." Five years later his brush failed, and friends paid their last visit to the Berkeley dwelling where his two dogs, Brownie and Hegel, guarded his casket. When it was taken away, Hegel tried to follow. Twenty-four girls, from twelve to twenty years old, dressed in white and each carrying a

St. Joseph lily, attended the casket to St. Mark's Episcopal Church. His widow was bequeathed $500,000. The remaining $500,000 was divided among his children and friends. San Francisco, Berkeley, and Oakland have streets named for Keith.

The modernistic movement has caused many of Keith's canvases, as well as those of Inness, which sold as high as $50,000, to be removed from museum walls and stored. His canvases in the lighter key still hold their own. His greatest are in the pre-Inness period, and certain later canvases, when he forgot Inness and was wholly William Keith. San Francisco has nearly eight hundred artists, many of high excellence, but none stands pre-eminent as did William Keith.

San Francisco has produced distinguished sculptors with national reputations like Robert Aitken, Arthur Putnam, Haig Patigian, and Edgar Walter. More recent are Ruth Cravath Wakefield, Keith Monroe, Robert Howard, also his wife, Adeline Kent. Sargent Johnson is a gifted Negro sculptor. Most controversial is five-foot-three Italian-born Beniamino Bufano.

"Is he a genius or a freak?" San Franciscans have asked ever since Bufano returned to his native Italy to spend several weeks at Assisi, St. Francis' birthplace. He roamed among galleries, museums, and churches, seeking every known likeness of the saint. Inspired by a vision of St. Francis, when he saw a 30-ton block of Swedish granite, he began working in Paris on St. Francis' figure, hardly eating or sleeping for a year and a half. Then he learned that his statue had been rejected by his patrons. For twenty-eight years it gathered dust in a Paris storehouse. Finally, art patrons raised $1,000 to pay Bufano's fare to Paris and they arranged for the transportation of St. Francis to San Francisco. A French liner transported the eighteen-foot statue freight free as a contribution to the Church of St. Francis. On St. Francis Day in October, 1955, Benny's giant statue was placed before the Church of St. Francis.

At Stanford is Benny's figure of Christ, carved from a tree. He gave all his work, valued by him at $1 million, to Stanford University.

In Moscow on the fortieth anniversary of the Red Revolution, the sixty-six-year-old Bufano had a long interview with Premier Bulganin which sounded like a summit meeting. They called each other "comrade" and argued about which country should be the first to destroy all weapons of war. Neither convinced the other. Bufano, however, exhibited a model of a statue 100 feet tall which shows an American and a Russian aviator shaking hands atop a shaft, a statue of Peace. He offered to provide the work if Russia would supply the material. Bulganin said he would take the matter under advisement. Bufano went on with his dream. The metal for the statue cost $1,200 and it took him three years to pay the bill. He says he is glad to work for the "Peace" statue, for his religion is the human race. He lives in a continual storm of controversy over his art. In 1961 his statue of St. Francis was taken to Oakland, but Benny wishes it to be given to the United Nations. British art critic Robert Fry calls Bufano's St. Francis the "most significant piece of sculpture in the past 500 years." Another critic says, "Bufano will be better understood, both as a man and as an artist, 5,000 years hence."

Maud Fay was San Francisco's first native daughter to have a leading role at the Metropolitan Opera House in New York. Daughter of Mr. and Mrs. Philip S. Fay, her voice attracted attention while she was a student at the Girls' High School. After graduating she enrolled at Madame Anna von Meyerink's School of Music. Madame Gadski, Walter Damrosch, and David Bispham advised her to go to Germany for vocal development.

After studying three years in Dresden, in 1908 she sang the role of Tosca at the Munich première of Puccini's opera, and appeared as Eurydice in Gluck's *Orfeo*. The Prince Regent of Bavaria heard her sing Wagnerian roles and bestowed upon her the title "Königliche Bayerische Hofopern Sängerin." Her career continued until World War I, when she engaged in Red Cross work in Germany, singing for the benefit of the wounded.

Back in San Francisco, her first concert, February 18, 1916, was with the San Francisco Symphony. Her numbers, largely Wagnerian, revealed the grandeur of her voice.

When she appeared at the Metropolitan Opera House after her San Francisco engagement, the critics wrote of her beauty, charm and temperament. After a triumphant tour, including New York, Chicago, and Philadelphia, she became the wife of the Baltimorean, Captain Powers Symington, U.S.N., and retired from operatic and concert stages to become a leader in social and musical activities in San Francisco.

San Francisco's newest diva is Lucine Amara, a former typist for the Southern Pacific Railroad and Bank of America clerk. This Cinderella prima donna earned vocal lessons by being an usher at the Opera House concerts. She is the daughter of Mr. and Mrs. George Amagani, and changed her name to the more euphonious "Amara." Born at Hartford, Connecticut, her childhood was passed in the flat over her father's Fillmore Street shoe repair shop. She made her debut in San Francisco in 1947 at a recital organized by the boys working in her father's shop who invited critics to come and listen to her songs.

Critics were enthralled and she began taking lessons with Madame Eisner-Eyn. In 1951 she won the Atwater-Kent Award in Hollywood over 1,500 contestants.

Three years after she made her debut as Nedda in *I Pagliacci* with the Metropolitan Opera Company and her brilliant, sympathetic, dramatic soprano voice enchanted New York. The audience interrupted the music at the end of the aria to salute her with applause. Her voice in *I Pagliacci* was recorded for Columbia records. In one year she appeared in fifty-three performances at the Metropolitan.

Usherettes at the San Francisco Opera House were proud of Lucine when they saw her as the cover girl of *Musical America,* and in 1951 she planed west from New York, for the fifth National Musical Festival of the Pacific Coast at the Opera House. When after the performance the usherettes gave her an ice-cream and cooky party they found her the same unspoiled girl that she had been before she was crowned with success.

She appeared at a concert with the San Francisco Symphony Orchestra at the Opera House where she had been an usherette, singing the first aria, "Mi Tradi," from Mozart's *Don Giovanni.* Like Tetrazzini in 1910, Lucine in 1953 serenaded the nation on Christmas Eve, singing from Union Square. Ten thousand acclaimed her later at Stern Grove, and no one was more proud of Lucine than her coach, Madame Eisner-Eyn. Her gratifications increased in 1959 when Lucine appeared for the first time as Aïda, at the Metropolitan in New York. Her performance enhanced and gave new distinction to her career.

"In the Garden of My Heart" sold two million copies, and its author was Caro Roma, an old Tivoli favorite who wrote more than a hundred songs. Another of her songs, "Oh, Can't You Hear Me Calling, Caroline?" was bought by 300,000. She also wrote many orchestral pieces and more than a thousand poems, the best known being "The Birth of a Lie."

Even at the age of three, in 1869, when Carrie Northey made her first appearance at Platt Hall, she sang a little verse of her own composition. Daughter of an East Oakland blacksmith, Vernon S. Northey, she changed her name to Caro Roma. After being graduated from the Boston Conservatory of Music, she appeared as a prima donna with the Castle Square Opera Company, singing before Queen Victoria and Emperor Francis Joseph. For ten years she sang at the Tivoli Opera House. Her last professional appearance was in New York's Lyric Theatre. Honoring her seventy-second birthday, a special broadcast of her songs went out through the air lanes. She was then paralyzed. Two weeks later, September 2, 1937, she died.

When two-year-old Yehudi Menuhin arrived in San Francisco in 1918 the family's capital was 32 cents. For a week the Moshe Menuhins had sat up day and night on local trains bringing them from New York City, where Yehudi was born. The Travellers' Aid Society assisted them on their arrival, for the teacher-parents had no money to pay the way to their brother's ranch.

Young Moshe Menuhin had only one year previously graduated from the New York University, where he majored in mathematics. Both he and his young Yalta-born wife taught Hebrew. They established San Francisco's first modern school, and he was director of the Jewish Educational Society. Hebrew was Yehudi's mother tongue, but soon he learned German, French, English, Italian, and Russian.

While still in swaddling clothes, the sturdy babe was taken by the music-loving family to a symphony concert. His parents said he sat up listening, and enjoying the music. Shortly before he was five he asked for a violin, "like that man who plays solos in the orchestra." He referred to Louis Persinger, who became his first teacher and gave him a technical foundation in music. Yehudi's father bought a small violin so that he and his two sisters could have lessons. None of the three ever saw the inside of a schoolroom.

San Francisco music lovers realized that a new genius had arrived when the self-possessed seven-year-old boy appeared and, tucking his small violin under his chin, charmed the audience. Sydney M. Ehrman gave him a fine violin and became his financial patron. At seven the lad's parents took him to Europe, where he studied with Georges Enesco and Adolf Busch. In Paris he had sensational success with the Lamoreaux Orchestra, but most memorable was his performance at Carnegie Hall in the city of his birth, where he gave a performance of Beethoven's Concerto with the New York Symphony Orchestra, enchanting the musical world. From that time he had no need of financial backers.

The Moshe Menuhins gave up their school to direct their son. For many years they have lived in the Santa Cruz Mountains on the Rancho de las Rosas, acquired by them from Playwright Richard Walton Tully. Yehudi flew many times to the Los Gatos ranch after plane trips around the world, but of late years he has come by train. In World War II he gave hundreds of concerts for American and British Red Cross and war victims. From his Stradivarius often came not only "Ave Maria," but simple songs the men in uniform loved, such as, "I Left My Heart at the Stage Door Canteen."

On tour of India Yehudi gave concerts, the proceeds of which were distributed among the charities of the young republic. At that time Yehudi and Nehru became fast friends. After the war Yehudi was the first American artist to give concerts in Russia.

Yehudi's first wife was Miss Nola Nicholas of Australia, mother of his two older children. Amicably divorced from her, he married Miss Diana Gould, a London ballerina, mother of his two younger children. He lives with his wife and four children in a villa at Gsaad, Switzerland.

In 1959 Yehudi, now in his forties, and his sister, Hephzibah, filled the San Francisco Opera House with a joint violin and piano recital. It was the first time they had appeared in San Francisco together since they had been child prodigies thirty years ago. Hand in hand, the famed brother and sister walked out on the stage for their joint recital. Yehudi is one of the world's great violinists and Hephzibah matched grandly the rapturous and lofty strains of her brother's violin.

For thirty-four years Gaetano Merola was San Francisco's most beloved man of music. It was Mrs. Sigmund Stern's influence that organized a group of sponsors for *Carmen* at the Stanford Stadium, from which flowered the San Francisco organization under Director Gaetano Merola that finally built the Opera House. He often discovered and trained San Francisco singers. Merola at the age of eighteen graduated from the Naples Royal Conservatory. His father, Giuseppe Merola, was a violinist at the court of Ferdinand II, and also a friend of Verdi's.

In August, 1954, Merola was on the podium at the Sigmund Stern Grove, his baton leading young Brunetta Mazzalini in the aria "Un Bel Di" (One Fair Day) from *Madame Butterfly*, by Puccini, whom he had known as a boy in Naples. Suddenly he slumped, as the singer's voice lifted on a high note. He fell to the floor as 10,000 listeners gasped with shock. Mrs. Stern rushed forward, cried, "My God, he has fallen!" A khaki-clad youth and a priest leaped upon the stage. Critic Alexander Fried started up from the press table, "Ladies and gentlemen, the concert is over." Gaetano Merola died as he would have liked—baton in hand.

An impressive Verdi's *Requiem* at the Opera House honored the memory of the founder and director of San Francisco's Opera House. Among those who sang, all had been brought to San Francisco by him and trained: Licia Albanese, soprano; Clara Mae Turner, contralto; Jan Peerce, tenor; and Nicola Moscona, basso. The San Francisco Symphony Orchestra and more than 120 singers contributed their talents. In the foyer of the Opera House a large bronze plaque bearing Gaetano Merola's likeness commemorates his thirty-four years' devotion to music in San Francisco.

CHAPTER 15

San Francisco Builds Museums

NO CITY had a more beautiful setting for its first adequate museum than San Francisco's Golden Gate Park, which was largely the creation of "Uncle John" McLaren. He made San Francisco a rhododendron city by bringing four hundred varieties from every part of the globe. The 1,015-acre park has 15 miles of roads and 27 miles of paths and trails. And yet, on March 8, 1866, when acquired by Postmaster Frank McCoppin, Golden Gate Park was only a waste of sand dunes. William Hammond Hall, landscape artist and engineer, planted *Arundo arenaria,* a creeping underground perennial that absorbed the salt, making the spot a home for blue and yellow lupines. Eucalypti, Monterey and European pines, and cypress were planted by the thousands. When Hall resigned in 1882, John McLaren took over the task of beautification. For half a century he was a familiar figure in the park, driving about in his sulky, helpfully criticizing workers and stimulating them with praise.

His skill was developed in Edinburgh's Botanical Gardens and on England's great estates. He was long in charge of the famous George Howard garden at San Mateo. McLaren planned to have forty-seven parks, one within walking distance of every San Francisco home. From Europe, South America, the Orient, he brought trees and shrubs for planting, but California's native growth was most emphasized. He avoided stiff formalism and developed naturalistic landscape.

He saw, however, beauty in the hybrid flowers, fuchsias, 125 varieties of camellias, tall tree ferns in the De Laveaga Dell, donated by Joseph De Laveaga, and he rejoiced when Alice Eastwood suggested the Shakespeare Garden containing every flower mentioned

158

by Shakespeare. James D. Phelan obtained for the garden a replica of the Girard Jansen bust of the bard in the Stratford-on-Avon church. McLaren was greatly pleased when gifts came for the park: the Spreckels Temple of Music in gray sandstone, the Academy of Sciences, sustained largely by the $2 million of James Lick. He would have been pleased with today's half-million-dollar Alexander Peter Morrison Memorial Planetarium, presenting three one-hour shows daily, the heaven's own theater, with real stars in the sky, and the half-million-dollar Hall of Flowers at 9th Avenue and Lincoln in Golden Gate Park. Here are held annual flower shows, and here garden clubs display their choicest flowers.

McLaren did not forget recreation: the Children's Playground donated by Senator William Sharon, with two young elephants, a gift from Allan H. Fleishhacker; the fly-casting pool; the athletic field for tennis, baseball, soccer, croquet, archery, bowling; the golf course established by Honora Sharp's $200,000 bequest; the $100,-000 Recreation Center, donated by Mrs. Mary Kezar; and the city's million-dollar Fleishhacker salt-water swimming pool, 1,000 feet long, the longest and most completely equipped pool in the world.

McLaren did not care for the park's twenty-two monuments and statues, thinking that they violated nature, and he tried to conceal them with vines. Mrs. Adolph Spreckels, however, gave a bronze statue of "Uncle John" to the park, and also donated his life-sized portrait to McLaren Lodge.

When Uncle John died on June 12, 1943, he had planted a million or more trees. His redwoods, grown from seed, were 40 feet high. In this world-famed garden was a greater number of varieties and species of trees, shrubs, and plants than in any other park in the United States. Annually, Golden Gate Park has more than four million visitors, and each spring Union Square sees a display of its glorious rhododendrons.

It was for this park that M. H. de Young, proprietor of the *Chronicle,* while acting as vice-president of Chicago's Columbian Exposition, planned the Mid-Winter Fair, at the close of the Chicago Exposition. He offered $5,000 to further the enterprise. By private subscription $365,000 was raised, the legislature appropriating a nearly equal sum. De Young was elected director-general.

When the Mid-Winter Fair opened, January 1, 1894, visitors were surprised to find that one hundred buildings had been erected in five months on sixty acres of land rescued from sand dunes and scrub brush. The main buildings were constructed around a depression, now surrounded by Claus Spreckels Temple of Music, the M. H. de Young Memorial Museum and the 2½-acre Oriental Garden.

When on July 9, 1894, the Fair closed, 2,255,551 visitors had passed through the gate. Surplus gains from the Fair was devoted to purchasing objects for the M. H. de Young Memorial Museum, a memorial not to a person but to the Mid-Winter Fair. At his own expense Mr. de Young gave an additional building. When Mayor James Rolph, Jr., as the city's representative, accepted the building, March 15, 1917, de Young closed his address with "I give to the city of San Francisco this building and all it contains, with only one condition attached, that no admission fee shall ever be charged."

Mr. de Young presented to the museum ancient relics from Egypt, ethnological material from the Sudan country and other parts of Africa and Asia, besides bronze replicas of works of Graeco-Roman art from Pompeii and Herculaneum. He later provided funds for construction of a new building, completed within three years, under the direction of Louis Mullgardt. The Mid-Winter Fair Building, finally considered unsafe, was razed.

Many additions have been made to the new building to house the gifts from its benefactors, who include San Franciscans Mr. and Mrs. George Cameron, Mr. and Mrs. J. W. Maillard, Jr., Mr. and Mrs. Walter Heil, Mrs. Herbert Fleishhacker, Mr. and Mrs. George Wagner, Mrs. Hans Benedict, Mrs. Peter Lewis, Mrs. James A. Bull, Mrs. William Hayward, Mr. and Mrs. Philip N. Lilienthal, Jr.; Mr. Chauncey McCormick of Chicago; Dr. Rudolph J. Heinemann, Irwin Untermeyer, and Mortimer Leventritt of New York. Magnificent gifts came from Mr. and Mrs. Roscoe Oakes, the William Randolph Hearst Foundation, and the Samuel H. Kress Foundation.

The Hearst Foundation gave four stained-glass windows of the first half of the sixteenth century. In 1954 the museum opened the Hearst Memorial Court following the presentation of a celebrated set of four Flemish Gothic tapestries depicting in allegorical form "The Divinity," the "Fall and the Beginning of the Redemption," the "Drama of the Resurrection," and the "Crucifixion." These tapestries were woven in Brussels in the early sixteenth century and at one time they hung in the Cathedral of Toledo in Spain. They were shown on Treasure Island in 1939 and are a distinguished permanent addition to San Francisco's art treasures.

In 1953 Mr. and Mrs. Roscoe F. Oakes brought to the museum the work of Peter Paul Rubens, one of the greatest artists of all time. No other American museum has any portrait of such quality as Rubens's "Portrait of a Gentleman," painted about 1615. During the same year Mr. and Mrs. Oakes enriched the museum by the gift of a large and magnificent French room dating from 1735, adding also a set of gilt and tapestry-covered furniture, signed by Jean Avisse, one of the foremost cabinetmakers of the Louis XV period, which came from the family of the Duc de La Tremoille. Mr. and Mrs. Oakes later gave two important paintings, "Diana and Callistro" and "Bacchantes," by the eighteenth-century French master, François Boucher, court painter to Louis XV, both pastoral scenes produced for Madame de Pompadour. Other offerings from Mr. and Mr. Oakes were the "Marchioness of Townsend" by Sir Joshua Reynolds and the "Painter Etienne Jeaurat" by Jean Baptiste Greuze.

In 1958 came another precious gift to the museum from eighty-eight-year-old Iowa-born Roscoe F. Oakes, one-time flashlight salesman in the Pacific northwest. It is Benvenuto Cellini's 30-inch-tall bust of Cosimo de' Medici, sixteenth-century First Grand Duke of Florence, valued at possibly a half million dollars. It is a statue elaborately detailed and depicting an arrogant, patrician, curly-bearded countenance. Dr. Walter Heil, curator, believes that the bust will be regarded as the most important High Renaissance sculpture existing in America, and among the major works of this type in the world. The Oakes Cellini was first on public view at the museum on Thursday, October 2, 1959.

The Samuel H. Kress collections of paintings, unveiled in 1922, inspired the new two-story structure of concrete built on the museum's main axis to house the Kress gift. A highlight of the Kress collection is the painting "The Meeting of St. Francis and St. Dominic," by Fra Angelico. Another is the supurb "St. Francis Venerating the Crucifix" by El Greco, especially acquired by Mr. Rush H. Kress for the museum as a particularly beautiful representation of the city's patron saint. An outstanding portrait of the Venetian school is Titian's expressive "Portrait of a Friend of Titian."

Another masterpiece is Claude Lorraine's "Classic Landscape with Figures at Sunset." Recent acquisition of the Kress collection is the Velásquez "Portrait of Queen Mariana of Spain." The Kress donation of paintings gave San Franciscans a new and unique opportunity to study European masterpieces.

In 1956 was shown the work of Morris Graves, an outstanding American painter from the Pacific Northwest, who currently lives in Ireland. He was born in Baker, Oregon, and grew up in the vicinity of Seattle. He left school and ran away to sea. Japanese art had a profound effect on him. He became absorbed in Zen philosophy. Out of this came an art of symbolism, making use of birds and fish, the moon and sea, painted in tempera on the thinnest of crinkled paper. Graves's art is rooted in his understanding of nature, and he has achieved wide recognition, his paintings being hailed as masterpieces of their time. His work has been sought after by such collectors as Duncan Phillips in Washington and Charles Laughton in Hollywood.

In 1959 the world's greatest collection of Oriental art was presented to the de Young Museum by the Chicago capitalist Avery Brundage. Chinese bronzes, some dated 1300 B.C., are in the collection. The ceramics were made by the best potters during 3,500 years. The jade has been called superior to the Bishop collection in the Metropolitan Museum, New York. Experts value these treasures at $15 million. In order to house the fabulous Brundage gift, the de Young Museum was remodeled by adding a rear wing of an Oriental character that is appropriate with the Chinese tea garden as décor. The cost of this remodeling was $2,725 million obtained by a bond issue instigated by Mayor George Christopher.

Also in 1959 was shown at the de Young Museum the first complete Mayan exhibition of art ever presented in the United States. Visitors saw a hundred examples of Mayan art dating from 1500 B.C. to A.D. 1500. It had been created in the highlands of Guatemala, the lowland jungles of Honduras and Yucatan. Sculpture in stone and terra cotta, decorated pottery, and carved jade interested not only many visitors but especially archaeologists.

Five rooms house English and Early American furniture and furnishings. There is also shown the Bravermann collection of minerals and California semiprecious stones. The west wing is devoted to California material. Prints at the entrance gallery show history and geography. Four period rooms have been arranged, 1850–1885, with original furniture and upholstery, draperies, rugs, and bric-à-brac. Costumes worn by California women during these periods are exhibited. Nineteenth-century paintings, ship models, arms and armor, fire engines, and articles for transportation fill the remaining rooms of the wing.

The art galleries are at the disposal of students. Temporary exhibitions take place in the east wing, where are also the children's room and the library. Exhibitions of special interest are arranged with art works borrowed from museums and private collections. The blind have been remembered in the exhibition rooms, where material is installed with Braille labels.

Schools of the Bay Area often send students on gallery tours as part of the classroom study. Art classes and special study groups for adults are regular events.

In the same year that M. H. de Young presented to San Francisco the museum founded by him, Mr. and Mrs. Adolph Spreckels gave the city of their birth a replica of the Palace of the Legion of Honor in Paris as a memorial to the 3,600 Californians who died during World War I. Lincoln Park was selected as the site for the structure. Near the driveway are three male bronzes by Rodin, standing with heads bowed and arms outstretched, a memorial to Raphael Weill, pioneer merchant and philanthropist.

Mrs. Alma Spreckels, descended from the aristocratic French de Bretteville family, suggested this generosity to her husband. Mr. Spreckels died before the Palace was completed. On the eve of Armistice Day, 1924, Mrs. Spreckels received a thousand guests for the first time in the Grand Court of the Palace, assisted by her late husband's brother, John D. Spreckels, and by the Marquis and Marquise Pierre de Bretteville. They beheld the beautiful art treasures lent by the French government and sixty Rodin plasters donated by Adolph Spreckels, Jr. The museum was formally opened after impressive ceremonies on the following day just before noon. At the sound of the bugle, throngs stood at silent attention for the soldier dead and for the deceased donor.

Mrs. Spreckels is the first San Francisco woman to found a museum, and she has been the most generous benefactor of the Palace of the Legion of Honor. She gave forty bronzes and marbles by Rodin, among them the immortal "Thinker." In the name of her children, Alma, Dorothy, and Adolph Jr., she donated a superb group of Tanagra figurines and an extensive collection of Egyptian art. One hundred bronzes by Arthur Putnam and the collections of the French sculptor Théodore Rivière were also her gifts. In recognition of Mrs. Spreckels's interest in French sculpture the government of France presented the museum with a set of Gobelin tapestries, commemorating the life of Joan of Arc, and a hundred pieces of Sèvres porcelain.

French art of the eighteenth century is shown in the distinguished Collis P. Huntington collection, donated by Archer M. Huntington to memorialize his foster father. His mother, a French student, assembled the paintings, sculptures, tapestries, and porcelains. Mrs. Anna Hyatt Huntington, his wife, one of America's great sculptors, is represented in the museum by "Jeanne d 'Arc" and "El Cid."

Mr. H. K. S. Williams and his wife, Mildred Anna Williams, presented the museum with more than a hundred works of the leading masters of the European School from the sixteenth to the twentieth century, a group of fine tapestries and choice examples of eighteenth century furniture. The Williamses provided an endowment fund of $1 million for increasing the collection and added notable canvases by Rembrandt and Renoir. They bought eight works by contemporary American artists: "Table with Glasses and Napkin," by Carlyle Brown; "Storm Coming," by John Langley Howard; "The Bridge," by John Koch; "Sticks and Stones," by Joe Lasker; "Woodstock Pastorale," by Jack Levine; "Artist's Studio," by Raymond Mintz; "Potatoes and Onions," by Bernard Perlin; and "Birds at Rest," by Lundy Siegriest. In its patronage of the work of living American painters the Cailfornia Palace of the Legion of Honor leads the field among western museums in the United States.

Also of inestimable value to the museum is the Achenbach Foundation supported by Mr. and Mrs. Moore S. Achenbach, who provided material for many imaginative exhibitions, both at the museum and at the public library. Their paramount interest has been in the graphic arts.

In 1943 Albert Campbell Hooper gave a collection of four hundred paintings, sculptures, and decorative arts, notably Dutch and Flemish paintings of the seventeenth century and English paintings of the eighteenth century. The late James D. Phelan left a fund for acquisition of drawings and paintings by contemporary California artists. Gifts of California Oriental art were made by Albert M. Bender. Gordon Blanding donated his choice collection of Keith paintings to the city of San Francisco to be displayed at the Palace of the Legion of Honor. Paolo Veronese's notable family group portrait was presented by Mortimer Leventritt in memory of his parents. In one of the large galleries is the Jacob Stern loan collection, largely of nineteenth-century European and American schools. Others who in recent years made gifts to the museum are Mr. and Mrs. Ralph C. Lee, Joseph M. Upton, Clarence R. Postley, Paul Dietrich, Milton H. Esberg, the late Catherine D. Wentworth, A. Sheldon Kenoyer, Mlle. Jeanne Cheron of Santa Barbara, Mrs. Frank J. Gould of Paris, Dr. and Mrs. James Ziegler of New York, Mrs. Thomas Carr Howe, Mrs. W. H. Slater, Jr., of Santa Barbara, Mrs. D. C. Ashley, the late Mrs. Julia D. Babcock, Mrs. James C. Bodrero, Mr. and Mrs. Garfield D. Merner and Mrs. Lester Goodman.

Efforts are constantly being made to reach as many San Francisco public school children as possible through the museum aid program and 10,725 children attended 194 lectures in 1954; these were given at the schools by two educational curators. The lectures were illustrated with slides furnished by the museum. Art classes for children enabled about 3,000 children the pleasure of painting and modeling. Members of the museum staff and exhibiting artists took part in twenty television programs. There were Saturday and Sunday organ concerts presented by Mr. Ludwig Altman and Mr. Richard Purvis. Twenty thousand children enjoyed motion pictures presented each Saturday afternoon at the Little Theatre. The pipe organ, costing $150,000, was the gift of John D. Spreckels.

In his book *Castles and Salt Mines*, Thomas Carr Howe relates how he, while serving as lieutenant commander in the United States Reserve in 1945–1946, aided by his associates, rescued from an Austrian monastery the art treasures of Rothschild and Mannheimer that had been hidden by Hitler. They also found in a salt mine Hermann Goering's loot: Michelangelo's world masterpiece, "Madonna from Bruges," and Hubert and Jan van Eyck's superb altarpiece, "The Adoration of the Mystic Lamb," Belgium's greatest art treasure. This fifteenth-century canvas had a familiar look, and its label on the back showed that it had been exhibited several years previously at the Palace of the Legion of Honor.

Most of the art objects were restored by General Eisenhower to their owners, but there being no adequate protection for the valuable contents of Kaiser Frederick's Museum at Berlin, they were shipped for safety to the United States. After being exhibited to the public, they were returned to the German people.

For his services to art, Director Howe received from the French government the decoration of the Chevalier of the Legion of Honor and the Dutch government gave him the decoration of the Order of the Orange Nassau.

Although during the year 1956 the California Palace of the Legion of Honor had exhibitions of masterpieces from seven centuries of French drawings, and treasures of the Jacquemart André Museum, Paris, and a hundred paintings from the collection of Walter P. Chrysler, Jr., no exhibition attracted so many visitors as the seventy-two paintings and one sculpture of the Gladys Lloyd Robinson and Edward G. Robinson collection visited by more than 60,000 admirers. Later a New York syndicate bought, for about $3,250,000, the collection made during twenty-five years by the Robinsons.

The Palace's most important acquisition in 1959 was the "Self-Portrait" by Jean Honoré Fragonard (1732–1806). It was purchased for the museum by Mr. and Mrs. Louis Benoist.

Both the Palace of the Legion of Honor and the de Young Museum specialize in old masters, but the San Francisco Museum of Art, founded by the Art Association in 1921, shows the work of the abstractionists. Moving into its quarters in the Civic Center in 1935 under the leadership of Mrs. Grace McCann Morley, it emphasizes advanced and controversial fields. Memorable exhibitions have been the works of Henri Matisse (1952), Les Fauves (1953), Fernand Leger (1953), José Clemente Orozco (1954), Raoul Dufy (1954). Among the San Francisco artists who have received national recognition are Sonia Gechtoff and Ralph du Casse. Local prize winners in recent times include Theodore Polos, Robert S. Newmann, Julius Wasserstein, Miriam Hoffman, Gurdon Woods, Roy de Forrest, and Robert Howard.

Much abstract art in San Francisco emanates from the California School of Fine Arts, whose students often use house paint with slapdash gusto to create a representation not of nature but of the immediate sensation it produces. A cliché concerning this school is that "Anything done next week is too old-fashioned."

Pranksters delight in having fun when abstractionists have an exhibition of canvases. A few years ago a caricature of abstract art was made and sent to an exhibition. It took the prize, but instead of the prankster's name, that of a stranger was given. Another prize was won by an inmate of Agnew's State Mental Hospital. The painting was greeted with enthusiasm by the abstractionists.

San Francisco's infant Maritime Museum is the youngest in the city. It began in November, 1949, when Karl Kortum, a former seaman, called together at luncheon publishers of the four San Francisco daily newspapers. He planned a new use for the Aquatic Park —it should become a repository for large-scale relics of California's shipping history. In the lagoon would be moored a full-rigged ship, a three-masted lumber schooner, an engine-aft steam schooner, and a stern-wheeler. On shore would be smaller craft in replica of an early-day shipyard. A Hyde Street cable car would be a feature of the park and one of the old brick warehouses would become a railroad museum. The Aquatic Park Casino on the shores of the lagoon was to become the Maritime Museum proper. The publishers were enthusiastic and the Maritime Museum Association came into being.

Mayor Elmer E. Robinson aided by arranging a dollar-a-year lease for the Maritime Museum building. The shipping companies gave much assistance, and labor unions contributed hundreds of hours of work. The largest individual supporter was Mrs. Alma de Bretteville Spreckels, who is honorary president. She had already founded the Palace of the Legion of Honor, but she contributed nearly $100,000 to the new enterprise. On May 19, 1951, the Maritime Museum opened its doors with Mayor Elmer E. Robinson and Edward H. Harms, of the Pope and Talbot Company, as principal speakers.

The museum, ably directed by Karl Kortum, has played host to hundreds of thousands of paying visitors. Income is received from displaying the museum ship, *Balclutha*, at Fisherman's Wharf. Completion of the Maritime Museum project has been ensured by the allocation of $2 million of State Tidelands revenues to the State

Maritime Historical Monument. This will include the display of the steam schooner *Wapama*, the historic three-masted lumber schooner *C. A. Thayer*, and the sidewheel ferryboat *Eureka*. These restored vessels will be moored at a reconstructed turn-of-the-century version of the city's old Broadway Wharf, which will act as protecting arm to a three-acre Victorian Park with Amundsen's *Gjoa*, a scow schooner, and a Chinese junk drawn up on its foreshore.

San Francisco is the only city on the Pacific coast with a Maritime Museum. It is a tourist attraction that recalls the colorful past of San Francisco's famed harbor.

Forty-two-year-old Karl Kortum was born in San Bernardino of pioneer parents. His German-born grandfather, Louis Kortum, in 1860 established the first permanent winery at the head of Napa Valley. Karl's great-grandmother on his mother's side was Sarah Fosdick of the Donner party, one of the survivors of the Forlorn Hope party that brought word to Sutter's Fort of the plight of the wagon train at Donner Pass. Sarah lost her husband, parents, and several brothers and sisters in the 1847 tragedy. After her recovery, she established a school for pioneer children in a brush shelter opposite the Bale gristmill in Napa Valley, said to have been the first American school in California.

A unique art exhibition in the San Francisco area has been held annually for nineteen years at San Quentin Prison. In 1959 more than three hundred paintings were shown in the Employees' Recreation Building. During two days visitors bought three hundred canvases, ranging in price from 25 cents to $1,200. Favorite subjects were abstract landscapes, with one portrait of a woman who recently had killed her daughter-in-law to regain her own son's affection. Ninety per cent of the $3,000 received from the sale of the paintings will go to the prisoner-artists when they leave San Quentin. The other 10 per cent is devoted to purchasing materials for the artists. It is believed by many that violence may be lessened by art in San Quentin.

CHAPTER 16

Social Clubs

SAN FRANCISCO'S pioneer "gentlemen's club" was the Pacific, founded in 1852, and progenitor of the Pacific-Union, now housed in the enlarged former Flood residence on Nob Hill. Their first rooms were at Montgomery and Bush Streets, and Major Richard P. Hammond was president. All members of the Pacific Club were Americans, but two years later the Union was established by English, French, and Germans. Pacific and Union Clubs found that their backgrounds and tastes were so similar that they merged in 1881, becoming the Pacific-Union—"P.U."

Only millionaires are supposed to belong to the Pacific-Union, but many members are in lower income brackets. Precedent was broken after the Fire when the Pacific-Union remodeled the Flood mansion and women were allowed to inspect the new rooms. At their centennial celebration in February, 1952, women were received as guests.

Like its emblem, a black cat, the Press Club has had several lives. In 1851 newspapermen clubbed together to provide hospitality for visiting pressmen. The organization soon went to sleep, not waking until the first year of the Civil War, when workers of thirteen daily papers, twenty-one weeklies, and six monthlies met informally at Ellen E. Moon's "Ivy Green" at 624 Merchant Street. Later they established themselves briefly at Harry Grim's "Arrion Halle," but again perished. The idea persisted, however, and today's Press Club was formed on July 4, 1880, with Hugh Burke as first president. They had rooms for a time at Sacramento and Spring Streets, but adjourned to Otto Norman's beer hall on Bush near Kearny. From there invitations went forth signed by the *Examiner's* J. C.

Klein and the *Chronicle*'s Walter B. Cook for a meeting on Wednesday, July 25, in the rooms of the State Board of Trade.

Joseph M. Ward was elected president, George Squires, vice-president, Fremont Older, secretary. The club quarters were in five small rooms on Ellis Street above Powell.

World celebrities have been guests of the Press Club. Their first show at the Baldwin Theatre in 1889 had Helena Modjeska as star. Sarah Bernhardt sailed in and out like a dazzling dream swathed in heavy white satin. Beautiful, blonde Lillian Russell was made an honorary member, accorded full privileges of the club, and given a golden key. Legend says that next morning she was found there smoking a cigar. "Am I not entitled to all the privileges of the club?" Another declares that she draped herself in a club portiere and sang *Carmen*, standing on a table at a jamboree. Ex-President Theodore Roosevelt, guest of honor in 1903, drank beer and learned with regret that he was not to be presented with the stein. It was to be retained as a historic souvenir. After the Fire in 1906, in which they lost many interesting mementos, he wrote a letter wishing "fellow members" all possible good luck.

Shortly after the Fire Lord Northcliffe was guest of honor at a "beer bust." President William Howard Taft assembled the full membership. Bright spots in later Press Club history were Gertrude Lawrence singing English ballads with member Barney Gould and Irving Berlin playing and singing snatches of his songs. James K. Hackett will always be remembered because he slid out of his shoes and did a Spanish dance. Other celebrities entertained by the club were Charles Lindbergh, Amelia Earhart, and Alice Marble. Helen Hayes was presented with a golden key.

In recent years Eleanor Roosevelt came to lunch. She dismissed secret service men and held a press conference. When offered a cigarette she said, "Must I? At the White House sometimes I smoked, for the ladies refused unless I did." So generous was she with her time that one of the members said to Miss Thompson, her secretary, "Does Mrs. Roosevelt know that a special automobile is waiting for her?" "Mrs. Roosevelt always knows just what she is doing." Eleanor Roosevelt was made an honorary member.

The Press Club dedicated their new building on Powell Street on September 6, 1913. At the Tivoli Show in 1916 Senator James D.

Phelan read President Wilson's telephone message, and the audience with earphones heard Caruso in Atlanta sing "The Rosary."

The Press Club has an annual "Scoop" party in November when they issue a paper, *The Scoop*. The redheaded reporter-dentist-detective William A. ("Doc") Mundell organized the "Late Watch" dinner. Given annually, on the Saturday evening closest to April 18, the anniversary of the great Fire, it is attended by those who have been associated with newspapers for at least twenty-five years. Doc presided the last time in 1947, and a few months later his friends took leave of him in a casket palled with gardenias.

The Press Club is now merged with the Union League Club, and as the Press-Union occupies the building at 555 Post Street. It was at an entertainment at the Press-Union Club that Mayor Robinson was motivated to invite the UN Conference to celebrate its tenth anniversary of the United Nations Assembly at San Francisco. During the conference in 1955 the Press-Union was host to many of the delegates. On one occasion General Carlos P. Romulo, ambassador from the Philippines, made a notable speech.

One of San Francisco's oldest clubs is the Olympic. In 1855 the two Nahl brothers, Arthur and Charles, began it by erecting a gymnasium in the rear of their home as a meeting place for young athletes. Five years later they organized the Olympic Club, meeting in the Hook and Ladder Firehouse on Broadway. The new club was named for Mount Olympus, mythical home of the Greeks, and a winged "O" became the emblem of the athlete members. The Olympians' first home was in a loft above a coal yard at the southeast corner of New Montgomery Street. Five hundred sport lovers wished to join, and larger quarters were sought.

They moved several times until President William Greer Harrison advised purchase of the present site. Ground-breaking ceremonies were held in 1891.

Their building was destroyed by fire and the cornerstone of the present structure was laid on May 6, 1911. President Harrison arranged with city officials to have salt water pumped ten miles for the Roman swimming pool. The city may use water, free of charge, for flushing sewers and extinguishing fires. Attorney William F. Humphrey became president shortly after the Fire and served forty years, during which time membership increased to 5,000.

The University Club was founded in 1890 by William Thomas, a Harvard graduate and its first president. In the organization was a large Harvard contingent, but charter members were Francis J. Carolan, Cornell; Elliott McAllister, California; A. N. Drown, Brown; Charles P. Eells, Hamilton; William H. Chickering, Amherst; Dixwell Hewitt, Williams; Sydney V. Smith, Yale; J. W. Carlin, George E. P. Harrison, and Frank Soulé, Navy.

In 1906 the first club headquarters at 722 Sutter Street were destroyed by fire and a new location was obtained at California and Powell Streets, on the site of Senator Stanford's stables. The clubhouse was built in 1909, and members may bring ladies into the dining room as guests. From time to time they are invited to special functions.

Six men brought about the founding of the Bohemian Club in March, 1872: writers Daniel O'Connell, Thomas Newcomb, James W. Bowman, and Joseph N. H. Irwin; Frank G. Kenny, special correspondent of the New York *Herald;* Frederick Whymper, artist, mining engineer, and editorial writer on the *Alta.* Some of those invited did not respond. They did not "wish to be called Bohemians." Eighteen answered, among them Ambrose Bierce. Thomas Newcomb was the first president, and actor Harry Edwards, the second. The club occupied modest quarters on Sacramento Street. At first, dinner was not served, only a 25-cent lunch. Members protested when the price was raised to 50 cents.

"Weaving spiders come not here" is the club's motto, and its symbol is the owl. Soon "High Jinks" were given monthly, with nonmembers invited. "Jinks" was taken from Sir Walter Scott, as well as the word "Sire." A subject like "Love" would be chosen for the "Jinks," and all speeches, poetry, and music devoted to the theme. "Low Jinks" burlesqued the High, and was ad-libbed by those ready with wit and humor, like Clay M. Greene, Joseph Redding, Frank L. Unger, Willard T. Barton and Charles Warren Stoddard.

In early days Daniel O'Connell recited Tennyson's "Locksley Hall," DeWolf Hopper "Casey at the Bat," and John McCullough brought tears with "Rover," addressed to his dog. The great Mansfield sat at the piano pouring out Irish, French, English, Scotch, and German songs. Edwin Booth came, speaking only in monosyllables when addressed.

Cartoons were frequently distributed at dinners. Tavernier did a picture of the redwoods for Charles A. Dana, editor of the New York *Sun*, who carried it in his arms to his hotel. Joseph D. Strong, first husband of Isobel Osbourne, Robert Louis Stevenson's stepdaughter, painted Charles Warren Stoddard in monk's robe and cowl and Raphael Weill in chef's cap and apron. Theodore Wores did a cartoon for the farewell "Jinks" of "Uncle George" Bromley when he left to be consul in China. A favorite after-dinner speaker, Uncle George never went to bed if he could help it. To friends departing at five in the morning he said, "It is so early, what shall I do with the rest of the evening?"

Among historic entertainments given by the club were those for Henry M. Stanley, who found Livingstone; historian James Anthony Froude and actors Henry Irving and Tomasso Salvini. At Salvini's dinner, Virgil Williams addressed him in Italian, and the actor courteously called his accent "pure Tuscan." After Henry Irving's dinner, lights were extinguished, and at the end of the room was a stage upon which appeared Bohemians representing Irving's great impersonations: Louis XI, Cardinal Wolsey, Becket, Hamlet, Shylock, and Macbeth. During the "Low Jinks" Irving gave a recitation and later sent club members specially printed passes to his London theater.

When the club gave a dinner for King Kalakaua of the Hawaiian Islands, Joaquin Miller declined: "I have never stood before monarchs, and were I to begin, I would select some other than the coffee-colored king."

Some Bohemians objected to the installation of the mummy of an Egyptian princess, Jerry Lynch's gift, but finally the dead lady was solemnly housed with chanted rituals. Charles Warren Stoddard wrote a poem, purporting to be a message from the princess:

> Feast well, drink well, make merry while ye may,
> For e'en the best of you must pass my way.

In 1899 President Vanderlyn Stow persuaded the club to buy the 280-acre redwood Meeker Grove on Russian River, where they could hold their annual "Jinks" and forget care. Joseph Redding wrote music for what is called the first "midsummer Jinks" play, Charles K. Field's *The Man in the Forest* produced in 1902. Among other authors of Grove plays were: Templeton Crocker, Louis A. Robert-

son, Newton Tharp, George Sterling, Herman Scheffauer, H. Morse
Stephens, Porter Garnett, Rufus Steele, J. Wilson Shiels, Frank
Pixley, Fred S. Myrtle, Richard M. Hotaling, Kenneth Ferguson,
Clarence B. Kelland, Howard A. Muckle, and Dan Totheroh. The
play in 1953 was *Romany Legend*, and author and composer were
Harry C. Allen and Antonio de Grassi. In 1958 the Grove play was
Aloha Oe (A Legend of Hawaii) by Earle C. Anthony in collabora-
tion with Carey Wilson. *Cortez* was the play of 1959, presented by
Howard A. Muckle with music by Hugh Brown. The 1960 Grove
Play, *Rip Van Winkle*, was written and directed by Dan Totheroh
and the music was composed by Charles Hart.

July was also the month when Deputy Premier Kozlov was given
special entertainment by President Clarke E. Wayland at a luncheon
in the redwoods, formerly owned by Russia. Kozlov was told that
four American presidents had been feted at the Grove: Theodore
Roosevelt, William Howard Taft, Herbert Hoover, and General
Eisenhower. When Montyn Thomas, a club member, sang "The
Freedom Song" from Borodin's opera *Prince Igor,* he received an
invitation from Kozlov to sing at the Bolshoi Theater in Russia.
The deputy premier promised to plant redwood seeds in a climati-
cally suitable area in the Soviet Union. Redwoods would serve as
a symbol of American-Soviet friendship. At the close of the luncheon
Kozlov announced that he had been taken into the Bohemian Club
as a member. "Of course only as a candidate now. I hope and expect
to be a full member."

Not all Bohemian Club members are admitted automatically to
the Grove. Sometimes candidates wait years to be voted upon.
Groups of members band together and share expenses. Camps must
be inconspicuous and not despoil the scenery. Men sleep and drink
in camp, but eat in the dining room—a wide clearing in which rustic
tables and benches have been made from fallen redwoods. During
meals club members furnish entertainment on the stage which is
only for "High Jinks." At night the members gather around a great
fire, sitting on long benches or redwood logs. Oil burners and camp-
fires take the place of electricity, which is used only for lighting
effects.

On the first Saturday night after the "Jinks" opening in July comes
the "Burning of Care." In the rear of the stage, burning before the

club symbol, is a large figure of an owl, before which is a perpetual flame. A wax figure of "Care" is punted on a barge across the pool to the altar by four naked acolytes swinging censers. "Care" is committed to the flames while from high in the trees someone is singing. "Low Jinks" takes place the following Saturday.

Two hundred tents provide shelter for members and guests who have been among the world's distinguished men—General Eisenhower, Wendell Willkie, Governor Stassen, and the King of Sweden.

Each camp strives for originality of name and design. "The Cave Men," an imitation cave, was occupied by ex-President Hoover, who in 1955 brought his son, Herbert Hoover, Jr., and young Hoover's son as guests. Former "Cave Men" were the late Ray Lyman Wilbur and Charles K. Field. "Stowaway" belongs to ex-President Eisenhower, who was a guest while he was a general. It is occupied by friends of the ex-President; among his guests have been William Randolph Hearst, Jr., and the late Garret H. McEnerney. The late William H. Crocker had "Land of Happiness," but the camp of his son, W. W. Crocker, is "Mandalay," which he shared with the late John Francis Neylan. "The Aviary" is inhabited by the chorus. "The Howlers" have a large sign showing coyotes yapping. Other colorful camps are "Cuckoo's Nest," "Poker Flat," "Semper Virens," "Silverado Squatters," and "Lost Angels."

An iron-clad rule is that women may not sleep at the Grove, but they are permitted to visit in May. One of the first women to visit the Grove as a picnic guest was Mary Garden, invited by Joe Redding. Only once was the ban lifted against the presence of women in the club rooms, and that was when Poet Laureate Ina Coolbrith was librarian for several years.

In the great Fire the Bohemian Club lost its collection of paintings and mementos gathered from the entire world. Immediately, Bohemians planned their new building on Post and Taylor Streets, which was completed in 1934 at the cost of $1 million.

About forty years ago a Bohemian coterie led by friends of the *Examiner*'s political writer, Edward H. Hamilton, remembered for his wit and distinguished appearance, decided that the club was too stodgy. They founded the Family Club with a stork as emblem. Despite its name and the circumstance that most of the members are family men, no woman may enter the club or the beautiful farm near Woodside, San Mateo County. On the Family Farm is a magnificent grove of redwood trees, among which are camps similar to those at Bohemian Grove. Their annual outdoor festivities are held at an earlier date than the Bohemian "Midsummer Jinks," and are called the "Family Row." Although they had separated forty years previously, in 1959 the Family Club entertained the Bohemians at their redwood home.

Founders of the Commonwealth Club were "Seekers after Truth." Five "seekers" dined at Marchand's French Restaurant, February 3, 1903, invited by the *Chronicle*'s Edward F. Adams—"Father" Adams. Others were the *Chronicle*'s managing editor, John P. Young; Benjamin Ide Wheeler, president of the University of California; Frederick Burk, of the San Francisco Normal School; William P. Lawlor, later justice of the California Supreme Court. "We should get the facts," said Founder Adams. "There is no such thing as a fact," President George W. Dickey frivolously remarked. The club's goal was to find the truth and reveal it to the world.

For some time the club was nameless, but Benjamin Ide Wheeler suggested "Agora"—Greek for "Market Place," where Socrates solved humanity's problems. "Are you Angora goats?" asked the irreverent. Following George W. Dickey's suggestion, the organization was christened the "Commonwealth Club." At the end of the year there were sixty members. Monsignor Charles Ramm, the last charter member, died in 1951. The club has 8,462 members—5,000 within a 40-mile radius of the city and the remainder all the way from Oregon to the Mexican border. At their weekly Friday luncheon at the Palace Hotel members listen to the world's best thought.

Ex-President Herbert Hoover has spoken there many times and other speakers have been ex-President Harry S Truman, King Albert of Belgium, Theodore Roosevelt, Woodrow Wilson, William H. Taft, Calvin Coolidge, Eamon De Valera, Manuel Quezon, Manuel Roxas, General Carlos P. Romulo, Alvaro Obregon, Elpidio Quirino, Mayor LaGuardia, Vice-President Nixon, Prime Minister Clement Atlee, John Foster Dulles, Dr. Yen; journalists Arthur Brisbane and Lincoln Steffens; musicians Walter Damrosch and Ignace Paderewski; singer and actor Paul E. Robeson; labor leaders Samuel Gompers and William Green; Harvard president James Conant. The table attendance at the Eisenhower dinner was 1,763. In addition, there

were perhaps 150–200 newspaper men in the French Room overlooking the Garden Court.

Recently the club has heard General Alfred M. Guenther, Governor Averill Harriman, Conrad Hilton, William Courtenay, Admiral
Arthur W. Radford; Paul-Henri Spaak, Secretary General of NATO;
Arthur Godfrey; Ambassador Sir Harold Caccia; William Randolph
Hearst, Jr.; Ambassador Gaganvihari Mehta; Secretary of Interior
Fred E. Seaton; President George Meany of the AFL-CIO; President Lee A. Du Bridge of California Institute of Technology; Admiral Arleigh A. Burke; Dr. Glenn T. Seaborg, Nobel Prize winner;
and Billy Graham. The largest attendance was for Graham—1,820.

Women speakers do not bring out large audiences, and so are
seldom invited to appear. The most popular woman speaker
was Queen Juliana of the Netherlands, who in 1952 had 1,589
listeners. When Clare Boothe Luce and her husband, editor of *Time*
and *Life*, spoke on China, they attracted 815 guests and her address was reported more effective than his. Dr. Aurelia Reinhardt
spoke several times, once having 427 listeners. The Hon. Florence
P. Kahn also gave three addresses, drawing 360 listeners in 1933.
Only 262 came to hear the Honorable Perle Mesta, minister to
Luxembourg.

At the annual Ladies' Evening of literature and music, gold and
silver medals are awarded to authors, residents of California, for
books published by them during the year.

Although the Commonwealth Club has entertained presidents and
royalty, no luncheon ever given by them in their fifty-six years of
existence attracted so much attention as did their dinner, September
21, 1959, held jointly with the World Affairs Council, for the
coal miner, Nikita S. Khrushchev, who became premier of Soviet
Russia and was touring the United States as President Eisenhower's
guest.

Even two weeks before the dinner the Commonwealth Club was
obliged to refuse requests for tickets; 1,833 were present at the
$10.50 Khrushchev dinner.

In Los Angeles Khrushchev had been so irritated by the mayor
that he threatened to go back to Russia. Riding up the California
coast in an 18-car special train, he was so warmly welcomed at
the stations where the train stopped that he calmed down.

The San Francisco AFL-CIO dinner at the Mark Hopkins Hotel on Sunday night had been boycotted by President George Meany of the Federation, saying that "he would not be caught dead in the same room with Khrushchev." Again there was a table-pounding argument between Khrushchev and the labor leaders, but it ended with the chairman's wish that "our two great countries work together for peace and the good of all mankind." On the following day, the Premier was up early for a before-breakfast walk and to admire the view from Nob Hill. Halfway down the steep Jones Street hill he retreated, realizing that hill-climbing is not for a sixty-five-year-old fat man. Then he visited "Comrade" Harry Bridges, the president of the International Longshoremen's and Warehouse Union, and was received like a comrade. He gave his fedora hat to a workman and departed with the longshoreman's cap on his head. At the cafeteria of the San Jose IBM plant, he carried his own tray for his 49-cent meal and said he would like to see cafeterias in Russia.

While the Premier toured San Francisco and visited a supermarket to ask prices, Mrs. Khrushchev saw the bay, crossed the famed bridges, enjoyed the view from Twin Peaks, and then, like a real American grandmother, shopped for toys for her grandchildren. She collected a Sears, Roebuck catalogue and was ready for the eight-o'clock dinner in the Garden Court of the Sheraton-Palace Hotel.

Two hours before the dinner, hotel halls were so crowded that only the police could force their way through the spectators. Police were on the hotel roof and also on other buildings across the street, facing the side of the hotel on the first floor through which Mr. Khrushchev was to enter and leave. Sixty plainclothesmen were scattered among the guests at strategically placed tables. At the extreme right of the speakers' table was one table entirely of ten plainclothesmen. Guests occupying the five meeting and television rooms were guarded by two police each, and in the lobby were other police. The added protection for the Premier cost San Francisco $19,451.

With the guest of honor and his family at the speakers' table were seated forty-five persons, including Governor and Mrs. Edmund G. Brown; Mayor and Mrs. George Christopher; Mr. and

Mrs. Henry Cabot Lodge, he being the President's personal representative. All at the table were introduced by co-chairman, Alvin J. Rockwell, president of the World Affairs Council of Northern California, except those who were later to give addresses. Mrs. Khrushchev won special applause with her friendly, smiling face. Women guests enjoyed Chairman Rockwell's remark that, while those at the speakers' table were using the historic gold service from which President Grant had dined at the end of his world trip, most of the ladies present did their own housework. A toast was offered to the Premier and to the people of the Union of Soviet Socialist Republics.

In saluting the Communist visitors Mayor George Christopher offered the prayer of San Francisco's patron, St. Francis of Assisi:

> Lord, make me an instrument of your peace.
> Where there is hatred, let me sow love.
> Where there is injury, pardon.
> Where there is doubt, faith.
> Where there is despair, hope.
> Where there is darkness, light.
> And where there is sadness, joy.

Governor Brown followed with a brief speech of welcome. Henry Cabot Lodge made a short address, and then Gardiner Johnson, president of the Commonwealth Club, introduced Premier Khrushchev. The audience rose and applauded.

The Premier read a prepared speech which was translated by Mr. O. A. Troyanovsky. After praising the beauty of San Francisco, he cited the horrors of war; urged an end of the nuclear arms race; and declared that Communists followed Christ's precepts, to love one's neighbors and fellow men. Then he laid aside his prepared speech. He explained his Los Angeles misunderstandings by saying that "the mayor got up on the wrong side of the bed." Facetiously he spoke about trying to solve the question of whether he should vote for Mr. Christopher for mayor. Of San Franciscans he said, "You are truly charmers, magicians, you managed to charm me, a representative of a Socialist state; you have charmed my heart, but in my head I still think our system is a good system. You evidently think that your system is a good one. Well, God be with you, live under it. Permit me to express the hope that my stay in the United States . . . will be of undeniable benefit and will bring our countries closer together."

When Mayor Christopher presented Khrushchev with a redwood gavel, the Premier again took the microphone and said that he would like to strike it after the signature of a treaty of friendship, non-aggression, eternal love between the people of the Soviet Union and the United States of America. He invited all present and all the citizens of this "flourishing and sunny city of San Francisco to come to see us in Moscow. We will be happy to welcome you there."

After a stay of 39 hours and 55 minutes in San Francisco, Soviet Premier Nikita Khrushchev shook hands with Mayor Christopher, climbed the stairs to the *Columbine III,* the President's Boeing 707 Jet, waved his large gray fedora to the crowd of airport workers and spoke the two American expressions he had learned—"Okay, very well." The huge aircraft headed for Iowa and Washington. In his speech to a welcoming throng six days later in Moscow Premier Khrushchev still extolled the beauty of San Francisco.

On April 27, 1960, the Commonwealth Club gave a historic banquet for President Charles de Gaulle of France. United with the World Affairs Council of Northern California and cooperating organizations—Society of France-Amérique and American Society of the French Legion of Honor—the soldier-President was their guest at the Civic Auditorium. Fourteen hundred and seventy-two San Franciscans paid $15 each for the dinner, and over 600 occupied the balcony.

From the time of his arrival at 12:15 P.M., at the San Francisco International Airport by military jet from New York, President de Gaulle was acclaimed by 250,000 people on his six-mile tour of the streets, through which he rode hatless and standing ramrod erect. Soldiers, sailors, and marines, showered with confetti, marched to music.

At the City Hall President de Gaulle was received by Mayor George Christopher and applauded by a crowd of 5,000. After a 21-gun salute, the national anthems of France and the United States were played by the Sixth United States Army Band. Mayor Christopher hailed President de Gaulle as "the living patriot symbol of France." The French President said that the "extraordinary welcome represented an unforgettable lesson which I shall tell all France when I return. Despite the distance, despite the time, the torch lit many years ago by our people—the torch of Lafayette, of Pershing and of Eisenhower is still aflame. It is the torch of Liberty. . . . We, the United States and France, wish all the people to have self-determination both within and without their borders. In bygone days certain countries have exerted their authority on others. But these days are over."

At the Mark Hopkins Hotel, where the President and Madame de Gaulle stopped, he had a half-hour conference with Governor Edmund G. Brown. After calling the view from the Top of the Mark "magnifique," he was driven across the Golden Gate Bridge to take a bay tour aboard a Coast Guard cutter. Later he was guest of honor at a reception given by the French consul general, Robert Luc, at the Palace of the Legion of Honor, which had been given by a woman of French extraction, Mrs. Alma de Bretteville Spreckels, and her husband, Adolph Spreckels. The reception was attended by 2,000 members of San Francisco's French colony. After brief remarks by President de Gaulle, fifty junior and senior girl students of Notre Dame des Victoires High School started singing the "Marseillaise" and the President joined most heartily in the song.

From the reception President and Madame de Gaulle were hurried to the banquet at the Civic Auditorium. The speakers' table was atop a base of red, white, and blue flowers. Before introductions, the President rose unexpectedly and offered a toast "to the President of the United States!"—the first toast ever given by him in English. Attentively he followed the speeches of Governor Brown, Mayor Christopher, Alvin J. Rockwell, president of the World Affairs Council of Northern California, and Lloyd E. Graybiel, president of the Commonwealth Club.

When Mr. Graybiel introduced the visitor, the audience rose. Standing erect before a mike, President de Gaulle paid a glowing tribute to San Francisco, observing that "the welcome of this magnificent city has touched me to the bottom of my heart." To the cheers of his listeners he remarked that "France is getting back on her feet. . . . I have full confidence in our future. Had it been our destiny to disappear, we would have done so. The bad days have now passed, the world remains dangerous but we have found ourselves and that is what counts. . . . America and France wish all people to freely choose their destiny; and it stems from one slogan well known—'Liberty, equality, fraternity.' . . . May our two peoples stand side by side in taking their decisions, and in the promoting of their influence all over the world. Long live San Francisco, long live the United States—a great friend and ally of France!"

The President spoke in French but his enunciation was so perfect and he was so eloquent that he was easily understood by most of those present, and they interrupted him several times with vigorous applause.

After a 26-hour visit in San Francisco and the Peninsula, President de Gaulle and his party took off for New Orleans by military jet plane. Before leaving he walked to a roped-off area at the International Airport, to say good-by to members of the press who had covered his San Francisco visit, while Mayor George Christopher and Police Chief Thomas Cahill beamed their appreciation of the visit of the courteous President of France.

CHAPTER 17

Memorable Social Events

PIONEER SAN FRANCISCO families still speak of the wedding of Senator Sharon's daughter, Flora, and Sir Thomas Fermor Hesketh, the city's first fashionable international wedding. Eight hundred guests, on that rainy afternoon of December 23, 1880, boarded special trains at Third and Townsend Streets, to go to fabulous Belmont.

Touring the world a few months previously, Sir Thomas Hesketh, of Rufford Hall, Ormskirk, Lancashire, arrived on his yacht, *Lancashire Witch*. At the Palace Hotel, where the Sharons lived, the baronet met brown-eyed Flora, who was not less attractive because her father's income was $2,000 a day. Henry Chauncey, who introduced the couple, told Flora that Englishmen liked dignified women. Perverse Flora sang rollicking California songs. After Sir Thomas entertained the Sharons on his yacht, where the chairs were covered with tiger skins, he sailed away, but was soon back in San Francisco and Flora was wearing his ring.

Palace Hotel chefs and twenty assistants went to Belmont for the wedding. Brother Fred Sharon came from Harvard to be best man. Guests were greeted at the station by members of the family in a violent rain. Inside the illuminated five-story house guests forgot the storm beating against the windows. Horns of plenty poured out camellias and roses. Great bouquets of exotic flowers were reflected in the large oval mirrors in the music room. From a large arch of flowers, lettered "H-S" in blue and white violets, hung a wedding bell of white carnations and camellias.

There was a slight delay in the ceremony. Smiling Senator Sharon ceased to smile. Consternation! No bridegroom. Where was he?

183

Asleep in his room. Sir Thomas was not unwilling—merely casual. He appeared as the orchestra began Mendelssohn's "Wedding March," and the Rev. Mr. Beers read the Episcopal marriage service. The lovely bride was in white corded silk embroidered with pearls, beads and chenille, holding a bouquet of lilacs, hawthorn, and orange blossoms. Sir Thomas fumbled for the ring. The nervous bride nearly fainted. Bridesmaid Bessie Sedgwick, in a reproduction of the Empress Josephine's gown, also was agitated; so was best man Fred Sharon. Finally Sir Thomas found the ring, placed his arm around the bride to support her, and the ceremony proceeded.

At eight o'clock several hundred guests poured into the house to congratulate Sir Thomas and Lady Hesketh. Sarah Althea Hill, the senator's alleged common-law wife, was among them, but her name was not given to the press. Gifts were shown, but Sir Thomas's present of his mother's jewels was in a safe-deposit box in England.

Toward morning eight hundred bedraggled guests ran in the rain from trains to carriages at Third and Townsend Streets, and one lady in a white dress fell into the mud. Within a week Sir Thomas and Lady Hesketh left in Senator Sharon's special car for New York, to sail for England. Although they were married in a storm, and the bridegroom was nearly missing, and the bride almost fainted, and the unwanted Sarah Althea Hill crashed the gate, the Heskeths were happy. So friendly were the relations between the California and British families that Florence Breckenridge, Mrs. Fred Sharon's daughter by her first marriage, became the wife of Sir Thomas Hesketh, nephew of Flora Sharon's husband, who succeeded his uncle. The third Baron Hesketh, great-great-grandson of Senator Sharon, is a half-orphaned schoolboy who lives with his mother and two younger brothers at the family home built by Sir Christopher Wren in North Hamptonshire, England. Sir Thomas Hesketh willed Rufford Hall to the National Trust and it is now a museum.

During this era of lavish hospitality San Franciscans went "down the Peninsula" to attend California's most fabulous party, the three-day golden wedding celebration given by the Martin Murphys, pioneers of 1844. It occurred on July 17, 1881, at their 6,000-acre Rancho Pastoria de las Borregas, Murphy's Station (Sunnyvale). Everyone in California was invited, and 7,000 accepted. A special train brought the guests from San Francisco. San Jose courts adjourned. From Notre Dame Convent came the sisters and from the University of Santa Clara the Jesuit fathers. Martin Murphy had helped found both institutions.

At 12:30 a band playing "Come, Haste to the Wedding," escorted the young-old couple under the trees to the table where a huge stuffed bear sat at one end. A white-flowered wedding bell hung overhead. The hungry 7,000 ate eighteen barbecued beeves, fourteen sheep, ten porkers, a carload of ham and another of roast chicken. They drank five hundred gallons of coffee, barrels of beer, kegs of whisky, and a freight-carload of champagne.

Grandchildren John T. Carroll and Elizabeth Carroll Whittier for many years occupied the 20-room dwelling that was brought around the Horn from Boston in 1849. After their deaths, all that remained of the 6,000-acre Rancho was the six-acre garden, with ivy-covered oaks, Castilian roses and palms, and the huge century-old fig tree. This dwelling has been continuously occupied by one family longer than any other frame house in California. In 1955 it was bought by the city of Sunnyvale, the garden to be a park and the house a historical museum—the only residence down the Peninsula to become a historical monument.

In the 1890's and at the turn of the century San Francisco's two great hostesses were Mrs. Eleanor Martin and her sister, Mrs. Peter Donahue, who rode through the park in a glass coach. These ladies entertained unceasingly. Their brother, Governor Downey, named Anaheim for his sister, Anna Downey Donahue. Mrs. Martin's first husband was Major Harvey, father of J. Downey Harvey, and her second husband was banker Edward Martin, father of long-time social favorites Peter, Andrew, and Walter.

Mrs. Martin and Mrs. Donahue entertained lavishly at their South Park residences, but in 1894 they erected a handsome dwelling at Broadway and Buchanan Streets. After her sister's death Mrs. Martin continued her social activities. One of her most notable receptions was for Secretary of War Taft when he and his party, the year after the Earthquake, were en route to the Philippines. "Princess Alice" Roosevelt was one of the guests. Unsophisticated San Francisco was agape when she used lipstick and smoked cigarettes. The press headlined her for plunging into a swimming pool completely dressed while aboard ship. On that trip she became engaged to Nicholas Longworth, afterward speaker of the House of Representatives.

Mrs. Martin came to be called "Queen Eleanor" and was seldom seen without a collar of pearls and diamonds. Debutantes and their families courted her and she graciously invited them to share her festivities. She generally bade guests an early good night and lived to be 101, dying without an enemy.

None of San Francisco's hostesses entertained more lavishly than Mrs. Phoebe Hearst, who had been an important social figure in Washington while her husband was in the Senate. First president of the Century Club and one of the founders of the Parent-Teacher Association, she had a Moorish palace, Hacienda del Pozo de Verona, which had developed out of a hunting lodge belonging to her son, William Randolph Hearst, at Pleasanton in Livermore Valley. Trainloads of social, scientific, artistic, and educational leaders came to her. Fairy godmother of the University of California, to which she gave many millions, she not only financed archaeological expeditions but herself went to Egypt to watch that institution's excavations, superintended by Dr. Reisner. No longer young, she lived in a tent with her secretary, thrilling to discoveries even more important than King Tut's tomb.

On one occasion she gave an Egyptian dinner in honor of Dr. Reisner. The patio surrounding the Verona well for which the house was named was transformed into the court of an Egyptian sheik. On the table eight brass boats of true Egyptian design carried hundreds of crimson lotus and roses. Guests received Egyptian jewelry. Attendants were in Egyptian costumes and music from *Aida* was played throughout the dinner.

Mrs. M. H. de Young was another hostess to have a salon. Her California Street residence had a large ballroom and stage where her four daughters, Helen, Phyllis, Kathleen, and Constance, with their friends, Ethel Hager and Pearl Landers, sang and danced like professionals, delighting guests. Later the town residence was used by the daughters on visits to "the city" from Burlingame, but it has since been razed. Mrs. George Cameron, the de Youngs' oldest daughter, who owns "Rosecourt" at Burlingame, is one of the few great hostesses today in the San Francisco area.

After the death of William C. Ralston, San Francisco's greatest host was Mayor James Duval Phelan, United States senator and the city's most eligible bachelor. Before the Earthquake and Fire he often entertained *al fresco* in the Phelan garden in the Mission or was host at large dinners in the Red Room of the Bohemian Club. After 1906 he planned "a little box in the country" near Saratoga, which proved to be "Montalvo."

This Mediterranean villa with a forested background was named in memory of the Spanish author, Ordóñez de Montalvo, in whose romance, *Las sergas de Esplandián* (1510), first appeared the word "California," a golden island presided over by Queen Califia. In the foreground a wide lawn swept down to an Athenian temple.

When Senator Phelan entertained a great company of guests a barbecue was served under canvas awnings. At one luncheon, during World War I, honoring Vice-President Marshall on Santa Clara County's famed Blossom Day, the guest of honor was ill in bed. Not only was the vice-president absent, but wind and rain had whipped every petal from the miles of white-flowering prune trees. The vice-president's place was taken by the unimportant assistant secretary of the navy, Franklin Delano Roosevelt, with his rosy-cheeked wife, Eleanor. Roosevelt made his only speech in Santa Clara County at "Montalvo."

Senator Phelan financed California playwrights, artists, and sculptors and their creations, together with European art and sculpture, filled his house and gardens. He would have preferred being a great poet rather than a millionaire, and in the redwood forest on the mountainside back of the dwelling he created a naturalistic shrine, placing in the circle of redwoods bronze busts of Joaquin Miller, Edwin Markham, and John Muir, using redwood stumps as pedestals. In the outdoor theater, back of the patio and swimming pool, his most enjoyable afternoons were experienced when poets read aloud their original verse. He, himself, contributed excellent sonnets.

World travelers were often welcomed at "Montalvo": the Grand Duchess Marie, the Duke of Alva, Princess Bibesco, Philip Guedella, Madame Melba. Gertrude Atherton called it her second home and never visited it after her host died.

Senator Phelan's last appearance as host was on April 26, 1930, when he honored Edwin Markham's birthday. The poet himself was absent, but the senator rose and brokenly quoted Markham's words:

> I dare not ask your very all:
> I only ask a part.
> Bring me—when dancers leave the hall—
> Your aching heart.
>
> Give other friends your lighted face,
> The laughter of the years;
> I come to crave a greater grace—
> Bring me your tears!

Those words were his farewell. The following day he was fatally stricken. Senator Phelan bequeathed Montalvo with its 160 acres, together with $250,000, to the San Francisco Art Association. For several years the property was under the management of the association and the dwelling and guest house were converted into apartments where writers, painters, and musicians might pursue their work, at minimum expense. Exhibitions of paintings are held in the library and concerts are frequent in the open-air theater. The old barn has been transformed into a studio for sculptors. In recent years the property has been transferred to the Friends of Montalvo, who carry on the spirit of its creator, James Duval Phelan.

CHAPTER 18

Notable San Francisco Women

IN 1860 bobbed, hatless, young Laura DeForce Gordon began the woman's suffrage battle in San Francisco with all the valiance of her ancestor, Ethan Allen, declaring, "Only idiots, Chinese, paupers and women are excluded from office." She began her long fight to be admitted to the bar after being refused admission to Hastings Law College. Demanding a hearing before the Supreme Court, she was finally admitted to practice in November, 1879. Then she knocked at the door of the United States Supreme Court and received permission to practice there in February, 1883. She was the second woman in the United States to be thus recognized.

In 1911, during the administration of Governor Hiram W. Johnson, the Woman's Suffrage Amendment became a law by a vote of nearly 4,000. San Francisco women continued to advocate national suffrage, among the leaders being Frances Jolliffe, Miriam Michelson, and Maud Younger.

Laura DeForce Gordon's spirit must have rejoiced when she saw Judge Annette Abbott Adams presiding over California's Third District Court of Appeals. Daughter of pioneer settlers of Plumas County, Annette Abbott taught school for thirteen years, becoming the wife of M. H. Adams. She received her degree in law from the University of California in 1912. Soon she came to San Francisco as a member of the firm of Adams and Ogden, her partner being Miss Margaret Ogden.

In 1914 Mrs. Adams was appointed assistant United States district attorney of the Northern District of California. The sudden illness of U.S. Attorney John W. Preston necessitated her being prosecutor in the German-Hindu conspiracy cases. One of the Hindu defendants was shot in the courtroom by another, and the assailant was promptly killed by U.S. Marshal Holohan. German Consul Franz Bopp, Vice-Consul Baron Eduard von Shack, and Attaché Wilhelm von Brincken were convicted of an attempt to set up military expeditions from the United States against England, to destroy shipping and foment revolution in India.

Four years later President Wilson appointed Mrs. Adams United States attorney for Northern California, and in 1920 she was named assistant attorney general of the United States—the first and only woman to hold either office. Another "first" came for Mrs. Adams when Governor Culbert L. Olson named her presiding justice of the Third District Court of Appeals at Sacramento. In 1950, the year of the hundredth anniversary of the Supreme Court of California, she had the distinction of being the only woman to serve as justice of that court during a trial when an associate justice disqualified himself. To women Judge Adams said, "Courage, courage, make up your mind what you wish to do and see it through."

Two San Francisco women followed Judge Adams's advice, Theresa Meikle and Lenore E. Underwood. During 1955 Theresa Meikle was a superior judge and the presiding judge, but is now retired.

Lenore E. Underwood is a municipal judge. She was born in Lithuania but came to this country in the arms of her parents. She was general chairman of "Bonds for Israel." After she helped roll up $350,000 bond subscriptions, the Israel Prime Minister Moshe Sharrett came from Israel to attend a banquet honoring her at the Fairmont Hotel. Judge Underwood's first trip to Israel was in May, 1959, to attend the world-wide convention there of B'nai B'rith, oldest and largest Jewish fraternal and service group.

As early as 1852 women were active as physicians in San Francisco, but they could not obtain a degree in medicine. Dr. Christina A. Cook occupied a three-story brick house on the site of Gump's art store. Her fan-shaped sign on the door read: "Christina A. Cook, Botanical Physician." She had learned healing and herbal cures from a highland Scotch uncle in Canada.

After practicing for fifty years Dr. Cook applied to Dr. Elias Samuel Cooper's Medical School and Dr. Hugh Toland's Medical School to be permitted to enroll. Dr. J. H. Crane of Petaluma expressed the faculty opinion: "Show me a woman who will straddle a mustang to ride fifteen or twenty miles on a dark stormy night to attend a man who has been shot, or some woman in confinement." Dr. Levi Lane reported to Dr. Cook: "They say they know that women will soon be admitted, but they'll be damned if they'll start it."

Dr. Cook carried the matter into court, and a law was passed permitting women to take the examination. Out of thirteen applicants, Mrs. Cook and two men passed. At last she had the legal right to call herself "doctor." Her daughter, Dr. Caroline Cook Coffin of Berkeley, received her degree in 1891 from Dr. McLean's Elective College and now resides in Santa Clara County, where at eighty-five she organized "Live Long and Like It" clubs.

Three years before the California Medical Society voted to admit women, Dr. Charlotte Blake Brown took her degree at Philadelphia, after reading medicine at Napa with her fellow townsman, Dr. Charles Nichols. Dr. Charlotte's husband became a San Francisco bank official, and soon the family established themselves in the city. Of distinguished appearance and friendly understanding toward all humanity, she was deeply revered. Chinatown knew her medical missionary work. The first ovariotomy by a woman on the Pacific coast was performed by her. The hospital for children and training school for nurses are her monument.

Dr. Adelaide Brown, daughter of Dr. Charlotte Blake Brown, was the only woman asked to serve on the State Board of Health during its first fifty years of existence. Dr. Philip King Brown carried on his mother's humanitarian work, and her grandson, Dr. Cabot Brown, continues the family service.

Few San Francisco women were so venerated as Madonna-faced Mrs. Sarah B. Cooper. A cousin of Robert G. Ingersoll, she denied the existence of hell-fire and was expelled from her church, where she had a Bible class. The Rev. Charles Dana Barrows invited her to bring her class to his Congregational church. Mrs. Cooper's class sponsored the Silver Street Kindergarten, already opened by Miss Emma Marwedel and Kate Douglas Smith, later Mrs. Wiggin, author of *Rebecca of Sunnybrook Farm*. Mrs. Cooper founded a free kindergarten in the heart of the Barbary Coast. Three years later the name was changed to the Golden Gate Kindergarten Association. In 1882 the San Francisco organization had twenty-two out of twenty-eight kindergartens in California.

Mrs. Cooper lived with her daughter, Harriet, on Vallejo Street. When the younger woman became mentally ill, friends advised her to have the daughter restrained. Mrs. Cooper had faith that the aberrations would pass. One morning the city was appalled to learn that Harriet had turned on the gas killing both mother and daughter.

From Sarah B. Cooper's Bible class stems the work of Elizabeth Ashe and Alice Griffith, who developed the Telegraph Hill Neighborhood Association. At this community club thousands of youngsters annually find wholesome recreation instead of getting into mischief in the streets. Betty Ashe, seated in her high-ceilinged dwelling on Sacramento Street filled with ancestral portraits, related that when she was fourteen San Francisco was talking about "that awful woman, Sarah B. Cooper, who said to her Bible class, 'It makes no difference whether you believe that the whale swallowed Jonah, or Jonah swallowed the whale. What you believe is useless, unless you do good deeds.'" Saying nothing to her mother, Betty stole into Mrs. Cooper's Bible class and listened to the heretic. Back home she confessed to her mother that she had heard Mrs. Cooper and was convinced that she must do good deeds.

Mrs. Ashe consulted the Rev. Dr. Foute of Grace Church. "Don't worry, Mrs. Ashe. I'll make Betty teach a Sunday-school class for poor North Beach children." "I don't know how to teach a Sunday-school class," said Betty. "You know more than the children do."

Betty's closest friend was Alice Griffith, daughter of a millionaire forty-niner. They were both Kings Daughters. The Bible class grew, but the girls decided that long-distance charity was futile. In order to attend Sunday school at Grace Church, Telegraph Hill children had to pass through the "street of bad women"—Dupont, now Grant Avenue. Betty Ashe and Alice Griffith opened a community center in a barnlike structure where Mrs. Cooper's kindergarten was being held. The two girls not only gave Sunday-school lessons but taught the children to wash dishes and sing while at work. The Telegraph Hill Neighborhood Association began. This was in 1890. After seventy years it is still an influence in the community. Both Miss Ashe and Miss Griffith are gone. When Mrs. Griffith died in 1959 at the age of ninety-four she bequeathed a portion of her million-dollar estate to the San Francisco Foundation to aid her many charities.

Similar in spirit was the work of Elizabeth Armor, foundress of the Sisters of the Holy Family, the only Californian to establish a religious order in the Roman Catholic Church. She was born at Sydney, Australia, in 1851; her mother was a native of Ireland and her father of England. As a child she came to San Francisco with her parents, and they became friends of Mr. and Mrs. Richard Tobin. After her mother's death, her father remarried and was obliged to leave for Australia. Before departing he asked his friend Richard Tobin to adopt Elizabeth.

That evening Mrs. Tobin was astonished when her husband entered and said, "Mary, I've adopted a little girl today." Mr. Tobin was a struggling lawyer and the Tobins already had twelve children. "Why, Dick," exclaimed the wife, "we can hardly feed our own." "God will provide, Mary" was his quiet answer. So Elizabeth Armor became big "Sister Lizzie" to the Tobin children.

The grave-eyed child attended the Academy of the Presentation and soon became concerned with problems of the poor. She welcomed the needy until the Tobin house overflowed. Once when Mrs. Tobin was absent on vacation her husband wrote; "You'd better come home, for Lizzie has a houseful of youngsters."

Elizabeth often visited Mission Dolores with Mrs. Tobin and she told the Rev. John Prendergast, the Mission pastor, that she wished to become a Carmelite. Father Prendergast dissuaded her, feeling that her work should be with poor children. Archbishop Alemany supported Father Prendergast's suggestion.

At twenty-two, Elizabeth Armor left the luxurious home of her foster parents on Nob Hill and on May 6, 1892, with one companion, opened a convent in a Pine Street flat. Elizabeth became "Sister Dolores," and working mothers left their children in her care. Six months later the sisters established their first Day Home on Post Street.

During Sister Dolores' lifetime, three large Day Homes were opened in San Francisco. Only fifty-four years old, she died in 1905. Archbishop Montgomery presided at the funeral and more than a thousand children attended the Requiem Mass. Agnes Tobin, foster sister of the founder, wrote a poem for the occasion:

All the Cathedral, wander where you will
Is filled with little children—aisle on aisle—
The church is a great garden for the while—
And in the windless air the flowers are still.
Of the bright eyes that pain and wonder fill—
The pearly throats astrain to watch the file
Of black-frocked acolytes go by! Beguile
Her not with odours from the heavenly hill—
Give way, dim seraphs—stop the misty rout
Of your soft dances on the floors of gold!
Press not so close upon her—let her be!
Oh, Sister! push the lattice—lean far out—
Bend thy grand auburn head enaureoled—
Thy cloud of witnesses, Beloved, see.

Sister Dolores' work has grown until now there are twenty-four
Foundations of the Holy Family in California, Nevada, Utah, Texas,
and Hawaii, instructing 75,000 children.

Chinatown's underworld for nearly fifty years called Donaldina
Cameron "White Devil" because she rescued girls from their masters, saving them from slavery and prostitution. New Zealand-born,
Miss Cameron's life had been largely passed on California ranches.
When she was twenty a friend suggested that she go to San Francisco to aid Miss Margaret Culbertson in the Chinese Mission
Presbyterian Home. Blue-eyed Donaldina, her pink and white face
framed in a pompadour of gold-tinted hair, appeared one gray morning in 1895 at 920 Sacramento Street, the first foreign mission enterprise in the United States. So ferocious were the white slavers
against Miss Culbertson that on the morning of Donaldina's arrival
a stick of dynamite had been planted in the hall of the home. Donaldina plunged immediately into the Chinatown war when the
police escorted her and Miss Culbertson to rescue a girl imprisoned
in an alley. Police axes bludgeoned down doors and prisoners
were taken. Donaldina found her lifework.

At that time Inspector John Banion was battling in Chinatown
with highbinders who were shooting one another on sight. He
helped Donaldina. "Sergeant Banion had neither moral nor physical
fear. Without him, I would have been helpless," said Miss Cameron.
Her work carried her through dramatic situations, even to passing

a night in jail with a girl arrested for stealing. For forty years she defied captains of prostitution, highbinders, and white slavers, taking her rescued victims to her mission, where they were taught useful work. Some of Miss Cameron's girls received diplomas from the best schools. The ablest went to China to assist in developing leaders among women. Through her efforts the slave trade was, to a large extent, eradicated. The Presbyterian Mission in Sacramento Street is now called Cameron House.

About fifteen years ago Miss Cameron retired to her Palo Alto cottage. There in her mid-nineties she is not far from the Ming Quong Home at Los Gatos, where live forty small boys and girls of broken families.

San Francisco realized that a small whirlwind had arrived when Katherine Felton, five feet tall, came from Oakland to San Francisco to direct the Associated Charities. Fair-haired Katherine wished to become a lawyer like her father, Judge John Felton. After graduating from the University of California, however, she took a course in political economy at the University of Chicago. Her lifework was determined after seeing the misery of the slums.

In 1901 Katherine Felton called the first State Conference of Charities held west of the Rockies. When she took charge of the Associated Charities, children were lodged in jail as vagrants. "Everyone's child is everyone's concern," she said, as she brought about the establishment of the juvenile court, presided over by Judge Frank J. Murasky. At that time more than half the foundlings in institutions—59 per cent—died annually. In 1908 the Foundling Asylum placed all babies under her supervision. The asylum became the Babies' Aid in a building made from two refugee shacks contributed by the Red Cross. Just inside its swinging porch a cradle was prepared every night with blankets and hot-water bottles. Above it was the sign: "Receptacle for Foundlings." When weight of more than two pounds was placed in the cradle, an electric bell rang in the nurses' quarters. The mother slipped away before the nurse could answer the bell. Miss Felton enlisted Native Sons and Native Daughters of the Golden West to find foster homes for foundlings, and their interest has never flagged.

With her carelessly piled braids, hat askew, in case she wore one (she often lost her hats), and her coat sometimes wrong side out,

Katherine Felton amazed governors and legislators when she appeared at Sacramento to obtain welfare legislation. She persuaded the police department to place woman officers on the force, was largely instrumental in having neglected children cared for in private homes, and also aided in the enactment of the widow's pension law. Problem children were her favorites. She inspired the Junior League to develop "Pinehaven" for children, and also Mrs. Sigmund Stern to support Recreation House.

San Francisco's death rate of foundling children dropped to less than 1 per cent. During the depression which bankrupted the Community Chest and brought the Associated Charities into debt, Miss Felton did heroic relief work, wearing out young assistants, who humorously spoke of themselves as "sold down the river as part-time slaves." She had no personal life. When one of her staff wished to go on a two weeks' honeymoon she said, "I should think a week-end would be quite sufficient." At the new and beautiful Associated Charities Home on Gough Street, her office was filled with toys to give children. Her orange Persian cat, Penelope, and the Siamese, Dhudeen, sat on her desk as "members of the staff."

On the day in 1939 that war was declared Miss Felton learned that she had cancer. She called her last year the happiest of her life. "Here I am surrounded by happiness and love." She asked friends to read poetry to her in the sunny garden. As her birthday gift she was taken back to the agency in a wheelchair. During her last months at the Stanford Hospital, she directed the Children's Agency until two days before her death. On the day she died, August 14, 1940, the flag of the United States hung at half-mast on the University of California campus. Grace Cathedral was thronged at the funeral of the modern saint.

Handsome Aurelia Henry was graduated from Lincoln High School and later from the University of California. After acquiring her Ph.D. at Yale, she returned to her native city and married Dr. George Herbert Reinhardt, college physician and professor of hygiene at the University of California. Suddenly widowed, she was appointed English lecturer at the same university.

Dr. Aurelia Reinhardt was named president of Mills College, which since its incorporation from Mills Seminary in 1866 has been the leading educational institution for women in Northern

California. During her twenty-seven years as president of Mills, Dr. Reinhardt was affectionately called "The Pres" and was often serenaded by the students. She traveled much, always seeking information. She toured South America and her interest in Latin America resulted in the development of the internationally known Mills summer course for Spanish- and Portuguese-speaking students. She retired voluntarily in 1943 to lecture and travel.

President Roosevelt appointed Dr. Reinhardt as special consultant to the UN Conference at San Francisco. On returning from Russia in 1947, she developed a heart ailment, and thousands of Mills alumnae lamented her death at Palo Alto, January 29, 1948, the same day that Dr. Donald B. Tresidder, president of Stanford University, died suddenly in New York City. Dr. Reinhardt's son, George Frederick Reinhardt, served as ambassador to South Viet Nam.

San Francisco's first native daughter to represent the city and also the first to represent California in Congress still lives here. She is Mrs. Mae Ella Hunt Nolan, widow of John I. Nolan, Progressive and Republican congressman for five terms from San Francisco's Fifth Congressional District. Mrs. Nolan was the fourth congresswoman in the United States.

She was chosen at a special election after Congressman Nolan's death to fill his unexpired term, January 23, 1923, and was re-elected the following term, although six men were her competitors.

Mrs. Nolan likes to recall that when her daughter, Corliss, was a child in Washington and King Albert and Queen Elizabeth of Belgium were guests at a joint session of Congress, the six-year-old girl was one of a hundred children on the floor of Congress. It is customary on such occasions to bring children. The Queen requested that the little girl with the golden curls and blue dress be brought to her. "What is your name?" said the Queen. "And where do you come from?" "I'm Corliss Nolan from California." "So you are the little girl who brought sunshine to Washington."

The incident, with the child's picture, was widely published. Corliss Nolan is now Mrs. Francis E. Guenther of Sacramento and mother of a son. She is proud that she is the only woman in the United States who had both a father and a mother in Congress.

San Francisco's second native daughter to represent the city in

Congress was Florence Prag Kahn, widow of Congressman Julius Kahn, a Shakespearean actor and lawyer who died in 1925. Elected to fill Mr. Kahn's unexpired term, she was returned several times, finally retiring in 1937.

A former school teacher and daughter of one of San Francisco's ablest educators, she became a force in Congress. Denounced by Representative Fiorello LaGuardia of New York as a "standpatter and follower of that reactionary Senator George H. Moses," she quipped, "Why shouldn't I choose Moses as my leader? Haven't my people been following him for ages?" Asked how she got more votes for her projects than anyone else in the House, she jammed her nondescript hat over her unpowdered nose: "It's my sex appeal."

She worked for and won the city's Marine Hospital Federal Building and improvements to the Post Office, Presidio and Harbor. She was largely responsible for the selection of Sunnyvale for the Naval Air Station, and she helped get the Naval Air Base for Alameda. J. Edgar Hoover called her "The Mother of the Federal Bureau of Investigation." Women generally draw slight attendance at the intellectual Commonwealth Club luncheons, but when Mrs. Kahn spoke there she had large audiences.

Alice Eastwood, botanical curator of the Academy of Sciences, was the only San Francisco woman whose birthday became a semi-public event, celebrated by groups of friends and clubs. A grove of redwood trees in Humboldt County has been named for her, as are many flowers, including a member of the sunflower family.

Canadian-born and self-educated, this clear-eyed, clear-skinned woman began her career as a Denver schoolteacher in 1887, when she botanized in the Rocky Mountains with Alfred Russel Wallace, coformulator of the Darwinian theory. She continued research over Colorado, Florida, the Pacific coast, Alaska, Hawaii, Mexico, and portions of Europe. Several years were spent by her at the Gray Arboretum in Cambridge, Massachusetts. She was an authority on garden flowers like fuchsias, and author of *Trees of California, Flowers of California,* and *Flowers of the Pacific Coast.*

She climbed Mount Santa Lucia (Mount Junipero Serra), alone, botanizing. She carried no blankets, but made a fire of pine cones and slept on the ground. At the time of the Earthquake she went to the Academy's building adjoining the Emporium, and mounted six floors over broken steps to save the botanical specimens.

At seventy she had her first vacation when, having been run down by a car, she was obliged to rest in a cast for thirteen weeks. She had a good time with the insurance company paying the bills, her friends showering her with flowers, books, and sweets—even cologne. "I enjoyed myself. The nurses were so interesting." Even when she was past ninety no maid looked after Miss Eastwood in her 75-year-old house on Russian Hill, which she described as "Old-fashioned like me. I was born before baths and showers, at the time of outdoor privies. I bathe in an unheated room on the porch, a daily sponge bath." She had never coddled herself and didn't intend to begin now. She did her own cooking and ground her own coffee.

When, after sixty years of service, Miss Eastwood retired, she taxied weekly to the Academy of Sciences to classify specimens and aid researchers in solving problems. At ninety-two she emplaned for the International Botanical Congress in Stockholm, where she, the eldest, was honorary chairman, presiding over 1,500 delegates. She loved flying and watching the sky and clouds. Returning, she flew to Washington to visit her younger sister, and she began a new book. She died in 1953 at age ninety-four.

Alice Eastwood never regretted being unmarried. "I don't need to look in the mirror. If I loved a man well enough to marry him, I'd lose freedom. I'm a happy old maid." She was guided by faith that something good would happen: "And it always does. Socrates says, 'There's no evil before a good man, whether alive or dead, nor are his affairs uncared for by the gods.' "

The Alice Eastwood Hall of Botany was dedicated in her honor at the California Academy of Sciences in Golden Gate Park, October 27, 1959.

CHAPTER 19

San Franciscans by Land and Air

THE HORSELESS carriage had long been an inventor's dream, but it was not until 1889 when J. W. Stanford disturbed the horse-drawn traffic on Market Street with his new Winton that motoring began in San Francisco.

The Winton if given the right-of-way could "tear along" at the rate of "5.05 miles per hour."

Soon other machine-age citizens were contesting the right-of-way with those newly invented gasoline buggies, the Duryea and the Haynes.

Progress on wheels was rapid from then on, despite frequent breakdowns, tire punctures, and the raucous advice from every side to "Get a horse!"

The smell of gasoline impregnated the salt-sweet San Francisco air.

Then on May 23, 1903, Dr. H. Nelson Jackson and Sewell Crocker set out from San Francisco in a Winton. On July 26 they arrived in New York after traveling some three thousand miles of dirt highway. They had made the first transcontinental trip by car.

Shortly after this a young engineer working for Mr. Edison's Illuminating Company, by the name of Henry Ford, was able to make a cheap workable automobile that put San Francisco and all the rest of the world on wheels.

Charles Fair, son of the Comstock senator, James G. Fair, imported a red, French runabout that stopped traffic on Market Street. Hill climbing was his goal, but impossible in San Francisco. After failing to struggle up even Oakland's gentle hills, he and his wife went to Europe, where their death in an automobile accident in France resulted in long litigation over their will, the question being, who had died first?

Hill-climbing history, however, was made in 1897 when William
Leonard Elliot, a blue-eyed bicycle manufacturer of Oakland, dis-
played his automobile at the Mechanics' Fair. Enterprising Bailey
Millard, the *Examiner's* Sunday editor, asked Elliot to drive his car
up Mount Hamilton, 4,209 feet, and take as passengers, Dr. David
Starr Jordan, president of Stanford University, and Professor Albert
W. Smith, of Stanford's Engineering Department. The momentous
start was made in San Jose. With horse and buggy followed the
Examiner's reporter, Charles Sedgwick Aiken (later editor of *Sunset
Magazine*), and artist Paul Heyman.

The following Sunday Dr. Jordan wrote in the *Examiner* that on
level Santa Clara Street in San Jose the machine "flew along" at the
rate of "12 to 18 miles an hour," but on heavy Mount Hamilton roads
it made 4 miles an hour. On the very heavy grade, the car "kicked
stoutly with its hind legs." City horses tolerated the new vehicle,
but a mountain horse backed its wagon in front of the automobile.
On the grade the team conveying Aiken and Heyman kept up with
the car, but was left behind on the level. Running time of 26 miles
was 5 hours and 20 minutes. The adventurers were cordially received and congratulated by Director James E. Keeler of Lick
Observatory.

On the return trip, the steering gear was thrown out of order
temporarily and the brake failed, but the emergency saved them.
The travelers boasted that they came down in 4 hours and 10 minutes. Mr. Smith said he enjoyed the trip up, but on the return "slide
into San Jose, the tingles ran up and down my back and up my
finger ends. I've had no such experience since the awful pleasure of
witches' tales many years ago. The horse must surely go, for the era
of automobiles is upon us."

Dr. Jordan said, "The cost of $1,200 places the Elliot car in the
luxury class, but automobiling will form the most delightful of all
modes of travel, especially in country charming in scenery and
equable in climate, as is the case in California."

Horse owners considered automobiles the invention of the devil,
and bitterly protested against their appearance in the park. Automobile missionaries came from the East, among them W. L. Emory,
with cars to sell. Ignoring the law against driving in Golden Gate
Park, he invited his friends and went. A mounted officer tried to
expel the intruder. Emory drove on, the officer racing after him.

Neck and neck, they tore through the park. After the officer "lass'ed" Emory, he was warned to keep out of the park. The "No Admittance to Automobiles" sign was not removed from the park until 1901, one year after the founding of the Automobile Club.

Drivers were obliged to have special park license. Mrs. Charles C. Moore first qualified, then came F. F. Rocket. Within a year 475 automobiles carried park-permit tags. By 1905 there were about 2,000 automobiles in San Francisco.

In early 1900 a "steam" car was invented by Charles C. Moore. John D. Spreckels liked "steamers" because they negotiated the hills. The late Herbert Fleishhacker had a Winton, but he said his thrilling experience was driving up the California Street hill with John D. Spreckels in a White "steamer." Mrs. Fleishhacker recalled that in going out of town he always took a dozen extra tubes and two spare tires. Dirt roads filled with chuckholes constantly snapped springs. A gallon of gasoline carried him five or six miles. He had to back up his car to make a 5 or 6 per cent grade. On a trip to Santa Barbara in 1903 his automobile caught fire and burned. His was one of the first limousines to reach San Francisco, a Pope-Toledo. During the 1906 disaster he lent his limousine to the authorities, but hard service wrecked it. At this time cars usually cost from $7,000 to $8,000 although there were a few at $1,000. James D. Phelan had a French car, William H. Crocker's was a Locomobile, Rudolph Spreckels chose a Columbia, and Eddie Bowes (radio's Major Bowes) also preferred a Locomobile.

Thirty unsuccessful trips across the continent had been attempted, but in 1903 occurred the historic "Ocean to Ocean Odyssey" when a San Franciscan, Sewell K. Crocker, left New York on May 23 with a thirty-one-year-old physician, Colonel H. Nelson Jackson, in a new Winton and headed for San Francisco. He wagered that he could cross the continent in three months. He surprised himself by doing it in 63 days. The trip cost him $8,000.

Success of the Crocker-Jackson-Winton journey was a challenge to Tom Fitch, plant foreman of San Francisco's Packard agency. Accompanied by Marius Krarup, sixty-one-year-old editor of the *Automobile Magazine*, he drove the Packard into the Pacific, re-christening the car "The Pacific," and set out for New York. People called Fitch and Krarup "drunk or crazy," but they reached New York in 61 days, breaking the Winton's record.

In Paris the Countess Boni de Castellane (Anna Gould) set the fashion for women to drive their own cars. Windshields had not been invented, and women plastered their faces with cold cream and powder and often donned caps and veils. Despite these precautions, they usually arrived at their destination windblown. Miss Sarah Drum, sister of banker John Drum, was one of the first San Francisco women to drive. Mrs. J. W. Leavitt first drove in 1902, and during the ensuing thirty-four years, had twenty-one different cars, driving 650,000 miles without accident or traffic violation. In 1936 Mrs. Leavitt was chosen as San Francisco's most representative safe driver. At fifty-seven, mother of six and grandmother of four, she drove to New York and back to attend the Safe Drivers' Conference. She said that her rule for driving was eternal watchfulness, and always expecting the other driver to do the wrong thing.

Mrs. Fred J. Linz, in 1902, was the first woman in the state to be registered. She became editor of the first automobile magazine on the Pacific coast and in 1906 formed the California Women's Automobile Club.

Motoring enthusiasts were so many that parking became a problem, and late in the thirties the Union Square Garage Corporation was formed, with Carlton H. Wall as president, to build the world's first four-story underground garage. The Reconstruction Finance Corporation made a first mortgage loan of $850,000 on the cost of $1,550,000 to be liquidated in twenty years. After the bond issue is paid in twenty-five years, the garage will be turned over to the city of San Francisco clear of indebtedness.

Ground was broken on March 31, 1941. General contractors were McDonald & Kahn, Inc., and Timothy L. Pflueger, architect. Beautiful shrubs and trees were removed and away went the Dewey Monument to be cleaned. Excavators took out 150,000 cubic yards of earth, but a 12-inch concrete roof, overlaid with asphalt and felt membrane was installed under a 6-inch drainage system of crushed rock 6 inches thick. Five feet of rich loam was placed thereon for shrubs and flowers to be replanted. Formal opening of the garage occurred on September 11, 1942. In Union Square each spring there is a rhododendron show of a hundred varieties from Golden Gate Park. Artists sometimes display their paintings in the square. Here occurs the Cable-Car Festival and also the annual Christmas Eve Festival of Song.

So successful was the Union Square garage and so great was the demand for parking that there was clamor for another municipal garage under St. Mary's Square. Cost of construction, $2 million, was borne by the S. E. Onorato Corporation and the W. B. Realty Company of Los Angeles. Land was leased for thirty-three years, at the expiration of which time it must revert to the city.

The project was completed after four years of intensive work. Back came lawn, trees, Bufano's statue of Sun Yat-sen, and the Chinese soldiers' Memorial Tablet were replaced on pedestals corresponding to their former position in the square.

First passenger to enter the garage was Mayor Elmer E. Robinson, who cut the ribbon barring the entrance and drove in a 1903 Ford, symbolic of long-gone days, followed by a new Chevrolet.

Beneath the Civic Center Plaza was constructed a third underground garage which was completed in 1960. Shortly after January 1, 1961, ground was broken for the fourth underground garage at Portsmouth Square, where the American flag was first raised in San Francisco. It is planned that this garage will be ready for occupancy in 1962.

San Francisco is the first city in the United States with underground garages. They not only help solve the parking problem, but they may serve as bomb shelters.

Even when motoring or the horseless carriage was only a dream, San Francisco was air-minded. British-born Frederick Marriott in 1856 founded the weekly *News Letter* to make sufficient money to perfect his flying machine, *Avitor*. Already in England he had experimented with a balloon driven by a steam engine. Marriott took his contraption to Shell Mound, Emeryville, July 2, 1869, and the crowd cheered when the *Avitor* went up five miles or more. San Franciscans saw themselves flying to New York. Later the *Avitor* crashed, and enthusiasts were glad to content themselves with the new, safe railroad.

An eleven-year-old boy, John Joseph Montgomery, saw and was thrilled by Marriott's *Avitor* and went home to Oakland and built what he thought was a model of the Marriott flying machine. As a child he had scared his sister's chickens to watch their motion, and in crossing on the ferry to attend St. Ignatius College he studied the sea gulls from the ferryboat. His interest intensified until as a professor at the University of Santa Clara, in 1883, he made the first glider flight at Otay, near San Diego. After fifty successful flights with his glider, Montgomery crashed to his death near San Jose on December 31, 1911.

In Montgomery Park on the hilltop from which Montgomery launched his first glider, San Diego citizens have erected a stone monument with a stainless steel wing 90 feet high. A plaque states that the aviator made the first winged flight in history, opening the highways of the air. He is also memorialized in Montgomery Airport, Montgomery School and Montgomery Street.

John Joseph Montgomery's glider was the parent of the modern plane. Twenty years later, in 1903, the Wright Brothers added a gasoline engine that they designed, aided by expert mechanics, and at Kitty Hawk, North Carolina, won aviation fame.

Glenn Curtiss flew his first plane in the San Francisco area on July 4, 1908. In France experiments were being made, and Louis Paulhan in 1910 soared 5,000 feet over Los Angeles. William Randolph Hearst, who had used balloons for *Examiner* publicity in the eighties, went up with Paulhan, the first San Franciscan to fly with the Frenchman. At Tanforan thousands crowded to see Paulhan fly, and soon youngsters were making gliders and flying them above the parkside sand dunes. Weldon H. Cook, an Oakland pilot, flew over Mount Tamalpais, delivering the first official "mail by plane" in California. He planned to start an Oakland-San Francisco Air Ferry, but crashed over Pueblo, Colorado.

Mayor James Rolph, Jr., enjoyed riding in the sky. He flew to Oakland, inviting its mayor to return with him, but the Oaklander had another engagement.

In spite of danger, in 1912 a birdwoman appeared at Emeryville —Miss Blanche S. Scott, in a wool-lined, black-satin skirt, red sweater, aviator's helmet, and puttees. Flying 90 miles an hour, the "tomboy of the air" stole the show, remaining aloft 15 minutes at an altitude of 1,000 feet. She saw birdman William H. Hoff dashed to the ground in the choppy air. "That is a part of the game," she said, trying to go aloft. Her managers forbade it. By this time Miss Harriet Quimby began flying in San Francisco. Soon Roy N. Francis took the Alcazar actress, Dorothy Lane, up 6,000 feet, the first woman to cross the bay by air. Champagne agent and cotillion leader Ned Greenway paid Francis handsomely to go up and sprinkle several bottles of his champagne over the Cliff House.

Lincoln Beachey's "upside-down flying" held Panama-Pacific Exposition audiences enthralled. Once he was given an "upside-down dinner" and was carried into the dining room upside down. Everything was served upside down. Beachey tried to eat standing on his head. His last upside-down performance was a dive to death over the bay in his new Taube, March 14, 1915. Art Smith took over and became the Exposition's daredevil of the air.

Lansing Tevis, a friend of Alberto Santos Dumont, had flown in Europe. His mother, Mrs. Will Tevis, was one of the first San Francisco women to go aloft. Tevis became president of the Christopherson Air Manufacturing Company in Redwood City, selling planes for delivering mail in China. He also did business with the President of Mexico. The company was dissolved when Silas Christopherson's biplane turned over in Redwood City.

Five of the Christopherson brothers were aviators. Goodsell met death at Long Beach in 1918, and Harvey at Yuma in 1929. In the $10,000 biplane invented by him, Silas held America's altitude record by flying over Mount Whitney, 15,723 feet. After three of his brothers had been killed, Harry P. Christopherson spent his sixties repairing automobiles on 32nd Avenue. He wanted "no more of that flying stuff. You put a plane together with baling wire, and flew with the seat of your pants."

No nonprofessional San Francisco birdman flew so many thousand miles as the late James Otis, son of Mayor James Otis and grandson of sea captain F. W. Macondray. He took off from any level place, often from the Marina. He flew to duck hunting, to lunch at Hotel Del Monte. Summers the Otises occupied a house on the Stanford campus so that he could commute to his office in a plane. Many times he hopped from continent to continent, desisting only when a heart ailment developed. In 1955, after his death his ninety-six-year-old widow flew to New York.

San Francisco's first birdwoman, Harriet Quimby, "little Miss Dresden China," took her first flying lessons in the city, and was the first American woman to soar over the British Channel: "It was just like sitting in a rocking chair." San Francisco was waiting to welcome their famous birdlady, but while piloting a white Bleriot over Boston Bay, she crashed 1,000 feet to death at sunset.

Honolulu beckoned flyers, and after Lindbergh's flight to Paris, pineapple king John D. Dole, offered $36,000 in prizes for the first transoceanic air race. The flyers set out from Oakland, August 16, 1927. The *Wolaroc*, carrying Art Gobel and Lieutenant W. M. Davis, and the *Aloha*, piloted by Martin Jenson, came through. The

Miss Doran, carrying little Miss Mildred Doran, a Michigan school-teacher, soared over the ocean with Augy Pedlar, pilot, and Vilas E. Knobe, navigator, but was lost. A similar fate met the *Examiner's Golden Eagle,* piloted by Jack Frost and Gordon Smith. President Coolidge ordered a ship to look for them, but no trace of the seven flyers could be found. Two army lieutenants, Maitland and Hagenberger, won the prize but they were not eligible, having started ahead of time.

In September of the following year memorial services were held for the intrepid flyers, 700 miles out at sea, on the Matson Liner *Maui.* Hawaiian leis and thousands of roses were tossed into the water.

In spite of the tragedy connected with flying, birdmen and -women continued to soar through the air. Amelia Earhart, the first woman to cross the Atlantic alone, flew from Honolulu to Oakland, January 11 and 12, 1935. She was on a world flight, and San Francisco and Oakland were again awaiting her when she disappeared somewhere near Holland Island, July 12, 1937. At the time of her death her own words were quoted:

> Courage is the price
> that life extracts
> for granting peace.
> The soul that knows it not
> knows no release
> from little things.

Twenty-one year old, red-haired Susan Bryant was not deterred by Amelia Earhart's disaster. She smashed all records for around-the-world flight in a commercial plane, 107 hours and 20 minutes, becoming "Miss San Francisco Airport." Chosen by the San Francisco Junior Chamber of Commerce, she was given a red globe studded with five diamonds, marking the stops here and at New York, Paris, Karachi, and Manila. She broke the previous global flight record set by Jean Marie Audebert of Paris, of 115 hours and 38 minutes. "I'm not tired a bit," she said. The only time she got for sightseeing was in Italy, where she had a salami sandwich, and at Saigon, where she had a 20-minute tour of the city. Cost of airline tickets for such a tour was about $1,200.

Milton Reynolds of Mexico, who now hunts tigers but once made $100,000 a day selling America's first ballpoint pen, set a round-the-world commercial flight record in 1960. He flew from San Francisco, across three continents, and back to San Francisco in 51 hours, 45 minutes and 22 seconds. This bettered the previous record by 9:09.36.

San Francisco's first flying machine crashed in 1869, but now this air-minded city has residents who commute daily to Los Angeles, 49 minutes by jet. Seven and a half hours via the "old-fashioned" nonstop airline is the time to New York, with 5 hours by jet. Honolulu takes a half an hour less. The average number of landings and take-offs is one every 2 minutes, or 720 plane movements a day. During peak hours there is a landing or take-off nearly every minute. They all come and go from the city's $75 million International Airport with 3,685 acres of land, or 2¼ times the size of Golden Gate Park. It is owned by the city and county of San Francisco and operated under the jurisdiction of the Public Utilities Commission. Fourteen miles, or twenty minutes, from downtown San Francisco, it is the most modern airport in the nation, and perhaps in the world. Thousands travel miles to dine or lunch at the airport. Do you want a hairdo, a shoeshine, a shower, a cocktail, candy, a magazine, a public stenographer, or a bank? They are all to be found at San Francisco's International Airport. There is even a resort-type Hilton Inn nearby, costing nearly $3 million. Twelve thousand employees, supported by the $75 million payroll, serve the public, and yet when the airport was begun it was called "the world's prize mudhole."

This description was accurate during Mayor James Rolph's administration in 1926–1927. Later the Board of Supervisors voted to have an airfield site chosen south of San Francisco. After much shopping for land, 160 acres were purchased with 1,000 acres of submerged land adjoining—Mills Field. The creators of the airport say it was made with "men, money and mud." Mills Field began operations on June 7, 1927. Five years later the airport had only 4,348 in-and-out passengers.

In spite of the fact that the airport was in the red, and it was so muddy that even Lindbergh's plane was stuck trying to take off on a transoceanic flight, the air-minded kept on striving to have the field improved. The federal government spent $1,675,982 trying to reclaim the land. During Mayor Roger D. Lapham's term, he campaigned for the $20 million bond issue. So much in earnest was he that he learned to fly in a single lesson, shrugging off the bump that his plane received when it struck the ground: "Flying is as easy as falling off a log."

The bond issue carried, and during the administration of Mayor Elmer E. Robinson the people again voted for a $10 million bond issue, making the envisioned airport become a reality.

There arose a splendid six-story administration building and the adjoining structures necessary to handle millions of passengers, tons of cargo, mail, express, and parking places for 4,500 automobiles. On May 1, 1954, the International Airport was officially opened with addresses by Mayor Robinson and Governor Knight.

After thirty-one years of being in the red, in June, 1958, director Belford Brown announced that the airport had a profit of $56,000 for the year, without tax subsidy.

Already, however, the present terminal is inadequate for handling the four million passengers arriving and departing annually. In 1956, during Mayor George Christopher's administration a $25 million bond issue won voter endorsement. Since March, 1959, the International Airport has been ready for jet age expansion. Welton Becket and F.A.I.A. & Associates are the architects and engineers to construct two new terminals, each with two piers, a three-level parking structure for 6,000 cars, and provision for sixty jet aircraft gate positions. Helicopters will land and take off at the westerly end of the new north and south terminal building piers.

Air freighters bring canaries from Japan, tropical fish from Hong Kong, monkeys from the Philippines and Singapore for medical research laboratories. Australia sends racing greyhounds to dog tracks in the United States, and race horses and elephants also are planed in. Until the development of the freight carrier it was difficult to transport flowers, but orchids grown near San Francisco were flown to Princess Elizabeth when she married the Duke of Edinburgh. Because of the expansion of the market by plane, the San Francisco flower industry brings more than $8 million a year to the Bay Area.

When human beings, animals, flowers, and freight fly through the air, one recalls Tennyson's vision in *Locksley Hall:*

> Saw the heavens filled with commerce,
>   argosies of magic sails,
> Pilots of the purple twilight,
>   dropping down with costly bales . . .

CHAPTER 20

Century-old Business Firms and Organizations

AFTER GOLD was discovered in 1848, business boomed and the Chamber of Commerce was organized, May 1, 1850, with Beverly Sanders, president. In 1961 the presiding officer is O. R. Doerr.

David Neeley Robison, a farm boy, set out for California from Lockport, New York. When he came across the Isthmus of Panama in 1848, he learned that if he bought bananas green, they would ripen on their way to San Francisco and find a ready market. After he reached San Francisco he had a fruit stand on the famed ship *Niantic*, beached in the harbor. On that stand he also sold monkeys, parrots and colorful birds. Robison could not foresee that he and his descendants would supply the city with pets, and as late as 1961 have a shop in Maiden Lane.

Robison's twenty-four-year-old son, Ansel Cobb, took over the business in 1874, often feeding Emperor Norton's dogs, Bummer and Lazarus. During the big Fire the Robisons gave away all the pets. Even in those anxious days people accepted them gladly. Soon there was a demand for replacements of lost pets, and Robison did a rush business at his home on Jordan Avenue.

When circus man Al G. Barnes ordered a female elephant, not more than four feet high, Robison cabled Singapore and Wells Fargo delivered her. Robison rented from Barnes the zebras used by Cecil B. DeMille in his picture, *King of Kings*.

Robison asked his friend Frank Buck ("Bring 'Em Back Alive!") to ship him 2,000 rhesus monkeys. Buck sent him everything from a canary to a python, all sold before they were unloaded. Once Buck telephoned Robison to come down to the steamer to help

210

catch a black panther hiding in the men's dressing room. Robison recalls the boa constrictor bought from a sailor some years ago. He placed it in a fish tank covered with chicken wire. Arriving at the store next morning, he found the place closed. "Shut the door! That darn snake has had babies all over the place!"

Eighteen baby boa constrictors were captured. Mama boa constrictor placed them in a neat little pouch under her chin. Newspaper publicity sold them within a week. An Oakland schoolteacher still keeps one in her living room. Her husband isn't quite pleased with having it on the bed.

Robison supplied animals for William Randolph Hearst's San Simeon Park, Wrigley's Catalina Zoo and the Zoo in Golden Gate Park. Ansel W. Robison, grandson of the founder, heads the business and thinks people are humanized by caring for animals.

Another '48 business family descends from the New York jeweler, George H. Tay. At that time, picks, pans, rockers and cooking utensils, more precious than jewels in San Francisco, were supplied by Tay at Montgomery and Washington Streets. Even the fire of 1851 did not discourage George Tay, and the firm Tay, Brooks and Backus did business on Montgomery Street for forty years. Tay married Backus' sister, Harriet, and they had as children, Charles Fox, Jeanie, Harriet and Irene. To the vexation of the Tay daughters, stoves manufactured by the firm at their 80-acre Alvarado plant, were named for them. In 1929 Tay absorbed the extensive business of Holbrook, Merrill, and Stetson Company, becoming Tay-Holbrook, Inc. Two great grandsons of founder Tay, Eugene F. Kern, Jr., and William D. Kern are with the firm today. Eugene is secretary and M. J. Burress is president.

Plug tobacco was the vogue when the '49 firm of Sutliff Tobacco Company on Washington Street was established by Baltimoreans Henry and Thomas Sutliff. Both were Vigilantes and members of the volunteer fire company. Tom wrote plays for the firemen's dramatic performances. The Sutliffs stimulated trade by having a man make cigars in their store window, also by presenting local editors with colored meerschaums. Free tobacco for Emperor Norton was paid for with "His Majesty's" Imperial Treasury Certificates.

Henry Sutliff, son of founder Thomas, and nephew of Henry, is chairman of the board of directors and Leonard Ruisinger is president of the company. Sons Henry, Jr., and Gordon Sutliff, servicemen of World War II, are both vice-presidents and help carry on the century-old business at 681 Market Street.

Forty-niner Andrew J. Pope came from East Machias, Maine, with a large shipment of lumber. Profiting from the sale, he went into business for himself, to be joined the next year by his brother-in-law, William Chaloner Talbot, who brought the schooner *Oriental*, loaded with lumber.

Captain Talbot's beautiful garden in the Western Addition became notable for two marble lions transported on one of his ships from Italy for the lawn. Pranksters often painted them green, decorating them with stripes. The lions now guard the entrance to the San Francisco Yacht Club. George A. Pope, Jr., grandson of Andrew J., is president of Pope and Talbot.

"I'm glad grandfather staked out a claim on California Street in 1849," says John G. Ziel, head of Ziel and Company. Founder Gustavus Ziel completed a seven months' journey from Hamburg when he arrived on the sailing vessel *Magdelena*. Already the young pioneer had formed a partnership with Caesar Bertheau, dealing in pianos, crockery and general merchandise, later adding insurance. When boxes of ice skates were forwarded from Hamburg, both boxes and skates were dumped into rut holes near the office at the water's edge, 94 California Street—excellent supports for filling.

In 1851 Ziel returned to Hamburg to fetch his bride. Later he became Consul of the Grand Duchy of Hesse for the Pacific Coast. In 1862 he was appointed Consul for the Free City of Hamburg. After Bertheau's death, Gustavus Ziel II carried on the business of exporting and importing, to be succeeded by his son, John Gustavus Ziel, who is still on California Street.

Andrew Kohler came up the coast in 1850 with Captain Talbot on the *Samuel Fales* and began selling musical instruments and toys near Clark's Point. When New Englander Quincy A. Chase joined the firm in 1853, toys were discontinued. Kohler retired in 1864, and Chase was in command until his death in 1902, when he was succeeded by his son, George Q. Chase, who is still president. Kohler and Chase have had only two presidents, and the stock is held entirely by the Chase family. They like to recall that they supplied Lotta, the child actress, with the piano purchased by an admiring group of friends.

For more than a century J. A. Folger and his descendants have furnished San Francisco with coffee. Three Folger brothers arrived from Nantucket, Massachusetts, in 1848. Young James went to the mines to sell coffee. He succeeded so well that in 1850 he established a coffee firm in San Francisco. J. A. Folger became a member of the firm of William H. Bovee and Company, later renamed J. A. Folger and Company and today headed by grandsons. James A. Folger III, president, and Peter Folger, executive vice-president. The firm's building on Howard Street was so well constructed that it stands upright after passing through the Earthquake and Fire of 1906, which left the surrounding business district in ashes and rubble.

No pioneer firm had a more picturesque beginning than that of the City of Paris. Arriving in 1850 on the brig *La Ville de Paris*, with its crest and motto, "It Floats But Never Sinks," Felix Verdier sold laces, shawls, bonnets and stockings to the ladies, and wines and liquors to the men.

Quickly exhausting his stock, Verdier returned to France, but came back to open the City of Paris in 1859. Fires compelled him to move to 150 Kearny Street. After his father's death, Gaston Verdier occupied his own building at Geary Street and Grant Avenue. His son and successor, Paul, learned the department store business at McCreery's, New York, and at twenty-four became manager of the City of Paris, sleeping on the top floor of the building. During the great Fire he became homeless, and slept in the stable.

First department store to reopen was the City of Paris in the Hobart mansion on Van Ness Avenue. Three years later the Verdiers were in their new home at Geary and Stockton. In the dome of the building is a panel by Arthur Brown, representing the historic brig, *La Ville de Paris*, with the motto "Fluctuat nec Mergitur." In 1958 Paul Verdier, who has been president of the Board of Trustees of the California Palace of the Legion of Honor, received from Consul-General Robert Luc for France the decoration of the French Legion of Honor.

For more than a century Nathaniel Gray and descendants have cared for the city's dead. In 1850 the New Hampshire-born founder arrived from New York, opening a funeral parlor in a small house on Sacramento Street. The first Gray hearse was a wagon covered with black cambric and drawn by two mules. Gray interred Senator Broderick, James King of William, and Gray descendants were summoned after President Harding died at the Palace Hotel. Nathaniel Gray's great-grandson, Kendrick W. Miller, is president of the company.

When twenty-year-old Bavarian-born Levi Strauss, creator of "Levis," arrived in 1850, he brought clothing and dry goods, making a quick sale. From the mines he wrote his two New York brothers to bring a supply of brown canvas, duck and denim pants. Fashionable "Levis," however, did not come until the late 1860's, when Strauss heard a Virginia City tailor, Jacob W. Davis, tell as a joke how he had repaired the pants of Alkali Ike with rivets that he had got from a harness shop. To Levi Strauss the "joke" was a business idea, and he had his lawyer obtain a patent for copper-riveted pants' pockets. They wore so well that one purchaser complained that his Levis had given out after ten years—they usually lasted fifteen. Since that time, 150 million copper-riveted Levis, stitched with orange thread, have been sold in fifty-one countries. When bachelor Levi Strauss died in 1902, his four nephews, Jacob, Louis, Sigmund, and Abraham Stern inherited the business. Walter Haas, grand-nephew of Levi Strauss, later became president, to be succeeded by his son Walter, Jr. Peter Haas, brother of Walter, Jr., is executive vice-president. Mr. Haas, Sr., married the daughter of Sigmund Stern. Mrs. Stern was Levi Strauss' sister.

Twenty-two-year-old New Hampshire-born Alfred L. Tubbs arrived in San Francisco in 1850, not "to make a strike," but to sell goods for a wholesale Boston firm. So promptly did he dispose of two cargoes that, although San Francisco was only a sprawling village, he wrote his father that it was destined to be the capital of the new American empire commanding the trade of the Pacific. He went into the ship chandlery business, forming a partnership with Captain William Folger. Both were members of the Vigilantes of 1852.

In 1853 Tubbs urged his older brother Hiram to sell his Boston hotel and come with his wife to California. Their vessel, the *Tennessee,* was grounded on the Marin shore. Traveling by mule cart to Sausalito, the Bostonians finally arrived. That year the Tubbs brothers bought Captain Folger's share and in 1856 manufactured the first rope in the west. They also operated whaling vessels and sent ships to the Orient.

The two brothers died within a few months of each other, just before the turn of the century. Austin C. Tubbs, son of Alfred, was elected president of Tubbs Cordage Company, to be succeeded upon his early demise by his older brother, Alfred S., who served until 1935. His place was taken by Henry D. Nichols who is chairman of the board of directors. F. P. McCann is president and Herman D. Nichols, son of Henry D., is vice-president. The Tubbs family still controls the business. Products of Tubbs Cordage Company helped build the bridges and also the Hoover, Bonneville, Shasta, Friant and Grand Coulee Dams.

Today the company operates cordage factories in San Francisco and Seattle as well as their Great Western Cordage Division in Orange, California, and a wholly owned subsidiary, the Manila Cordage Company in the Philippines.

The oldest historical society in California is the California Pioneers, formed by a group of six who met in 1850 for refreshments at Delmonico's on Montgomery Street. They elected president William D. M. Howard, the large, handsome, popular merchant, captain of the first California guards, for whom Howard Street was named. Vice-president was Samuel Brannan, California's first millionaire. He was a Mormon who not only preached, but published San Francisco's first newspaper, *The Star*. Other vice-presidents were Jacob Rink Snyder and George Frank Lemon. Also at the meeting were General Henry W. Halleck, Jacob Leese, Talbot Green, Ben Lippincott, William Swasey, and James C. L. Wadsworth. Today's San Francisco president is Alexander Arguello, a descendant of Don Luis Arguello, California's first native son to be governor.

Wilson and George Meyer & Co., West Coast distributors of agricultural and industrial chemicals, are proud to belong to the California State "100 Year Club," an organization composed of firms that have been in business a century. The honor was accepted by Wilson Meyer, grandnephew of the founder of the business in 1850. Pioneer Meyer was treasurer of the Vigilantes. Shortly after the firm was organized under the name of Rogers, Meyer and Wilson, they chartered a fleet of sailing vessels for export and import trade. The firm became Meyer, Wilson and Company until 1928, when industrial and agricultural lines were transferred to the present organization. They have specialized in these products ever since. Wilson Meyer is chairman of the board of directors. He is also past president of the Cow Palace. In 1961, Jeffery Meyer is president of the company.

In 1959 Wilson Meyer received King Olav V of Norway the Knight's Cross, First Class of the Royal Order of St. Olav. The decoration presented to Meyer by George K. Thestup, Acting Consul-General of Norway at San Francisco, was in recognition of Meyer's promotion of friendly cultural and trade relations between Norway and the Pacific Coast of the United States.

Haas Bros., importers of green coffee and wholesalers of liquors, celebrated their centennial in December, 1951. Bavarian Charles A. Haas arrived in 1851 with a fellow-Bavarian, Leopold Loupe, and the two founded the grocery firm, Loupe & Haas. Loupe retired in 1875, and William Haas, a cousin, became a member of the firm of Haas Bros. Julius Marx and Joseph Triest, members of the original Haas family, are still active in the organization. Today's president, Ernest Lilienthal, is the son of Alice Haas, daughter of the firm's first president, William Haas.

When Ernest Gabriel Lyons, founder of Lyons-Magnus, Inc., reached San Francisco in 1851 from Paris, he was off immediately for the Tuolumne mines, but not for long. Monsieur was soon back in San Francisco where in 1852 he tickled palates by introducing grenadine. Soon he added more fruit syrups, cordials and wines. After Lyons' death in 1893, his sons, Edmund and Roger, with their relatives, the Raas boys, took over. Grandson Ernest Gabriel Raas retired several years ago and J. H. Voorsanger is president and general manager.

From Rip Van Winkle land, Catskill, Greene County, New York, came L. H. Bonestell with partner Henry Williston. The mines held them only briefly. In San Francisco, they purchased a route of the *Alta California,* and in 1852 they founded *The Wide West,* a weekly. After having had several partners, Bonestell became sole owner of Bonestell & Co., the oldest paper business west of Chicago. His son, Cutler L. Bonestell, succeeded him, and his widow with her husband's cousin, H. S. Bonestell, Jr., managed the company. The firm celebrated its centennial in 1952. D. K. Beswick is president and H. S. Bonestell, Jr., is chairman of the board of directors.

When Massachusetts-born Henry Mayo Newhall, in 1852, stood on a barrelhead in San Francisco, auctioning the contents of his trunk, the firm of H. M. Newhall and Company began. After mining in Placer County, he decided that auctioneering was less hazardous and more profitable. The business expanded into shipping, import and export trade, and insurance. Investing heavily in real estate, he founded the town of Newhall in Southern California. George A. Newhall, grandson of Henry Mayo, was the company's president until he died in 1958. Today's president is Harold J. Steele with Ruthie Newhall Melone, vice-president.

Six hundred pounds of Ghirardelli's chocolate were brought to San Francisco from Lima, Peru, by neighbor James Lick, setting out for San Francisco in 1847. Even before the gold discovery, Lick wrote urging his friend, Domingo Ghirardelli to come to California. On the *Rosetta* he arrived in 1849, but left for the mines. Back in San Francisco, he set up a store in a tent where he grubstaked miners. June 18, 1852, found "Ghirardely" and Girard selling candy, syrups, ground coffee, pastes, fruit and pastry in the Verandah building.

After Domingo's wife arrived, the business was listed as "Mrs. Ghirardelli and Company," with Domingo as director. Their two-story brick building on Jackson Street served as residence, office and factory until 1895 when the factory was moved to the present site on North Point Street. Domingo returned to his native Rapallo, Italy, where he died a naturalized citizen of the United States; he had requested burial in California. His descendant, H. T. Ghirardelli, is the company's president. Among 115 employees are many whose parents and grandparents worked for the company as far back as 1860.

In the office of Lewis W. Sloat, son of Commodore John D. Sloat, at 129 Montgomery Street, was organized the California Academy of Natural Sciences. Present on the evening of April 4, 1853, were Dr. Andrew Randall, Dr. Henry Gibbons, Dr. Albert Kellogg, Col. Thomas J. Nevins, Dr. John B. Trask, Dr. Charles Farris, and Lewis Sloat. Dr. Randall, who was chosen chairman, later became president. After the Academy was legally incorporated, members met in the office of Col. Nevins, San Francisco's first superintendent of schools, and founder of California's common schools.

Drama entered the new institution three years later when President Randall on July 24, 1856, was shot by gambler Joseph Hetherington, who was soon lynched by the same Vigilantes that disposed of Casey and Cora. Members of the Academy attended the funeral of Dr. Randall, and then held their regular meeting.

Celebrated scientists were elected honorary members, including

Louis Agassiz, Sir William J. Hooker, and Napoleon's nephew, Prince Charles Lucien Bonaparte, author of *American Ornithology* and other scientific works. Soon it was decided by the Academy that they approved of the aid of "females" in every department of natural history. It was the first scientific institution to encourage women in scientific spheres, and even to appoint them curators.

Dr. George Davidson persuaded James Lick to endow Lick Observatory. Lick also gave property on Market Street to the Academy and to the Society of California Pioneers. Here for fifteen years the Academy had its home. Destruction of the building, museum and library came during the Fire of 1906. All that could be saved was loaded into a spring wagon by Miss Alice Eastwood who lost her own possessions in trying to help the Academy. Since the disaster of 1906 the Academy of Sciences has been located in Golden Gate Park.

This is an appropriate setting for the first large public aquarium in the West, which the Academy opened through the generosity of Ignatz Steinhart. Leslie Simson also gave the first unit of Simson African Hall with its unsurpassed groups of African mammals.

Closest, perhaps, to the hearts of Californians is Alice Eastwood's herbarium, which through her efforts grew from 1,000 specimens she saved from the Fire in 1906 to 275,000 specimens.

The California Academy of Sciences is daily expanding under Director Robert C. Miller.

Since 1854 the Weill family has supplied San Franciscans with choice dry goods and household furnishings. In that year young Raphael Weill arrived from Paris and was soon taken into the firm of Davidson and Lane. After they retired, Raphael's partner was his brother, Henri, and later came Eugene Gallois and Albert Roulier. The name The White House was adopted in 1875, being the Americanized form of La Grande Maison de Blanc in Paris. Michel D. Weill, nephew of Raphael, is president.

A family that has been for a century in lumber, shipping, real estate and banking, is that of John A. Hooper who arrived in San Francisco in 1854. Three of his children are still living, the youngest being Arthur W. Hooper who heads the John A. Hooper Company.

In faraway Paris, Morris Greenberg heard that gold could be picked up in San Francisco streets, and so he set out with his wife and children. They were shipwrecked in the Straits of Magellan, but arrived in 1851. Finding no gold in the streets, Greenberg worked at his trade. Three years later he started the Eagle Brass Foundry. Busy supplying hydraulic mining equipment, he found time to invent a new type of fire hydrant. At first, the Greenbergs lived next door to Fort Gunnybags, but they moved to Rincon Hill as soon as the sons grew to manhood. In 1867 the firm became M. Greenberg's Sons. After the father died, Joseph took over and saw the business through the 1906 disaster. Within three weeks business at Greenberg's was as usual. Joseph's sons followed him, first Maurice, now dead, and then Stuart M., who heads the company.

All Stuart's life, except when he left the University of California in World War I to be an Air Force pilot, has been given to Greenberg's. He knows the name of each of his 1,000 employees, who have their own insurance pension plan. His hobby is taking motion pictures, and he sometimes flies to New York to see a ball game. Fourth-generation Greenbergs, Stuart, Jr., and Maurice's son, John, hope to carry on for the next century.

Robert Watt Miller represents a family that for 100 years has been banking in San Francisco. His grandfather, Albert Miller, was one of the original San Francisco Accumulating Fund Association that developed into the billion-dollar American Trust Company. It began in 1854 in a one-room Phoenix Building office at 174 Clay Street. The depositors, called "members," were obliged to make regular monthly deposits. Loanable funds were available to members only, all loans to be adequately secured by real property. The American Trust vault contains a copy of the Association's constitution. E. W. Burr was president of the Association, as he was of the Savings and Loan Society, the first bank to incorporate in California. In Vigilante days Burr was also mayor. After a series of acquisitions of other banks, the name was changed in 1927 to the American Trust Company.

Albert Miller, who began with the Association, was succeeded by his son, C. O. G. Miller as director of the Savings Union. He was board chairman of the American Trust until his death in 1952. His son, Robert Watt Miller, has for over thirty years been a director of the company, which in 1960 was merged with Wells Fargo and Union Trust, which celebrated its centennial in 1953. On the ground floor of their offices at Montgomery and Market Streets is their famous museum, containing Vigilante medals and a replica of the

gold spike driven at the completion of the Central Pacific Railroad.
A unique exhibit is one of bandit Black Bart's original verses left by
him after committing a robbery:

> Now I lay me down to sleep
> to wait the coming morrow
> perhaps success perhaps defeat
> and everlasting sorrow
> let come what will I'll try it on
> my condition cant be worse
> and if there's money in that box
> TIS MONEY IN MY PURSE
> Black Bart P.O.8

Since the merger the name Wells Fargo Bank American Trust
Company is used. Ransom M. Cook is president and Robert Watt
Miller continues as a director.

St. Mary's Hospital was founded by a group of eight Sisters of
Mercy, under the guidance of Sister Mary Baptist Russell, who arrived in San Francisco from Ireland on December 8, 1854, after
crossing the Isthmus of Panama. The Sisters had hardly unpacked
before a cholera epidemic hit the city. They had fought the disease
in Ireland and so, from their past experience, were able to save many
lives. After the cholera fight had been won, the city asked the Sisters
to take charge of the County Hospital on Stockton Street. Two years
later, this building was purchased from the city and named St.
Mary's Hospital. In 1861 the Sisters built a larger and better
equipped hospital on Rincon Hill. The Fire in 1906 destroyed the
building. After five years in a temporary hospital, the present St.
Mary's Hospital was opened on Hayes Street as a nonprofit institution to care for all, regardless of race, creed, or color. More than
800,000 persons have been treated by the Sisters of Mercy.

"Go West," said Horace Greeley to two young printers, Francis
Blake, a State-of-Mainer, and James Moffitt, an Emerald-Islander.
employed on the New York *Tribune*. They set out for California.
Moffitt came overland in 1848 via Galveston. Another printer,
James W. Towne, arrived by a different route, and in 1852 became
a member of the firm, Witten, Towne and Company, which printed
the *Bulletin*, the *Call*, the *Alta* and also Bret Harte's first book of
poems. Blake and Moffit became Towne's partners in 1855. The

firm's trademark was the California Grizzly. One of founder Moffitt's sons was Dr. Herbert Moffitt, and another, James K. Moffitt, was a regent of the University of California and president of the Blake, Moffitt & Towne Company until his death in 1955. Arthur W. Towne is president of the company, and heirs of the founder's family hold a controlling interest in the organization.

Charles Brown and Sons began 1957 by celebrating their 100th birthday. Founder Brown, a Bavarian-born tinsmith, arriving on a sailing vessel a century ago, noticed that San Franciscans needed buckets badly because water was distributed by mule back. Bucketless housewives bought water and carried it home in pots and pans. The enterprising young tinsmith set up a shop in a two-story frame building on Kearny Street and soon was turning out not only buckets, but tin roofs for miner's shacks and steel pans for panning gold. The Fire of 1906 destroyed the Browns' store at 815 Market Street, but soon it was reopened. Later Brown and Sons also developed a hotel supply firm at 712 Mission Street. Recently they discontinued the retail business on Market Street. President S. Walter Newman and vice-president Edwin S. Newman are members of the Brown family who still are controlling owners of stock.

When in 1858 the Walter brothers came from Reckendorf, Germany, the D. N. & E. Walter and Company began. In New York they combined their assets of $15,000 and decided that new San Francisco with its 60,000 people was where they should begin business. David Nathan, the oldest brother, was president of the company when Emanuel, the second oldest, came in. The company took in the remaining brothers, Isadore, Herman N., Moritz and Isaac. They have been in the city ever since, expanding and establishing branches in Portland, Seattle, Los Angeles, Fresno and Honolulu. Furniture and household decorations are supplied by them. Eighty-one-year-old Edwin J. Walter, a son of founder Moritz Walter, is still active in the New York office and chairman of the board of directors. Vice-president Stephen Walter is his son. Stanley H. Sinton, Jr., president of the firm, is the son-in-law of Mrs. John I. Walter. He has established branches in Chicago, Denver, Houston, Salt Lake City, Phoenix, and Dallas.

Dunham, Carrigan & Hayden Company has distributed hardware for a century; the business has been in continuous operation for 113 years. Two Irish forty-niners, James C. Conroy and John F. O'Connor, came around the Horn and set up their business in a tent on the waterfront, supplying miners with equipment. In 1859, Benjamin Dunham and Andrew Carrigan took over the business organizing Dunham, Carrigan & Company with twenty-three-year-old Brace Hayden of Buffalo, New York, as their eastern buyer. Twenty-nine years later the firm was incorporated as Dunham, Carrigan & Hayden Company. Dunham was president, Hayden, vice-president, and Carrigan, treasurer. After the death of Carrigan and Dunham in 1897, Hayden came from New York and became president. When he retired twenty-five years later, he was succeeded by Duane Bliss, son-in-law of founder Dunham. At his death, Curtiss Hayden, Sr., son of Brace Hayden, became today's president. The treasurer is Hayden Shuey, grandson of Brace Hayden.

Many century-old firms have passed out of control of family founders. San Francisco's oldest drug company began in 1849 when Bostonians John H. Redington and Dr. E. S. Holden arrived, founding Coffin-Redington. Associated with them was another Bostonian, H. P. Livermore, who was, for a long time, president. The Brunswick Drug Company absorbed the forty-niner firm.

One of San Francisco's most famous restaurants, The Poodle Dog, dates from 1849 when it began in a tent. Its present-day owner is Louis J. LaLanne.

Another forty-niner business was the Selby Smelting Works, established by a New Yorker, Thomas Selby. In 1865, he erected the famous "Shot Tower," at Fifth and Howard Streets, and he also became the city's mayor. The Selby Smelting Lead Company is now a part of the American Smelting and Refining Company. A neighbor of Selby's at Menlo Park was the Scotsman, Frederick W. Macondray, another forty-niner who sold insurance. The Macondray firm continues as Rathbone, King & Seeley.

In 1850, M. P. Jones established the Jones-Thierbach Coffee Company, of which George C. Thierbach is president. During the same year, came today's Dohrmann's, which was founded by Bernard Nathan and now has many branches retailing hotel supplies. Another development of 1850 was the grocery of Charles R. and Henry A. Bowen, the beginning of Goldberg Bowen, today managed by James H. McDonald. In the same year arrived Thomas Day, selling coal lamp fixtures. San Francisco's Municipal Opera House was lighted by the Phoenix Day Company which is headed by Joseph Guglielmo.

Also in 1850 came druggist Charles Langley with Philadelphia's Dr. Augustus Hogge and Boston's H. B. Kirk. With a capital of $43, they founded a firm that developed into Langley and Michaels. The business was taken over in the 1930's by McKesson and Robbins.

"Can't Bust 'Em" work clothes that "can't be ripped apart even by a horse team" are the pride of the Eloesser Heynemann Company who celebrated their centennial in 1951. The organization is presided over by Charles Madsen.

Bostonians George C. and Samuel S. Shreve came around the Horn in 1852 and established Shreve and Company which supplied jewels to potentates and multimillionaires. A proud memory of the firm is that although their building was gutted in 1906, they managed to save the jewelry and silver. Today Howard Hickingbotham is president of the company.

Bullock and Jones sell ready-to-wear women's garments. The organization has had many owners since it was founded in 1852 by Frank D. Bullock and John Luther Jones who tailored for multimillionaires. Today's owner is William E. Steen.

In 1854, C. C. Hastings established the clothing firm that bears his name, but his business also has passed into other hands and is headed by G. Stroud.

Parrott and Company had their centennial year in 1955. One century before that time, John Parrott, a Virginian, who had been United States Consul at Mazatlan, engaged in banking in San Francisco. In recent years banking has given way to dealing in wine, but the founding family is not in the company. Kingwell Bros., Ltd., a brass foundry, also had their centennial in 1955. The firm began as Weed and Kingwell.

San Francisco's only daily newspaper to have a centennial is the *Call-Bulletin* which had its 100th birthday party in 1956. Consolidated with the Scripps-Howard *News* in August, 1959, it is now the *News-Call Bulletin*.

Famous historian Hubert Howe Bancroft, from upstate New York, published his first law book in 1857. Although Bancroft's family has passed on, the Bancroft-Whitney Company still publishes law books.

Celebrating their 100th birthday in 1957 are tanners S. H. Frank and Company whose boast was that they had not changed their business location in a century. At that time it was the waterfront of San

Francisco. None of the families of the original founders are there today. President Joseph Salomon started as the office boy.

Gustav and Charles Sutro came in 1858 and founded the first securities brokerage firm in the West, handling the business of the Big Four railroad builders. Today's senior partner is A. C. Hall succeeding Sydney L. Schwartz who joined the firm in 1906. Mr. Schwartz was president of the Stock Exchange nine terms.

On March 6th, 1858, the *Monitor,* today's official organ of the Roman Catholic Church, was published by James Marks, James Hamill, and Patrick J. Thomas at Washington and Kearny. Thomas A. Brady bought control of the paper in 1860. Five years later, Dennis Lyons and John T. Barry purchased it. The *Monitor* became the official organ of the Archdiocese on April 1, 1877, when the announcement was made by Archbishop Alemany. The oldest existing copy of the *Monitor,* dated March 20, 1858, is in the University of California Library in Berkeley. Today's editor is Monsignor Walter J. Tappe.

One hundred years ago, the Hibernia Bank began as the Hibernia Savings & Loan Society, composed of men whose descendants are well known in 1961: John Sullivan, Robert J. Tobin, D. J. O'Callaghan, William MacCann, John C. Horan, Michael Cody, N. K. Masten, Ino Mel, James Ross, John McHugh, C. D. O'Sullivan, Richard Tobin, L. L. Lawrence, Michael Reynolds, Thomas J. Broderick, Michael Kane, M. Guerin, Thomas England, P. McAran, and J. P. Buckley. The Hibernia Savings & Loan Society was incorporated on September 6, 1864 and on December 10, 1947, became the Hibernia Bank. There are nine branches, and Joseph O. Tobin, descendant of one of the founders, is president.

St. Ignatius Academy, which began in 1855, celebrated its centennial in 1959 because its charter was received in 1859. During the Diamond Jubilee celebration of 1930, St. Ignatius became the University of San Francisco. Rev. John B. McGloin is president.

CHAPTER 21

The Bridges and Farewell to the Ferries

MAD EMPEROR NORTON laid down his check for $3.5 million and ordered the mayor of San Francisco, "Bridge the bay." San Francisco grinned at the madman's command. The Emperor's dream, however, became reality when the Hoover-Young San Francisco Bay Bridge Commission met at Sacramento, October 7, 1929, in cooperation with the Department of Public Works. Their plan was to build the San Francisco-Oakland Bay Bridge.

The route selected was from Rincon Hill, over the west channel of San Francisco Bay, through Yerba Buena Island, and thence over the east channel, parallel with the Key System. From terminal to terminal the distance was eight and a quarter miles, the bridge itself being four and a half miles long. Chicago's bridge builder, Ralph Modjeski (son of the great Polish actress), and John Vipond were employed as engineers.

On the proud day July 9, 1932, Mayor James Rolph, Jr., held the golden shovel that lifted the first dirt for the official ground-breaking for the world's longest bridge. Then came Nevada's Governor Balzar. At Washington at 12:58 P.M. President Franklin D. Roosevelt pressed the golden telegraph key and three blasts of explosives roared—one on Rincon Hill, another at Army Point, Yerba Buena Island, and the other at the foot of 14th Street, Oakland.

At the ceremony on Yerba Buena Island, presided over by Earl Lee Kelly, state director of public works, there was an invocation by Archbishop Hanna and another by Dean Gresham. In his first speech after retiring from office, ex-President Hoover said, "This marks the physical beginning of the greatest bridge ever erected by the human race."

Early in its construction, Eugenio Cardinal Pacelli, the papal secretary of state and future Pope Pius XII, blessed the bridge when he visited San Francisco on his tour of the United States. With him were the Most Rev. Francis (now Cardinal) Spellman, Archbishop John J. Mitty, and Mayor Angelo J. Rossi.

Commuters on ferryboats thrilled over the longest pier ever sunk, 235 feet below water. Tunneling Goat Island also excited them, the world's longest bored tunnel—540 feet long, 70 feet wide, and 58 feet high. Into the work went 54,850,000 man-hours of labor, and 23 lives were lost. After the last rivet had been driven on October 23, 1936, San Francisco prepared for its greatest day jubilation on November 12 of the same year.

Some arrived at midnight to see the opening, and by dawn crowds had gathered on roofs, fire escapes, and bluffs. Three battleships steamed in for the three-day party. At 12:38 P.M. Governor Frank F. Merriam severed the gold chain guarding the gate at the San Francisco approach. Three thousand miles away President Franklin D. Roosevelt turned on the green starting signal. Warships fired a 19-gun salute and 250 Navy planes zoomed over the city. With cameramen as passengers, Walter Reed drove the first official car. His mother, Mrs. D. A. Reed, and his sister, Doris, had waited from midnight. It was worth the long wait.

Governor Merriam and former President Hoover came next. Six radio- and newsmen occupied the first car to pay toll. Sonny Boy, owned by Don Leavenworth, was the first dog to walk across. Movie star Wendy Barrie dropped flower leis on the bridge. All day cars crossed and recrossed—65,000 vehicles.

At the Civic Center, Mayor Angelo Rossi reviewed the parade of 60,000 marchers up Market Street. "Now the Bay Cities are made one," said John Francis Neylan as he addressed the civic luncheon of 1,500 guests at the Palace Hotel. There was a night parade, a regatta, a cruiser race, and an automobile show. Coit Tower was lighted up and Oakland had fireworks on Lake Merritt.

Cost of the Bay Bridge was $77.2 million, financed by sale of 4¾ per cent bonds issued against prospective bridge revenues. These bonds were purchased by the Reconstruction Finance Corporation. The gas fund also lent $6.6 million for building approaches to be paid out of tolls.

Although the original debt on the Bay Bridge has been paid, additional indebtedness has been incurred for certain improvements and to reimburse the State Highway Fund for maintenance and operating costs previously paid from that fund. Under present state law tolls must continue to be collected to cover current costs of operation, maintenance, and insurance. When the Bay Bridge was opened to traffic the automobile toll was 65 cents, but it has been reduced to 25 cents. From the day of the opening, November 12, 1936, until December 31, 1960, 616,041,459 vehicles have crossed the bridge bringing a revenue of $189,681,180 from traffic tolls. Records show that 45 suicides from the Bay Bridge have taken place.

At present the Bay Bridge is being altered so that it will eventually have one-way traffic in each direction on each deck.

Six months after the Bay Bridge was opened San Francisco had another great party honoring the Golden Gate Bridge. When pioneer Lieutenant Juan Manuel Ayala on his little San Carlos beat his way through the rocky Golden Gate on August 5, 1775, it was called "Yulupa," or "Sunset Strait," by the Indians, but in 1848 it was rechristened "Golden Gate" by John C. Frémont. These explorers could not have envisioned that one day there would be a bridge 8,940 feet long, and 220 feet in the air, over the swirling waters. The legislature took the first step by creating a Bridge District. It included the city and county of San Francisco, also Marin, Sonoma, Del Norte, and portions of Napa and Mendocino Counties, which were empowered to issue $350 million worth of bonds for construction.

One of the world's great engineers, Joseph B. Strauss, a Chicago bridgebuilder, was employed; he was also a poet and only five feet tall—"a little man with big dreams." Strauss and five other engineers chose the bridge site: from Fort Point, on the Presidio side, slightly northwest to Lime Point at Fort Baker, on the Marin side. Both terminals were owned by the United States government.

On January 12, 1933, a mechanic perched on the arm of a machine, pulled a lever and a gargantuan mouthful of dirt was torn from the hillside. Ground had been broken. Official opening, however, was on February 26, 1933, before 100,000 spectators at Crissy Field. Flashing a golden spade, William D. Filmer turned up the

Presidio's brown earth, followed by engineer Strauss. (Both spades are preserved in the de Young Memorial Museum.) Governor Rolph said, "The bridge will stand as a monument to California's farsightedness and progressiveness." Mayor Rossi added, "We are breaking the ground for the greatest bridge ever designed by man."

In the waters on the Presidio side, running like a millrace, deep-sea divers met more difficulty than in construction of the San Francisco-Oakland Bridge, but they valiantly continued. On the Marin side the tower rests on solid rock, 1,125 feet out from shore. Eleven men lost their lives in the construction; 24 million man-hours of labor went into the work. Charles H. Segerstrom of Sonora donated the final gold rivet driven by Shirley Brown, daughter of Supervisor Arthur H. Brown. Edward Stanley a steelworker, who had driven the first rivet, stepped forward with his hammer, and the super-bridge was complete. Engineer Strauss, who had suffered a nervous breakdown before the last rivet was hammered in place, said, "Now that the bridge which could not be, is, I'll be glad to take off my war paint, drop my responsibilities, and say to California, 'Here is your bridge.'"

For the opening, May 27 to June 13, 1937, poppies had been sown on both approaches to the bridge, and they blazed their golden welcome to the party to which all the West, Canada, and Mexico had been invited. Schools were closed for the celebration. The bridge was opened to pedestrians on May 27 before vehicles were allowed. Thousands dashed over, some skating and some on stilts, others wheeling babies.

Early in the day Governor Merriam, Mayor Rossi, and guest governors crossed the bay to participate in the dedication ceremonies on the Marin side. Two huge redwoods were thrown across the highway as barriers, but three champion woodsmen swiftly sawed them in two. "Kindly remove the obstruction," ordered Governor Merriam. "Long may this approach serve him who would reach the other side. May it always be a happy crossing."

Again chains were severed. In the first southbound car was Dean Kintner, the district engineer, who fell from the high approach viaduct on the final day of riveting. "I got banged up in that fall but, golly, this was worth it!"

The electric moment came. President Roosevelt at Washington gave the green-light signal that the highway was clear to cars parked behind the barrier. Shouts of people on the sidewalk drowned the sound of 500 planes soaring overhead from Admiral Hepburn's fleet of 122 ships—cannon boomed. Acetylene torches burned imaginary chains at the North Tower as the car containing Mayor Rossi and Governor Merriam moved forward. President Filmer of the Golden Gate Bridge and Highway District severed the gold chain; Mayor Rossi, the silver; Frank P. Doyle, treasurer of the Empire Redwood Association, the copper. At the beautiful floral gate Chief Engineer Strauss formally presented the bridge to the public. "The bridge needs no encomium, neither praise nor eulogy, it speaks for itself."

Queen Empress Vivian Sorenson of San Francisco, assisted by ladies in waiting, opened the floral gates. Admiral Hepburn's capital ships moved beneath the bridge into the harbor. The Chilean battleship led visiting foreign vessels. Mrs. Ethel Olson, of 40 Capistrano Street, paid the first official toll. Francis Terry was led over by a seeing-eye dog. Seven-year-old Margaret Little of El Cerrito crashed the gate, and 32,000 automobiles crossed the first day.

At Bal Tabarin there was a luncheon for a thousand guests. In the streets were men from the fleet, cowboys in ten-gallon hats, Mexicans in sombreros and serapes, and cave girls from Oregon clothed only in wolfskins. In the parade there were 150 floats. A ball was held at the Civic Auditorium for the families of the eleven workers who lost their lives building the bridge, and memorial exercises for them were held on Crissy Field. President Ubrico sent a giant marimba from Guatemala. Twenty-six-year-old Bernardine King flew up from Los Angeles and risked discipline by darting her black and yellow biplane under the bridge. In Polk Gulch an up-to-date Joaquin Murietta, in costume, staged holdups.

Night brought a gorgeous pageant to Crissy Field: Wilbur Hall's *The Land of Gold* presented on a 300-foot stage with redwood grove background. On bleachers, 20,000 people listened while John Charles Thomas sang the leading male role. Climaxing the last scene, the bridge itself was flooded with blazing rockets shooting upward.

For erecting something that had never before been accomplished by man, engineer-poet Joseph B. Strauss received $1,080,000. Inadvertently he wrote his own requiem:

> Launched 'mid a thousand hopes and fears,
> Damned by a thousand hostile sneers,
> Yet ne'er its course was stayed.
> But ask those who met the foe
> Who stood alone and took the blow,
> Ask them the price they paid.

One year later he died at Los Angeles of a heart ailment. At his funeral in Glendale his poem "Redwoods" was sung. At the request of the Golden Gate Bridge and Highway District, Frederick W. Schweigardt executed a monument to Strauss; it was placed near the plaza at the south tower. When it was unveiled, May 28, 1941, by his widow Annette Strauss, traffic stopped for a minute—a tribute to the master engineer who had erected four hundred bridges.

The bridge was financed by a $35 million noncallable bond issue, final bond maturity date is July 1, 1971. Since its opening on May 27, 1937, tolls over Golden Gate Bridge have been reduced to 25 cents. Highest day's traffic on the bridge was 75,063 vehicles, Sunday, August 21, 1960. Traffic in the fiscal year which ended June 30, 1959, totaled 17,592,396 vehicles, a new record. Receipts from 1937 to November 30, 1960, approximate $85 million.

For sight-seers Golden Gate Bridge is the most popular, but grim records in 1960 state that more than 200 persons have died by leaping from the span and more than a hundred suicides have been prevented by patrol officers and passers-by. Many of those rescued were mental patients, others were alcoholics. Several of them later committed suicide in the city. A young girl with a broken romance was saved. A few months later she returned to thank the officer who patroled the bridge. She told him she was happy and about to be married.

In 1942 lovesick twenty-one-year-old Cornelia Van Ireland leapt from the bridge, but was rescued. Her sweetheart, Sergeant Henry Blencke, had gone to war. After twelve weeks in the hospital Cornelia, a San Francisco ice-skater, walked about. She said, "I'll skate again." At her side Sergeant Blencke told pressmen, "I want to marry her more than ever." Playing Cupid, United States Senator

Sheridan Downey aided the sergeant to leave the army. Three months later when the pair were married at Albuquerque, New Mexico, the bride said, "I'm as good as new."

Some have survived a leap from San Francisco-Oakland Bridge, among them Ray Woods, who liked the thrill and danger of high diving. His mother came from Los Angeles on May 22, 1937, to watch him plummet 185 feet from the bridge. He was rescued by lifeguards. He had smashed several vertebrae, but he said, "I'm going to get well." At his home in St. Louis after a year and a half he took the first faltering step and continued to drive a car. While on a Florida fishing trip five years later, in seeking to disentangle a fishing line, he fell overboard and was drowned in St. John's River.

Athens' pride was in her Parthenon; that of Rome was in her Coliseum; and San Francisco's glory is her bridges. This is not only because the bridges, as man-made wonders, attract tourists from the entire world but for the reason that they afford quick and easy transportation to freedom of life in the country. San Franciscans, however, were so proudly conscious of the noble San Francisco-Oakland Bridge and the one spanning the Golden Gate that they scarcely realized that the bridges' younger brother was being built at the cost of $68 million to connect Richmond and San Rafael. The Judson-Pacific-Murphy Corporation was in charge of construction.

The bridge was begun on March 2, 1953, and was completed on May 10, 1956, when the last rivet was driven by James Austin, who had lost a leg in an accident on the bridge in 1954. The lower deck was dedicated August 31, 1956, when Governor Goodwin J. Knight spoke and Mrs. Knight unveiled the bronze plaque presented by Alfred J. Peracca, president of the Native Sons. Then the governor led across the cavalcade of cars. The upper deck was completed in 1958. The toll is 75 cents, but in time passage will be free.

The new bridge replaced a ferry system founded in 1915 and saves 28 minutes in crossing. This bridge gives San Francisco Bay four of the ten longest bridges in the world. The Golden Gate Bridge ranks sixth at 8,940 feet; Carquinez Bridge spans 4,482 feet. The Richmond-San Rafael Bridge, 21,343 feet in length, is second only to the San Francisco-Oakland Bridge, which is 22,720 feet long.

In April, 1959, 6,052,435 vehicles crossed the bay bridges, paying $2,004,879.50 in tolls.

Many persons shed nostalgic tears for the "good old days" on the ferries when coffee could be enjoyed on the deck. They took a farewell ride July 30, 1958, on the last ferry, the *San Leandro*. Among the guests were acting Mayor Henry Rolph of San Francisco, Mayor Clifford Rishell of Oakland, and representatives of nine bay cities. Pat McGarrigle piloted the *San Leandro* on her last run, and a fireboat sent out plumes of water. As the ferry moved out of its San Francisco slip to the sound of the final dirge played by the San Francisco Municipal Band, mourners on the crowded bow sank a white model of the boat as radio, television and newspaper representatives recorded the last run of the *San Leandro* and the end of the ferries. Others, less sentimental, said, "The ferries are dead. Long live the bridges!"

CHAPTER 22

Expositions

SAN FRANCISCO'S first fair was held by the Mechanics' Institute in September, 1857, in conjunction with the California Horticultural Society. A large pavilion in the shape of a Greek cross was erected on Montgomery Street between Post and Sutter, later site of the Lick House. There was an astonishing display of fruit and flowers from Captain Sutter's Hock Farm, gardens and vineyards, the San Jose Fruit Nursery, the orchard of George B. Briggs of Marysville, and D. J. Staples's ranch in the San Joaquin Valley. For the first time Californians realized that they had a new bonanza in the soil. Vineyards were set out, orchards planted, flowers imported, and land was cleared for sowing grain, but it could scarcely be imagined that California crops in 1960 would lead the nation in cash receipts of $1,946,582,000.

In midwinter of 1893–94 came San Francisco's next imposing fair. It resulted in the reclamation of 60 acres of land and founding the M. H. de Young Memorial Museum. In 1909 there took place the colorful celebration of the arrival of the Portolá expedition which discovered San Francisco Bay. Don Nicholas Covarrubias of Santa Barbara was Portolá with statuesque, blonde Virginia Bogue as reigning queen.

Next came the $50 million exposition celebrating completion of the Panama Canal. Aboard the first ship steaming through the canal was played "I Love You, California," the official song of the exposition-to-be. Later it became California's state song. All nations were invited to participate in the Panama-Pacific Exposition, of which Charles C. Moore was president. On October 14, 1911, President Taft broke the first earth.

Harbor-view tidelands were chosen as the site for the Panama-

233

Pacific Exposition, and this necessitated filling in 184 acres by hydraulic dredges. Creation of the great spectacle was entrusted to San Francisco's architects, Louis Mullgardt, George W. Kelham, Willis Polk, William D. Faville, Clarence E. Ward, Arthur Brown, Jr., and Bernard A. Maybeck, assisted by McKim, Mead and White, Henry Bacon, and Thomas Hastings of New York, with Robert Farquhar of Los Angeles. Golden Gate Park Superintendent John McLaren directed landscape engineering.

Mayor James Rolph, Jr., and Governor Hiram W. Johnson led the parade, two and a half miles long, that marched to the exposition on the opening day when 150,000 persons saw the fairgrounds. The marshlands had been so transformed that they seemed always to have been a paradise: "All the beauty in the world is here assembled."

The exposition told California's story from the discovery of Panama to 1915. Visitors were dazzled by the central structure, the "Tower of Jewels," 453 feet high, sparkling and flashing in the sunlight and at night a blinding beauty. Most splendid of the garden structures was the Byzantine dome on the Palace of Horticulture, larger than St. Peter's at Rome, and formed like an overturned fruit basket. There were 1,000-year-old Microcycas from Cuban swamps, gigantic flowers, and a tropical jungle. W. D. Faville's "Walled City" had Spanish-Moorish houses with avenues, fountains, and pools with bottoms tinted blue. In the great central Court of the Universe, designed by McKim, Mead and White, were Robert I. Aitken's heroic figures, "Fire," "Water," "Air," and "Earth."

Although hidden away in the arcade, Frank Brangwyn's murals, "Fire," "Water," "Air," and "Earth" drew throngs. Happily the murals never left San Francisco; they adorn the Veterans' Memorial Auditorium.

Two women contributed beautiful fountains: Gertrude Vanderbilt Whitney's "Fountain of Eldorado" and Edith Woodman Burrough's "Fountain of Youth." Ralph Bernard Maybeck's Palace of Fine Arts, standing among water and trees like an ancient Roman villa, housed what the International Jury called "the most important collection of contemporaneous art at that time assembled in America."

Unhappily the Palace of Fine Arts, which attracted so many visitors, fell into disrepair, but the public declared that it should not be demolished. In May, 1959, San Francisco's most beautiful structure found a savior. Civic-minded seventy-four-year-old millionaire Walter S. Johnson came forward with $2 million for its preservation. "I fell in love with that building forty-four years ago. It is a building with a soul. It refused to die." San Francisco will supply $1.8 million for rehabilitating and perpetuating Maybeck's masterpiece.

In traditional mission-style was erected the largest structure of the exposition—the California Building. Mission Santa Barbara's Sacred Garden, forbidden to women, was reproduced. Oregon erected a characteristic structure with forty-eight columns hewn from their largest trees. Virginia showed Mount Vernon, with original replicas of the Washington family belongings. Denmark made very real Hamlet's Castle of Elsinore. France reproduced the Palace of the Legion of Honor for Louvre treasures, including Rodin's "Thinker." Relics of Lafayette and Rocheambeau were lent by their descendants. For the first time the Mikado permitted his private garden to be reproduced, and he also sent a collection of art. Holland contributed ten carloads of conifers, rhododendrons, and bulbs, with landscape architects to install them. Masterpiece among foreign buildings was Italy's Pavilion by Piacentini, with Michelangelo's bust of the Virgin and Cellini's enamels.

The Court of the Universe contained a sunken garden seating 7,000 persons. In the Joy Zone were boxing, baseball, wrestling, field games, polo, and automobile racing. The only tragedy of the exposition was when Lincoln Beachey fell to death while stunt flying over the Bay.

Much of the exposition beauty remains. In Golden Gate Park's Arboretum are the floral collections of England, Belgium, and Holland. The Palace of Fine Arts has been used for tennis courts and conventions. The exposition itself created a large, new, delightful residential district—the Marina.

Twenty-four years passed before San Francisco had another exposition. This was to celebrate the completion of the world's longest bridge and of the longest suspension span in history. After considering Golden Gate Park, the Presidio, Lake Merced, China Basin, and Candlestick Point, Mayor Rossi, the Chamber of Commerce, and other groups decided to create an island on 735 acres of shoals separated from Yerba Buena Island, midway in the bay, by a 900-foot channel. This idea, presented by Harmon S. Butler, stirred the imagination of the city. "Fantastic," said the critics.

San Franciscans, however, voted for creating an island on the shoals discovered by Don Juan de Ayala in 1775, always a menace to navigation. Construction cost was to be about $18,987,000, but the Work's Progress Administration gave $5,587,830. Leland W. Cutler headed the new exposition. W. P. Day was director of work, and George W. Kelham was chief of architecture for the "city-to-be."

For eighteen months eleven gigantic dredgers pumped black sand, lifting Treasure Island from depths of from two to twenty-six feet below the sea to an elevation of thirteen feet above mean low-water level. At last 400-acre Treasure Island was a reality, with a three-mile-long sea wall. The job cost $4,100 less than estimated.

A causeway, 900 feet long and 100 feet wide, was constructed leading to Yerba Buena Island. Salt was drained off so that trees and flowers would grow. Shiploads of rich loam were transported from the Sacramento River delta and mixed with tons of commercial fertilizer. Water was brought from San Francisco through a gravity pipeline from Yerba Buena Island.

In 1936 Governor Frank F. Merriam broke the ground. Although construction was only half completed, seven months before the exposition opened President Franklin D. Roosevelt was entertained at luncheon in the Administration Building. To the thousand guests he said, "I think you people out here on the Pacific coast, when you start to do something, do it better than anyone in the United States . . . I await the passage of months before I can come back to your exposition."

The President, however, was never to return to San Francisco. After Governor Culbert L. Olson flung open the gates on February 18, 1939, from faraway Florida came the President's voice in congratulation. On that day Mayor Rossi proclaimed Fun as King. He had a white carnation in his lapel, wore a black sombrero, and packed two guns. Bank president Parker Maddux also went "Wild West." *Polk Gulch, Marina Coast, Old Mission Trail,* and *Covered Wagon* were a part of the play week.

Visitors arriving over the causeway at Treasure Island saw that "Uncle John" McLaren and his assistant, Julius L. Girod, had repeated their success of 1915. Trees weighing 40 tons each had been brought 40 miles. A floating forest had come up the Bay on barges and been hauled into position by caterpillar tractors and placed in holes. There was a 25-acre carpet of ice plants—pink, white and yellow. For each season there were blossoms: 250,000 tulips, 200,000 iris, 200,000 tuberous begonias, 10,000 hyacinths, with hundreds of thousands annuals and perennials. Louis P. Hobart's Court of Flowers had a constant note of red and gold in the blossoms. Flowering peaches, rhododendrons, eucalyptus, calendulas, golden violets, bronze pansies, orange and red tulips, contrasted with blue lobelia, agapanthus, and white chrysanthemums and begonias. In the Court of Reflection, bougainvillea and red passion vine cascaded into the court from niches high in the wall.

The Court of Pacifica attracted most attention. "Pacifica" by Ralph Stackpole had a backdrop behind a showering curtain of metal, 100 feet high and 48 feet wide. From the base of Pacifica ever-changing water cascaded into the fountain. In this court were the California state colors shown in bachelor buttons, ageratum, anemones, iris; and yellow marguerites, marigolds, calendulas, zinnias.

Many women contributed to the exposition. A notable mural "Peacemaker" was done by Margaret Helen and Esther Bruton, a cross between sculpture and painting. Adeline Kent symbolized the South Pacific islands, "Girls in the Sun," listening to a youth improvising music. Ruth Cravath Woodfield did the Alaska group. Cecelia Graham offered South American figures. Chinese musicians were by Helen Phillips. In the Hall of Science and Vacationland Buildings, Helen Forbes had two panels on canvas and Dorothy Puccinelli decorated the walls.

Japan sent the first large ship to enter the port of the man-made island; it brought an exhibit of silk manufacturing. The French Indo-Chinese Pavilion showed lacquerwork and ivory handicraft. A Hindu-Japanese temple of the East Indies displayed native workmanship of Sumatra, Bali, Borneo, Java, and New Guinea. The Hawaiian Pavilion, with native flowers and fruits, always had many visitors. A Philippine band of 180 pieces gave daily concerts on the lagoon. Grace Church lent its carillon of forty-four bells to hang in Arthur Brown's 40-foot Tower of the Sun. Alec Templeton, blind pianist, often delighted the crowds by playing classical themes on the carillon.

Visitors never failed to enter the large French Building, which reproduced the Café Lafayette. At the entrance to the exhibit pavilion stood Rodin's famed "The Shadow," while within was a collection of the works of well-known painters and sculptors. Norway's Ski Lodge attracted sport lovers. The Argentine Café was thronged with visitors enjoying delectable coffee.

World masterpieces were exhibited in the Fine Arts Palace by Director Walter Heil of the M. H. de Young Memorial Museum. Here were seen Botticelli's "Birth of Venus," Raphael's "Madonna of the Chair," and canvases by Michelangelo, Titian, Tintoretto, and Donatello. American, Mexican, and Canadian art was shown as well as masterpieces from China, South Asia, the Pacific Islands, and South America.

In the Science Building the University of California gave the public its first glimpse of Dr. Ernest O. Lawrence's cyclotron, in miniature, for which he received the Nobel Prize.

Religion had its own temple with Camille A. Solon's "Creation in Europe," Peter Ilyn's "Rise of Religious Freedom," and José Moya del Pino's "Life of Man in Relation to God," showing more than a hundred plants mentioned in the Bible.

Indian, army, and navy life were shown in the Federal Building, the exposition's largest structure, standing on a seven-acre site designed by Timothy E. Pfleuger especially to display WPA projects.

Disaster struck the exposition when fire broke out on September 24, 1940, in the California State Building. Sailors from the *Montgomery* and the *Ramsey* and two hundred soldiers from Treasure Island's Camp Hunter Liggett saved nearly all works of art, also historical objects and valuable equipment before the flames destroyed most of the structure. Within three hours the executive officers had opened new quarters and that day gave a scheduled luncheon for seven hundred guests.

World-famous women were exposition guests. Author and lecturer Mademoiselle Eve Curie of Paris; also Mademoiselle Nadia Boulanger, symphony composer; Signora Amanda La Baroa, Santiago educator and sociologist, and Madame Sigrid Undset, Nobel Prize winner and Norwegian refugee from the Nazis. They were entertained by the Yerba Buena Club, decorated by Frances Elkins of Monterey, which was called by many the charm spot of the exposition.

Women's Day, October 25, 1939, brought 110,000 visitors. Its success caused it to be repeated on September 18 of the following year, when at a luncheon nationally famous California-born women were honored at Treasure Island's Women's Club: Gertrude Atherton, Dr. Aurelia Henry Reinhardt, Kathleen Norris, Julia Morgan, Anna Klumpke, Louise A. Boyd, Dorothy Arzner, Annette Adams, Dr. Margaret Smythe, Maud Fay, Florence Prag Kahn, Dr. Mariana Bertola, and Helen Wills Roark. Each woman was introduced by a prominent man instead of a toastmaster.

Two million people saw Billy Rose's *Aquacade*, with Morton Downey, John Weismuller, and Esther Williams. "America, Cavalcade of the Nation" grossed close to half a million dollars in 1939, but music and song were Treasure Island's magic. San Salvador's marimba band repeated its triumph of 1915. On an overcast day 50,000 people gathered at an open-air concert, but no one quite equaled Bing Crosby as an attraction. The American Society of Composers, Authors and Publishers gave a musical festival at the Coliseum before an audience of 17,000. Among those appearing were: Dr. Howard Hansen, conducting his own third Symphony; John Charles Thomas; Bill Hill at the piano, playing his "Last Round-up"; Carrie Jacobs Bond at the piano for "The End of a Perfect Day"; Joseph Howard singing his "Goodby, My Lady Love"; Jerome Kern at the piano with "Smoke Gets in Your Eyes"; George M. Cohan, singing his own songs, climaxed by Irving Berlin, giving his new American anthem, "God Bless America."

Treasure Island throngs would have had the show go on forever, and the closing attendance on March 29 topped all others—147,647. At 11:45 P.M. President Cutler at the microphone spoke the final words, "Memories come from God and live forever, so will our memory of this beauty live till time's end."

The last note of taps sounded. The 35th Infantry band broke into "The Star-Spangled Banner," and the national colors on the exposition standards were hauled down from their lofty poles. The fiesta had become a memory.

A few buildings had been erected for permanent use. They were shortly to be made useful as administration offices and hangars for the military. Over Treasure Island, in two more years, crept the shadow of the Japanese planes at Pearl Harbor.

CHAPTER 23

War-Time San Francisco

THE SPANISH-AMERICAN conflict had marked the emergence of the United States as a major world and colonial power.

Wartime excitement stirred San Francisco when tension arose over sympathy in the United States for the insurgent revolt in Cuba. On January 4, 1898, the U.S. battleship *Maine* was dispatched to Havana harbor to make a courtesy call. Relations between Spain and the United States were thought to be improving when on February 15, 1898, the *Maine* was destroyed by a magazine explosion and 260 of her crew lost their lives. "REMEMBER THE MAINE!" became the battle cry. War was declared April 25 of the same year.

A fleet was assembled in Hong Kong under Commodore George Dewey. Ordered to seize the Spanish fleet at Manila, he staged a surprise invasion on May 1. Steaming past the guns of the old Spanish fort at Cavite, he seized the naval base and set up a blockade of Manila harbor.

Dewey's flagship, the *Olympia*, was built at San Francisco's Union Iron Works. From the same company came the most-storied vessel of the navy at that time, the battleship *Oregon*, famed for her race around South America to share the action that occurred when Admiral Cervera's four fast, heavily armored cruisers of the Spanish fleet, on July 3, 1898, made a running fight to escape from the harbor of Santiago de Cuba. This epochal race helped convince authorities of the need for the Panama Canal.

During the Spanish-American War San Franciscans watched the troops drilled in the roads at Golden Gate Park and the Presidio. A planing mill whistle was seized upon by a former calliope player,

240

to play "Good-bye, Dolly, I Must Leave You," and other patriotic numbers. A cannon was mounted in the cupola of the Spreckels Building and soon it boomed out news of American victories.

In Cuba new heroes were developed. Colonel Theodore Roosevelt led his Rough Riders up San Juan Hill so gallantly that later he became president. Captain Richmond Pearson Hobson sank the Merrimac to block the entrance of Santiago harbor and prevent the escape of the Spanish fleet. This daring exploit made Hobson the so-called "kissing hero," because so many women embraced him when he returned to the United States.

After the Spanish fleet had been destroyed the war was concluded by the Treaty of Paris, signed December 10, 1898. Dewey returned to the United States to be made an admiral and to receive the gift of a handsome dwelling from the government.

One of the picturesque heroes of the Spanish-American War was Colonel Andrew Rowan, a Virginian who was to become a part of San Francisco. A graduate of West Point in 1881, Rowan volunteered to carry to the Cuban General Calixto Garcia a message from President McKinley, advising that the United States would supply an invading army in the battle for Cuba's freedom. Already Garcia had spent half his life in fighting for the overthrow of Spanish rule in Cuba.

On this hazardous trip, had Rowan been captured by the Spanish forces he would have been shot as a spy. Landing from a small boat and swimming rivers, he fought his way through jungles, periled by wild animals and snakes, but finally made contact with Garcia. During the war he served on the staff of General Nelson A. Miles. Many years later he was given the Distinguished Service Cross, the second highest award bestowed by the United States. Elbert Hubbard made Rowan world-famous with his little book, *The Message to Garcia,* which sold 11 million copies and was translated into many languages.

In 1904 this hero came to San Francisco and married Mrs. Josephine Morris de Greayer. They had a home on Russian Hill and also a summer place in Mill Valley. In San Francisco, Colonel Rowan wrote two books, *The Island of Cuba* and *How I Carried the Message to Garcia.* He died in San Francisco in 1943.

The greatest figure of World War I was General John Joseph

("Blackjack") Pershing, who commanded the AEF (American Expeditionary Force) in France and had close, yet tragic, ties with San Francisco.

Returning from the Philippines in 1914, the year the war started in Europe, General Pershing was stationed at the Presidio in San Francisco. With him was Mrs. Pershing, daughter of Senator Warren of Wyoming, and their three daughters and a son. Shortly after their arrival the Mexican border trouble started, and General Pershing headed the expedition into Mexico to find Pancho Villa. While he was there, in August, 1915, the Pershing house caught fire at night and Mrs. Pershing and the girls died in the flames but Warren, the boy, was saved. Later he became an engineer and served as major in World War II.

Great was the opposition to the United States' entering World War I. A Preparedness Day Parade was fixed for July 22, 1916, in order to stimulate enthusiasm for the war. Before the parade, warnings had come to the newspapers and police that trouble might be expected. Feeling was running high at the time, with members of the German consulate unusually active. Some were later convicted of violating the neutrality law and sent to jail. Sea raiders had been outfitted in San Francisco; ammunition barges blown up in the Northwest. There had also been bomb explosions, all thought to be traceable to German agents or their representatives in the United States. Unusually heavy precautions were taken by the police on the day of the parade to protect the marchers. Policemen were at all intersections. Others guarded the wire cables strung along the sidewalks. It was almost impossible for anyone to cross the lines without a card signed by Thornwall Mullally, marshal of the parade, and yet someone did. A bomb was thrown at Steuart and Market Streets which killed ten marchers and injured forty or more spectators. Who did it? was the horrifying mystery.

In the absence of any direct proof the police, urged on by the district attorney, arrested two radical labor leaders, Thomas Mooney and Warren Billings. A strong case of circumstantial evidence was presented, and Mooney was convicted and sentenced to death. Life imprisonment was for Billings.

Fremont Older, and others, doubted the guilt of the convicted men and appealed to President Woodrow Wilson to save them. The President asked Governor Stephens to grant executive clemency. On November 29, 1918, Mooney's sentence was commuted to life imprisonment. Twenty years of investigation proved that the people's case was a fabric of falsehood. Governor Culbert Olson pardoned Mooney on January 7, 1939, and Billings received his pardon the same year.

In spite of opposition the United States entered the war on April 6, 1917, and on June 13 of that year as commander in chief of the Expeditionary Force, Pershing reached welcoming, grateful France. On July 4 Paris had a great parade which was reviewed by Pershing with Ambassador Sharp, General Joffre, Lieutenant Colonel Charles E. Stanton of San Francisco, and many officers and soldiers. After reviewing the parade at Les Invalides, they went to the little cemetery of Picpus. There they placed a wreath of American Beauty roses on the stone slab above the Marquis de Lafayette's grave. This dramatic gesture recalled that Lafayette, at nineteen, had come in 1777 to help the American colonies when their affairs were at a low ebb. Stanton, as a representative of Pershing, made the eloquent address in English, thanking Lafayette and saying, "Lafayette, we are here" (*Nous sommes ici*). This phrase became a slogan for groups of persons wishing to pay tribute of honor in return for past services rendered.

In World War I prominent San Franciscans were in the "California Grizzlies," a field artillery regiment. They trained at the old Tanforan race track before going overseas. Thornwall Mullally was colonel, and later brigadier general. Peter B. Kyne was their captain.

The city became the war center on the Pacific coast. Headquarters of the army were at the Presidio, where hundreds of second lieutenants were turned out from the Officers' Training Camps. The 363rd Infantry was recruited and became part of the famous 91st Division. One of the heroes of this division was Phil Katz, the first San Franciscan to be awarded the Congressional Medal of Honor.

Fort Scott in San Francisco and Forts Baker and Barry in Marin County were the coastal defense posts, and on the lookout for German raiders. The big guns were constantly manned, but no raiders were destroyed, although they operated in the Pacific for several years. The late Harry Coleman of the *Examiner* went out on a tug, boarded one of these raiders, and came back with wonderful pictures.

At the University of California there was a school for training aviators. Among the famous men who attended this school was Jimmy Irving, winner of the Distinguished Service Cross, as one of the first "aces" in the war. He also served as a colonel in the Air Force in Italy in World War II. Another in training was Ernie Smith, the first civilian to fly from San Francisco to Honolulu before the Dole Flight. Down the Peninsula, at Camp Fremont, troops were trained, then later sent to Siberia. Yerba Buena Island was a naval training center and supplied escort vessels for convoys that went from San Francisco through the Panama Canal with troops.

Employment soared to 16,000 at the Union Iron Works. Sixty-six destroyers and 18 submarines were built by the San Francisco Yard for World War I.

San Francisco had its spy excitement in World War I, as well as in World War II. The German consul, Franz Bopp, and Baron Wilhelm von Brincken were charged with espionage and jailed. Von Brincken was married to one of the society beauties of the time, Milo Abercrombie, but they were later divorced.

In 1918 came the great flu epidemic. Everyone on the streets had to wear a mask. On street corners were barrels of Dobell Solution for anyone to use. People were supposed to gargle it daily. Wartime prohibition went into effect—but for men in uniform only. No man in uniform could get a drink.

Civilians grew "Victory Gardens," raising vegetables. There were "Meatless Days" and "Wheatless Days," and the use of sugar was sharply curtailed.

In the war hysteria people with German names were suspected of being spies. The famous old Hof Brau Café changed its name to the "States." Hamburger steak became "Liberty steak," and sauerkraut was "Liberty cabbage." The symphony orchestra would not play the music of Bach, Brahms, Wagner or other German composers.

Shortly after the war began Fritz Kreisler, one of the greatest violinists of all time, gave a concert but his appearance was protested because he had served in the Austrian army.

This war was brief, from April 6, 1917, to November 11, 1918, but there were 4,744,000 men in service. Killed in action were 131,000 Americans. Mr. and Mrs. Adolph Spreckels erected the Palace of the Legion of Honor as a memorial to them. Today there are approximately 300,000 World War I veterans living in California.

San Francisco will always remember one veteran of World War I —Colonel Charles Egbert Stanton. Stanton was born in Illinois, and after his father's death he and his mother moved to San Francisco, where he attended Lincoln School. He studied at the University of Santa Clara in 1874–1875, later taking a postgraduate course at Yale. In 1930, after he retired from the army, the University of Santa Clara conferred upon him the honorary degree of Doctor of Laws. Later the university's drill field was named the Colonel Stanton Drill Field.

In San Francisco Mayor James Rolph appointed Stanton a commissioner of the Board of Public Works. The war hero remained active in public service and social life during the remainder of his days.

When the Japanese bombed Pearl Harbor, December 7, 1941, World War II became inevitable. The "blow in the dark," wholly unexpected, brought blame to the officers in charge of the fleet. Even the President was criticized for not having foreseen the Japanese attack.

Once more San Francisco became the shipping point for most of the war activity in the Pacific. The Union Iron Works increased its new construction and repair facilities. They built 72 ships, of which 52 were combat vessels for the navy. They also repaired, or reconverted, more than 2,500 naval and commercial craft, including British, French, Russian, Dutch, Danish, Swedish, Greek, Yugoslav, Spanish, Mexican, and captured Italian and German vessels, in addition to those under the control of the U.S. navy and the War Shipping Administration.

So pressing was the need for troopships in the early part of the war that the San Francisco Yard was asked to arm in only four days the luxury liners *Lurline, Mariposa, Monterey,* and *Matsonia,* which had been ordered to San Diego to pick up a detachment of marines. The job was completed on time.

When this war came Americans realized what tyranny was like.

Restrictions were placed on new construction, unless it was for the armed forces. Building material could be secured only if the authorities ruled that the purpose was justified. Rents were controlled, as were wages and prices. There was a "black market" for automobiles and liquor. Gasoline was rationed, and automobiles bore labels, "Is This Trip Necessary?"

San Francisco's war hero was a native son—Admiral Daniel Judson Callaghan ("Uncle Dan" to his men), commanding the U.S.S. cruiser *San Francisco*, built at the Union Iron Works. Uncle Dan's *San Francisco* engaged two Japanese battleships, a cruiser, and eleven destroyers fighting at point-blank range in an action lasting only twenty-four minutes, one of the most furious sea battles ever fought. In the fray Admiral Dan lost his own life, as did 98 of his gallant shipmates. The *San Francisco* received 45 hits, but turned back the Japanese at Guadalcanal. The invincible cruiser fought on in the Aleutians, at Wake, in the Gilbert, Marshall, Caroline, and Palau Islands off New Guinea, and in the Marianas. For four years the *San Francisco* battled before she returned to her home town to receive the presidential citation and be inactivated. San Francisco memorialized Uncle Dan Callaghan and the *San Francisco* by placing a portion of the superstructure, its battle flag and bell, in a monument at Land's End, dedicated on November 12, 1950.

Memories of Pearl Harbor lessened regrets for the violence of ending World War II on August 6, 1945, by the atomic bomb carried by the superfortress *Enola Gay*, piloted by Paul W. Tibbits, Jr., with Thomas W. Ferebee as bombardier. Designed by Captain William S. Parsons, the bomb laid waste Hiroshima so completely that San Franciscans shuddered, and yet were thrilled by the realization that the weapon which hastened the surrender of Japan was largely the product of the University of California's cyclotron that had ushered in the atomic age.

After peace was declared, the agreement in Cairo stated that Korea, after having been occupied by the Japanese for forty-five years, should be independent. It was solely for the purpose of receiving the Japanese surrender that the 38th parallel was established as a line separating the northern zone, which the Soviet forces dominated, and the southern zone, protected by the United Nations. Both zones were placed under a provisional government. In the north, Russians encouraged the Koreans to set up their own administration under the Communist party.

On June 25, 1950, North Korea launched a full-scale attack on South Korea. Seoul was 60 per cent destroyed. Then, with the approval of the United Nations, President Truman sent soldiers on a "police mission." Clearly the Soviets intended taking over Korea, as well as China itself. The police action became a new war. Before ending it was to engage a total of 5,720,000 men from all branches of the service. There were 33,629 battle deaths; 20,617 deaths from other causes; 103,284 wounded—total casualties 157,530.

Most controversial figure of the Korean War was General Douglas MacArthur. Washington said that he did not follow directives. He proposed bombing the sources of the North Korean supply. Washington was alarmed, fearing that such action would involve the United States with Communist Chinese, and eventually with the Russians. Instead of bluntly ordering MacArthur to report to him, President Truman offered to meet him halfway. The general chose Wake Island. Mid-term elections of 1950 would be held in less than three weeks, but it was said that the general sensed a political implication in the meeting. Truman was charged with fearing that MacArthur would be a candidate for president.

Arriving first, MacArthur met the plane bearing the President and his advisers. For an hour the President and MacArthur talked privately. Truman feared Chinese and Soviet interference. MacArthur returned to Japan. It was hoped that the war was nearly over.

Neither MacArthur nor the public had any intimation of the startling message from President Truman at Washington that came on April 10, 1951:

I deeply regret that it becomes my duty as President and Commander in Chief of the United States military forces, to replace you as Supreme Commander, Allied Powers; Commander in Chief, United Nations Command; Commander in Chief, Far East; and Commanding General, U.S. Army, Far East.

You will turn over your commands, effective at once, to Lieutenant-General Matthew B. Ridgway. You are authorized to have issued such orders as are necessary to complete desired travel to such place as you select.

My reasons for your replacement will be made public concurrently with the delivery to you of the foregoing order, and are contained in the next following message.

On the same day the President gave an explanation of the change of command: "General Douglas MacArthur is unable to give his wholehearted support to the policies of the United States government and of the United Nations, and matters pertaining to his official duties. In view of the specific responsibilities imposed upon me by the Constitution of the United States, and the added responsibility which has been entrusted to me by the United Nations, I have decided that I must make a change of command in the Far East. I have, therefore, relieved General MacArthur of his commands and have designated Lieutenant General Matthew B. Ridgway as his successor. . . ."

This statement was a verbal atomic bomb. Many called MacArthur's removal "the crime of the century." Republicans asked that Truman be impeached. Soon MacArthur was on a plane flying to Washington.

Before leaving Tokyo, MacArthur had agreed to a public reception in San Francisco. However, he was not prepared for the warmth of the crowd of 3,000 that met the five-star general, April 18, 1951, at San Francisco's International Airport. Escorted by the motorcade of 200 police, the MacArthurs passed through miles of cheering San Franciscans and rested for the night at the Hotel St. Francis.

On the way to the plaza the following morning, so many flowers were thrown at the general's automobile that they threatened to smother him, Governor Warren, and Mayor Robinson. Some tried to embrace MacArthur—others merely touched him. "God bless you, General!" was shouted by many. At the City Hall the Muncipal Band played, "California, Here I Come." He shook hands warmly with Archbishop John J. Mitty, who had served as chaplain at West Point when the general was commandant.

San Francisco stopped everything and gave everything in a vast outpouring of admiration for the lean, erect seventy-one-year-old General Douglas MacArthur. They cheered until their throats were hoarse. Fifty thousand were gathered before the City Hall. Finally John Francis Neylan succeeded in quieting the tumult and opened the meeting by saying, "Douglas MacArthur, soldier and statesman, is home!" The audience whooped, yelled, and waved. When Neylan was able to continue, he said, "There was nothing comparable in the history of civilization that three days ago the Emperor of Japan joined with millions of his people in expressions of gratitude to their conqueror for the rebuilding of a nation dedicated to freedom."

Governor Earl Warren, the next speaker, brought one of the greatest cheers of the day when he began, "Isn't it great to have General MacArthur home?" After the governor finished, Mayor Robinson said, "General MacArthur, as mayor of San Francisco, I have proclaimed this as GENERAL DOUGLAS MACARTHUR DAY. . . . I present to you the people of San Francisco."

General MacArthur began by saying, "I cannot tell you what it means to me to be home. . . . My emotions almost defy description as I find myself once more among my own people—once more under the spell of the great American home which breeds such magnificent men as I have just left fighting the battle in Korea. . . . In Japan it has been my privilege to welcome California's own division, the 40th, sent there not for a commitment to Korea but to serve a no less vital purpose, to defend the bastion we have helped erect there in the pattern of American Democracy. . . . Speaking for both Mrs. MacArthur and myself, I cannot tell you how deep is our appreciation of the wonderful hospitality with which this great city has welcomed us. The memory of it will live in our hearts always. . . . I feel like a native son."

Robinson, Warren, John Francis Neylan, and 3,000 others were at the International Airport for the farewell to MacArthur. He stood at rigid attention and held a salute the full minute and twenty seconds, while 77 cannons boomed out a 17-gun salute. When asked before departing whether he would be a candidate for president, he replied, "No, I do not intend to run for any political office, and I hope my name will never be used in a political way. The only politics I have had is known to all of you, *God Bless America*. Again my sincere thanks."

The big Constellation *Bataan* soared up into the skies for the flight to Washington. Eight days after the general was deposed he made his historic address before Congress, but the entire nation listened. "In war there is no substitute for victory . . . History teaches with unmistakable emphasis that appeasement but begets new and bloodier war. . . . Why, my soldiers asked of me, surrender military advantages to an enemy in the field? I could not answer. I am closing my fifty-two years of military service. When I joined the army even before the turn of the century, it was the fulfillment of all my boyish hopes and dreams. The world has turned over many times since I took the oath on the Plain at West Point, and the hopes and dreams have long since vanished. But I still remember the refrain of one of the most popular barrack ballads of that day which proclaimed most proudly that—'Old soldiers never die; they just fade away.' And like the old soldier in the ballad, I now close my military career and just fade away; an old soldier who tried to do his duty as God gave him the light to see that duty. Good-by."

In the San Franciscan area is another dramatic figure of the Korean War—General William F. Dean, who since his retirement has lived in Berkeley. Three years he was a prisoner of the Korean Communists and his family did not know he was alive.

Dean was born in 1899 at Carlisle, Illinois. When he was five the family moved to California. He tried to enlist in World War I, but he was under age. As a student he took military training at the University of California, winning his regular army commission after graduation.

During World War II he commanded the 44th Infantry Division, which he led through France and Germany. In 1947 he became military governor of South Korea. After the Korean War broke out, he was in command of the 24th Division.

When Taejon fell to the Communists in 1955, Dean said he did not surrender but was captured. Communists ordered him to reveal defense plans for Japan. He refused, and then was compelled to sleep on floors; he was kicked, called a thief, a murderer, and a Wall Street dog. Suffering from dysentery, he was starved until he lost a hundred pounds. The Communists threatened to cut his tongue out. They told him they would drive bamboo splinters under his finger nails and then set fire to them.

After peace negotiations began, Dean was treated in a more civilized way. Now General Dean says that his three years as a Communist war prisoner taught him that we must prove to the Communists that ours is a better world than theirs, and this we do every day.

CHAPTER 24

Picturesque Financiers

SAN FRANCISCO is the home town of the world's largest privately owned bank. In San Jose, a historical marker indicates the birthplace of its creator, Amadeo Peter Giannini, son of a Genovese orchardist. Near San Jose the boy saw his father, Luigi Giannini, shot down by a violent neighbor. Amadeo's stepfather, Lorenzo Scatena, found work with the San Francisco Commission Merchants and moved the family to the city.

Soon Scatena was in business for himself, with his stepson assisting when not at the Washington Grammar School. After six months in a commercial college, the fifteen-year-old youth quit school. Grown to be six-feet-two, at nineteen he had a third partnership in the Scatena business. He fell in love at first sight with Clorinda Cuneo, a singer in the old Spanish church. After marriage their home was in San Mateo.

An executor of the estate of his father-in-law, Joseph Cuneo, a director in the Columbia Savings and Loan Society, Amadeo entered the banking world as director. After a dispute as to policy, Giannini and six other directors left the loan society to found the one-room Bank of Italy, at the corner of Columbus Avenue and Washington Street, October 17, 1904. Amadeo Giannini was vice-president and general manager.

San Francisco bankers felt it undignified to solicit new accounts, but "A.P." didn't worry about dignity. He solicited accounts in the produce district, and was called a "vegetable peddler." Within a year the bank had resources of nearly half a million.

Giannini was at his San Mateo home when the Earthquake of 1906 shook him from his bed. Hastening to the burning city, he found the Bank of Italy open for business as usual. Driven from their quarters by the Fire, A.P. and his assistants heaped all the gold and bank furniture on trucks and transported everything to the apartment of his brother, Dr. Attilio Giannini, on Van Ness Avenue. That night a white mare, Dolly Gray, harnessed to a buggy, took A.P. to his San Mateo home with $300,000 in pouches. The money was concealed in the chimney.

He drove back to town next day behind Dolly and put up the sign "Bank of Italy" on the Washington Street front, but the main office was Dr. Giannini's apartment. While San Francisco was ablaze, Giannini sent a circular letter telling depositors and stockholders that their money was available. During the panic of 1907 he shocked bankers by advertising for borrowers. He erected a new building at Clay and Montgomery Streets. Then he opened the first branch in the Mission. Not all states permitted branch banking, but Bank Commissioner Alden Anderson interpreted the California law favorably. Between 1922 and 1925 A.P. opened thirty-two new branches, backed by a holding company that he formed.

Bancitaly stock rose so rapidly that many people, especially Italian-Americans, gambled in its shares, although Giannini warned against it. He told employees to save 5 per cent a month from their salaries to pay for their stock or sell their shares. His advice went unheeded.

The crash came June 11, 1928, while Giannini was at Milan. Bank of Italy fell 160 points; Bancitaly, a corporation, 86; Bank of America, N.A., 120; United Security, 80. Stricken by acute neuritis, three months passed before Giannini was back at his San Francisco desk. With stock at its lowest, he decided to consolidate his various companies under Delaware corporation laws. He retired from the presidency and his place was taken by Elisha Walker, a New York banker, with a salary of $100,000. In a few months Trans-America sold at a new low of 18¾ cents per share.

While Giannini was taking the cure at Bad Gastein, his son Mario wrote him that Walker was trying to toss branch banking out the window by ceasing to pay dividends "until better times." Giannini's neuritic hands were in such pain he could not write, but he spent $10,000 to cable protests to James Baciagalupi, who was one of the few Giannini men left on the board of directors. New Yorkers were in control.

Giannini came back to California by way of Canada to battle

Walker for proxies. His speakers were everywhere looking for proxies, and so were Walker's "Wall Street boys." At Dreamland Rink, San Francisco, Giannini's representatives asserted that Walker entered the organization to dismember it from within for Wall Street bankers. In turn, Walker's speakers accused Giannini of intimidating his employees, compelling them to pay for a dead horse, and stock trickery.

Senator Hiram W. Johnson represented Giannini at Wilmington, Delaware, February 15, 1932, where the election took place. Victory was won by nearly three to one. A.P. telegraphed the San Francisco bank, "Tear down the spite fences. Now we are going to build."

Walker's series of small offices was removed. Giannini sat in the open and received people without secretaries, in his usual "vegetable-peddler way," talking with New York and London. When Bancitaly Corporation presented him with a bonus of $1.5 million, he asked that it be used to endow the Giannini Foundation of Agriculture and Economics, and to build Giannini Hall at the University of California. At his death in 1949 his personal fortune amounted to less than a million dollars.

A.P.'s son, Lawrence Mario, served as president of the bank until he died. Today's president of the Bank of America is Seth Clerk Beise. Claire Giannini Hoffman, A.P.'s daughter, is on the board of directors. San Francisco's Chinatown branch is presided over by a woman, Miss Dorothy Gee, who has been in the banking business since she was fourteen, when she went out to solicit accounts.

In 1960 branches of the Bank of America were being opened at the rate of two or three a month. There are 710 throughout the United States and abroad, employing 28,062 people. Total assets of the bank, announced as of 1960, were $11,941,981,258, the largest of any privately-owned bank in the world.

Bankers shy away from wildcat schemes, but in August, 1926, the late James J. Fagan, vice-president of the Crocker First National Bank, listened to a "wildcat scheme to end wildcats" when George Everson, a Community Chest organizer from the east, told him about nineteen-year-old Philo T. Farnsworth. This farm-boy genius, born in Beaver, Utah, had solved the problem of how to transmit messages by electricity, instead of mechanical devices producing only flickering smudged pictures.

"Well, it is certainly a darn-fool idea," said Fagan, "but somebody should put money into it who could afford to lose it." "I've invested all my savings," replied Everson. "The boy is a genius. As a kid he won prizes for scientific articles. At fifteen he astounded his high school professors at Rigby, Utah, by explaining how he would transmit messages through the air, as electricity sends the voice through the radio receiver. I'm not an engineer, but my partner, Leslie Gorrell, is a Stanford graduate, and he also has invested in Phil's invention."

Perhaps television's most astonishing story is that Everson was able to sell the idea not only to Fagan but to Jesse B. McCargar, executive vice-president of the Crocker First National Bank. Fagan talked the matter over with W. W. Crocker, son of president William H. Crocker. Young Crocker was so much interested that he consulted Roy M. Bishop, an engineer and capitalist, to see if he thought it practicable. Bishop became enthusiastic.

Everson hurried Farnsworth up from Los Angeles. The youth's suitcase had been stolen on the way. He arrived in shabby clothes, looking so like a poor inventor that Everson fitted him out with a new suit for the Fairmont Hotel luncheon. When the shy, blue-eyed youth met the potential backers he was not at his best, but when asked whether other men had been working on television he lost self-consciousness.

"Yes, but they are barking up the wrong tree. There is Dr. Ives at Bell Laboratory; Dr. Alexanderson at the General Electric; Jenkins, the Englishman, in Baltimore, and Baird in London. Baird has transmitted recognizable pictures. To obtain clear unsmudged pictures, you must have greater speed, and that can only be brought about by manipulating electrons in a vacuum tube."

After several conferences, W. W. Crocker, Bishop, McCargar, and Fagan decided "to take a flyer." "How much money will you need?" asked Bishop. "About a thousand dollars a month for a year," said Farnsworth. "You will need twice that," replied Bishop. "And that won't be enough." Bishop was correct.

In a loft at 202 Green Street, Philo T. Farnsworth began work. After daily adjusting, experimenting, one year later he produced his first electron picture, a triangle. Gazing at it in awed silence, he shook hands with his friend Everson, the first to believe in him.

Two years passed and $60,000 was spent before he had a picture good enough to show his backers. When Crocker, Bishop, Fagan, and McGargar came to the laboratory in the fall of 1928 to look at the picture transmitted by Farnsworth, Bishop said, "The pictures justify the money spent, but it will take a pile of money as high as Telegraph Hill to carry it to a successful conclusion. Your idea ought to be incorporated and sold to one of the big electrical companies." Phil was disappointed, but Television Lab, Inc. with 20,000 shares was incorporated in March, 1929. Farnsworth, Fagan, McCargar, Everson, and Gorrell kept control of the stock.

Shortly after the incorporation, from the roof of the Green Street laboratory, Farnsworth transmitted through the air to the Merchants' Exchange Building, one mile distant, the first picture ever sent through air by electronic television.

One of Farnsworth's favorite subjects for television was a scene from *The Taming of the Shrew* with Mary Pickford and Douglas Fairbanks. Miss Pickford came from Hollywood to see herself televised, and congratulated him.

Five years after the laboratory at 202 Green Street had been leased, the Philco Company, largest radio manufacturer, became interested in the Farnsworth development and made a contract with the inventor for licensing television receiver sets. Most of the staff went with him to Philadelphia, but the Green Street laboratory continued with selected engineers to supplement Philco operations. It took thirteen years and $1 million for Philo T. Farnsworth to perfect electronic television, for which $3 million was received in April, 1939. The Farnsworth Radio and Television Corporation has been changed to the Farnsworth Electronics Company. Farnsworth is vice-president in charge of research and lives at Fort Wayne, Indiana. At the age of fifty he had received more than a hundred patents.

No invention is a product of one mind, but when television audiences of countless millions witness world events and see history in the making they can thank the farm boy, Philo T. Farnsworth, who at fifteen fixed his goal, and they can also thank his San Francisco backers, who made possible this modern miracle.

Not only was San Francisco the scene of the first picture ever sent through the air by electronic television, but on August 23, 1955, there occurred the first public demonstration of a two-way videophone, developed by the Kay Laboratory of San Diego. Pacific Telephone and Telegraph Company provided transmission facilities. Mayor Elmer E. Robinson, in the Civic Auditorium, was seated before a large panel. A pink French telephone rested on a built-in ledge in front of him. Just above it were two television screens, one seven inches square and the other ten inches.

A camera seated behind a third rectangle began taking his picture and transmitting it to the seven-inch screen, as he dialed a number. Mayor Noel Porter of Palo Alto was about a mile away in the Fairmont Hotel, seated before a similar panel. Each mayor saw himself talking on his own small screen and watching the other's facial expression on the screen.

One-way closed circuit systems, which produce at only one end, are in use in several places, but it is predicted that the new elaborate two-way gadget will have an important place in American life in the 1960's. Probably the first installation would be in factories and hospitals. Two-way systems at present would cost $5,000, with $2,500 for each additional panel. Doubtless the cost will be reduced so that two-way videophones will be as common as today's TV.

CHAPTER 25

World History Made

MAYOR JAMES D. PHELAN was one of the pioneers of 1906 who saw San Francisco as the "City Beautiful." Son of a forty-niner and himself born on the site of the St. Francis Hospital, in 1904 he organized the "Association for the Improvement and Adornment of San Francisco." As president of the organization of four hundred members, Phelan brought to the city D. H. Burnham, Chicago's famed architect, to outline a plan. Burnham's beacon was beauty. He said that the Panhandle should be extended to Market Street or Van Ness, where should be placed the Civic Center, with one group of public buildings and another for educational and cultural purposes.

"Impossible," said the critics. "Too many buildings to be purchased!" No sooner had they spoken than the disaster of 1906 reduced most of the city below Van Ness to ashes, and the project became feasible.

At the election in 1912, during the administration of Mayor James Rolph, Jr., a bond issue of $8 million to aquire land for the Civic Center building site, carried nearly 9 to 1. Rejoicing was great when ground was broken for the Auditorium, the first building in the Civic Center, erected on land purchased by the city. Mayor Rolph also expedited work on the City Hall, which was completed in record time and without hint of graft. Building and land cost $4,761,525. The mayor's pride was that the City Hall, for which he broke ground with a silver spade on April 8, 1913, had spires on the gold-embellished 308-foot dome that are 6 feet and 2⅝ inches higher than the Capitol in Washington. In this building Mayor Rolph welcomed Queen Marie of Romania, Eaman de Valera, Presidents William Howard Taft and Woodrow Wilson. Here took place the funeral of President Warren G. Harding, and here Rolph himself lay in state.

The year 1914 saw great activity in the Civic Center, for the library was rapidly completed, with George W. Kelham as architect. In 1961 the public library contains 869,298 volumes. In addition, 5,000 documents, state, federal and local; 6,000 pamphlets and 7,500 photographs are housed in the main library building. The San Francisco Public Library has 25 branches. The next one will probably be the McCreery Branch, replacing the one badly damaged by the 1957 earthquake. Three years after the library was completed, a unit was erected for accommodation of the Central Emergency Hospital, costing $90,682.

San Francisco has always been a "city of song." Between 1880 and 1906 the Tivoli Opera House, owned by Joseph Krelling and brothers, presented light and grand opera. After the old Tivoli was burned, Luisa Tetrazzini and Mary Garden appeared at the New Tivoli. Efforts were made soon after the great Fire to build a Municipal Opera House, but the project seemed defeated.

Then Major Charles H. Kendrick, chairman of the American Legion, presented the idea of building an opera house as a war memorial. Major Kendrick began raising funds for the War Memorial Opera House. The block bounded by Hayes, Franklin, Fulton Streets, and Van Ness Avenue—then the athletic field of the High School of Commerce—was bought for $3 million. Lawrence W. Harris, auctioneer for the occasion, raised a million dollars at a mass meeting in the Exposition Auditorium on May 1, 1920. Later $600,-000 was subscribed. At the end of thirty days $2,150,000 had been pledged. First ground for the war memorial was turned on the St. Ignatius Church lot.

Selected as architects were Ernest Coxhead, John Galen Howard, Willis Polk, Arthur Brown, Jr., Bernard Maybeck, Fred Mayor, John Reid, Jr., and G. Albert Lansburgh.

Soon the veterans realized that they needed a separate building for their official use, and the opera house design was altered to fit a two-block plan. By bond issue, an additional $4 million was raised, supervised by a board of trustees: General Hunter Liggett, Frank L. Belgrado, James I. Herz, Charles H. Kendrick, Herbert Fleishhacker, Kenneth R. Kingsbury, Robert I. Bentley, George T. Cameron, George Hearst, James W. Mullen, and Jesse C. Coleman.

Cornerstones of both buildings were laid on the thirteenth anniversary of the signing of the Armistice. They were dedicated September 9, 1932. Separated by Memorial Court, they are harmonious architecturally, with the noble group of buildings in the Civic Center. San Francisco was the first city in the United States to have a municipally owned Grand Opera House.

When the curtain rose for *La Tosca* on the night of the first performance, October 15, 1932, every one of the 3,286 seats and 25 boxes was occupied. The first voice heard was that of the San Franciscan, Marsden Argall, in the role of Angelotti, the escaped prisoner, whose entrance marks the beginning of the opera. Artists who followed were Claudia Muzio, Dino Dorgioli, Alfredo Gandolfi, Louis d'Angelo, Merick Wendheim, Eva Gruminger and Austin Sperry. Other guest artists of the season were Richard Bonelli, Arnold Gabor, Mary Lathrop, Queena Mario, Tandy MacKenzie, Ezio Pinza, and Lily Pons. Nearly every artist of importance has appeared on this stage. For two decades Maestro Gaetano Merola guided the spirit of the opera, searching the world for artists, and developing many young singers.

In the Veterans' Building, nearly 150 veterans' organizations meet and often look at the many war trophies. An ever-burning light shines down on a bronze urn filled with earth from the graves of Californians who died in France. On Armistice Day, San Francisco school children march in silence past this urn.

The classical white and gold Opera House with walls of cast stone, marble floors, in 1945 saw world history enacted when it became the setting for the United Nations Conference. Previous conferences had been held at Casablanca, Teheran, Cairo, and Yalta, but this was the first on American soil. For a month San Francisco seemed the world capital. Only a few weeks previously President Franklin D. Roosevelt had been interred at Hyde Park. This assembly was to complete the work which had cost his life. Although they realized that Woodrow Wilson's League of Nations had failed in its purpose, gravely delegates from fifty nations came together to be architects of a new world. They were impelled by their realization that during the five years' conflict Europe suffered a loss of 14 million dead, and 45 million wounded or captured. The United States also had lost one million.

Long before the historic moment fixed for the opening, April 25,

1945, the crowd opposite the Opera House had to be held back by police. Up the steps of the building strode the delegates. Soldierly Field Marshal Jan Christian Smuts, with goatee, wore the British uniform. Admiral Chen Sao-kuen, commander in chief of the Chinese navy, dripped gold braid. India's white-and-gold-turbaned delegates supplied romance of the East. Strayed from biblical days seemed Saudi Arabians headed by Prince Raisal. British Secretary of State for Foreign Affairs Anthony Eden, brought glamour as he arrived hatless, in black coat and gray trousers. A sleek, shining limousine adorned with Russia's hammer and sickle purred to a halt. Preceded by four bodyguards, appeared the man from Moscow, Foreign Commissar Molotov, square-headed, with inscrutable smile, representing 190 million people. Undaunted, an American seaman thrust forward a big hand. Molotov greeted him, passing on to the side entrance. Mrs. William P. Roth, one of San Francisco's richest women and chairman of Red Cross Volunteers, stood at the door, admitting press and radio representatives.

Under the gilt dome, against the azure-blue background, with flags of fifty nations, the World Conference began. First to step forward was Secretary of State Stettinius, tall, middle-aged, graying. Three major raps of the gavel: "The Conference of the United Nations on International Organization is now convened." A moment of silent meditation was requested.

Across the nation from Washington there came by radio President Truman's voice: "In the name of the great humanitarian who surely is with us in spirit, I earnestly appeal to each and every one of you to rise above personal interests, and adhere to those lofty principles which benefit all mankind. President Franklin D. Roosevelt gave his life while trying to protect those high ideals."

Mayor Roger Lapham and Governor Earl Warren also spoke in welcome. Seven thousand had begged for seats, but after delegates, press, radio representatives, and distinguished guests had been provided for, only five hundred could be accommodated. The public understood and thronged outside the building, listening to speeches through the microphone.

At the Opera House Canteen Mrs. David Luenergardt and her volunteers served 80,000 meals. Mrs. James Flood turned over her Mark Hopkins penthouse to the Big Three for a conference with

China's T. B. Soong. Never had so many women appeared at a similar conference. From Britain came Florence Horsbrugh of the Ministry of Health and Ellen Wilkinson of the British Ministry of Home Security. Delegate Cora Castleman was a member of Canada's Parliament. Madame Wu Yi-fang, president of Ginling College, was one of China's representatives. The Dominican Republic sent Minerva Bernardino; Peru, Bertha Lutz; Uruguay, Isabelle de Vial. Delegate Dean Virginia C. Gildersleeve, president of Barnard College, said at a large luncheon given in her honor, "The millennium will not dawn the day after the charter is ratified, but good will come of it."

Molotov was photographed at a dinner he gave for Stettinius and Eden, drinking a toast to them. With ever-present bodyguards he tramped through the Kaiser shipyards. On a visit to Stanford University, he stopped at a restaurant where the proprietor, a woman, sought his autograph. "No, lunch first," insisted the interpreter. After lunch the woman said, "All right, cutie, sign." Molotov signed. Although delegates paid their own hotel bills and traveling expenses, the conference cost the State Department $2 million, far less than the cost of equipping one destroyer.

After a month's session, the Charter was formulated, and President Truman arrived by plane. At the closing session of the conference, he entered the Opera House with Stettinius and stood before the delegates. "Oh, what a great day this can be for history This Charter, like our own Constitution, will be expanded and improved as time goes on. No one claims that it is a final and perfect instrument. . . . Changing world conditions will require adjustment, but they will be adjustments of peace, and not of war." Greatest applause met his words: "I know that I speak for every one of you when I say that the United Nations will remain united."

"The Charter is adopted," said Lord Halifax to wild applause.

On a circular Copenhagen-blue rug on the main floor of the Veterans' Building was a large blue table framed by a blue curtain. Here delegates signed the Charter. Representing China, Wellington Koo was first with a Chinese brush. British, Russian, and French delegates followed, others coming in alphabetical order. As host, the United States was to have been last, but in order that the President, who was planing to Washington, might see the signing, this country numbered 38. E. R. Stettinius, Cordell Hull, Tom Connelly, A. H. Vandenberg, Sol Bloom, Charles A. Eaton, Harold E. Stassen, and Virginia C. Gildersleeve were signers. The Charter was flown from San Francisco to Washington, to be ratified by the Senate.

After five years the eyes of the world again were focused on the War Memorial Opera House when history was made at the conference for signing the peace treaty to end war with Japan. Although men of the United Nations were dying on Korean battlefields, for eleven months Ambassador at Large John Foster Dulles had carried on negotiations that brought together world-ranking diplomats by train, water, and plane.

Mayor Elmer E. Robinson greeted President Truman on September 3, 1951, when he disembarked from the presidential silver and blue *Independence* at the International Airport. All the way into town people cheered and honked. From his rooms at the Fairmont Hotel, the President spoke five minutes, and that evening dined on fried chicken with the California veterans of the 129th Field Artillery of World War I—another old soldier.

India, Burma, and Yugoslavia were absent, but there were 51 flags on the stage of the War Memorial Opera House representing 51 nations. For the first time history making was observed by an audience of forty millions, made possible through television. From coast to coast they saw in action Britain's sturdy Herbert Morrison; France's chunky, smiling Schuman; Japan's ailing minister of foreign affairs, Shigeru Yoshida; unsmiling Andrei Gromyko, and 36 Communist followers who came up from their rented million-dollar mansion at Hillsborough.

When at the beginning Secretary of State Dean Acheson, as president of the conference, asked a moment of prayer and meditation, Gromyko became a man of ice. After welcoming addresses by Acheson, Governor Warren and Mayor Robinson, President Truman said, "As we approach the peace table, let us be free of hate to the end that from here on there shall be neither victor nor vanquished among us, but only equals in the partnership of peace. . . . We're trying to build a world where there is justice and freedom for all men and all nations." Although Japan would be restored to the family of nations, he warned that the past was not entirely forgotten and any future acts of aggression would be ruthlessly punished. After closing his address the President shook hands with a thousand at the hotel reception and in the morning rolled out of town toward Kansas City to inspect flood damage.

Tall, gray John Foster Dulles, the treaty's architect, said, "The Japan of today is transformed from the Japan of yesterday." He spoke in appreciation of General MacArthur, who had educated the Japanese in democracy. "This treaty is an act of enlightened self-interest. . . . It will restore to Japan equality and opportunity in the family of nations. . . . No nation is bound to sign the treaty. The only compulsion is the moral compulsion of grave circumstances. They unite to say, 'Let us make peace.' "

Although Russia had been at war with Japan only six days and the other nations for four years, delegates from Russia, Poland, and Czechoslovakia tried to rewrite the treaty and to confuse and complicate, but they did not succeed. Ceylon's delegate, J. R. Jayawardana, quoted Buddha: "Hatred ceases, not by hatred, but by love."

Buddhists, Christians, and Moslems stood together, and at 10:00 A.M. of September 8 began signing the beautiful blue-vellum book lying on the modernistic table. Beginning with Argentina, Acheson called the nations in alphabetical order. For the United States, he signed first, followed by John Foster Dulles and delegates Alexander Wiley and John Sparkman.

After the last signature an almost religious feeling swept through the audience when Minister of Foreign Affairs Yoshida took up the pen to affix his signature for Japan, making enemies into allies. Now Japan's white flag, with the scarlet rising sun, flew proudly among the banners. At a press conference Yoshida said, "We shall strive in all good faith to assume our full responsibility for peace in the Pacific."

After the pact had been signed, Acheson said, "We must live the treaty from this day on. It depends on each nation, each individual of each nation, to make it what it is in words. . . . May the Peace of God which passes all understanding be amongst us, and remain with us always."

Later at a press conference, Gromyko stated, "The treaty is a separate peace that will breed war."

Minister of Foreign Affairs Yoshida had arrived with his daughter and five delegates on the plane *Bold Eagle*, but after signing the treaty the plane was rechristened *Monarch of the Skies*. Amid cries of "Banzai!" from their assembled countrymen, the Japanese delegation emplaned for their peaceful homeland.

After the treaty had been ratified by the Senate it was signed by President Truman, April 28, 1952, the fifty-first birthday of Emperor Hirohito. After more than six years of military occupation, Japan was proclaimed a sovereign nation. Celebrating the new era, the Emperor addressed his subjects before Tokyo's Imperial Palace. Throughout the land temple bells rang and sirens sounded. Once again the joyous voices of 80 million people sang the national anthem, "Kimigayo."

In 1955 again San Francisco's War Memorial Opera House made history. The supervisors voted $150,000 for the city's greatest birthday party, to commemorate the founding of the United Nations. Even in that war-scourged year, 1945, General Eisenhower was clinching the victory over the Germans; Mussolini was captured; Hitler died; United States troops were advancing on Ishan; the Japanese were withdrawing from Wenchow; but world leaders assembled April 25, 1945, to find a way for nations to live in peace.

In 1955, after ten years, the world asked how the nations had lived up to the noble language of the Charter. The Iranian question had been solved; the Greek Civil War brought under control; and disputes between Arabs and Israeli calmed. Prompt action had been taken in Korea in 1950, but the blood of thousands of Americans had been shed before the Armistice was completed in 1953. There was still tension between East and West, when the date was fixed in 1955 for the United Nations' San Francisco birthday party.

First to arrive in midweek was the 175-page Charter, flown out from the State Department in Washington. Bound in blue morocco, trimmed with gold, printed in five official languages—Chinese, French, Russian, English, Spanish—it was placed on display at the San Francisco Museum of Art. The 80-man Russian delegation came early and was installed in the 39-room Hillsborough mansion of Neal McNeil, where they toasted their visit in vodka.

In the Civic Auditorium 7,000 teen-agers of the Young People's Luther League, prayed that the world would "win with Christ." At the Cow Palace 16,000 men and women held a Festival of Faiths on Sunday attended by Buddhists, Moslems, Jews, Hindus, Confucianists, and Christians. New Zealand's Leslie Monro spoke and so did Secretary of State Dulles, who said, "The successes of the United Nations have been largely due to those throughout the world who believe that there is a God, a divine creator of us." The Catholic Church invited all delegates to gather at St. Mary's Cathedral for a special Mass.

President Eisenhower's huge silver presidential plane, *Columbine III*, touched wheels to the runway at the International Airport on Sunday evening before the opening of the birthday party. With sirens blasting the way, one hour later the President was greeting callers at the St. Francis Hotel. Among them were Mayor and Mrs. Robinson and Secretary Dulles.

Next morning 5,000 persons milled around when the President entered the automobile with Governor Knight. Cheers and "Hello, Ike!" were heard as, trim, fit and smiling, he stood in the car driving from the St. Francis to the stately, white War Memorial Opera House. Other cheering thousands surrounded the building when he entered.

The curtain rose on a gathering of diplomats from sixty nations. Dulles represented the United States; Macmillan, Great Britain; V. M. Molotov, the Soviet Union; and Antoine Pinay, France. Eelco N. van Kleffens, a courtly diplomat of the Netherlands, called the meeting to order and asked for a moment of prayer or meditation. The President bowed his head, Secretary of State Dulles's chin touched his chest, but Russia's Molotov stared straight ahead.

When the President appeared the audience rose to its feet. He set the session's keynote. "Global war has come to pose for civilization a threat of shattering destruction and sodden existence on the survivors of a dark and sodden world. The basis for success is simply put; it is that every individual at this meeting to be loyal to the United Nations and to the principles of the Charter. . . . I can solemnly pledge to you here, and to all men and women of the world who can hear or read my words, that those who represent the United Nations will strive to be loyal, thus dedicated. . . . We and the majority of all nations are united in the hope that every government will abstain from itself attempting, or aiding others to attempt subversion, coercion, infiltration or destruction of other governments, in order to gain political or material advantage, or because of differences of ideologies."

After laying the foundation of the summit meeting, he shook hands at a reception with Molotov and chatted pleasantly. The President's whirlwind tour ended, and in 8 hours 7 minutes he was back in Washington.

Later in the day Mayor Robinson and Governor Knight welcomed the delegates. Ex-President Truman arrived the latter part of the week. In 1945 he had rejoiced over the Charter with, "Oh, what a great day this can be for history! . . . You have created a great instrument for peace and security and human progress in the world." Five years later, however, he had been obliged to send troops to Korea to resist Communist invasion. When he appeared at the birthday party he received a spontaneous standing welcome. Among other things he said, "Some nations have become so accustomed to living in the dark that it isn't going to be easy for them to live in the light. . . . The choice must be between United Nations and international anarchy. The UN is a beacon of hope to a world that has no choice but to live together or die together."

Russia and her satellites lined up against the "Spirit of San Francisco." When Molotov spoke it was Communist propaganda, proposing measures that would divest the free world of means to oppose Communist activities.

After the birthday party was over, people began asking, would the United Nations live another ten years? It was realized that no country would wish to leave the United Nations. If the organization should disappear, it would be necessary to start over again in the struggle for peace. Governor Goodwin J. Knight named October 24 "United Nations Day."

CHAPTER 26

Pioneers of 1906

WHAT HAVE they accomplished—the pioneers of earthquake and fire? Have they been worthy of the city's founders?

In 1776 Captain Don Juan Bautista de Anza, a fighting Spanish frontiersman, led from Mexico San Francisco's first 240 pioneers, valiant descendants of Cortez' soldiers. On March 28, 1776, at today's Fort Point, Anza established the Presidio. Three miles distant near Twin Peaks, on June 29th of the same year an altar was set up and Mass was first said on the site of Mission Dolores. On that day the metropolis-to-be, San Francisco, consisted of fifteen tents. Pioneers of 1906 remember the city's founders. They have collected funds to restore the 246-year-old birthplace in Majorca of Padre Junipero Serra, founder of the twenty-one missions and the colonizer of California.

English-speaking San Francisco began in the village of Yerba Buena when the British seaman, William A. Richardson deserted his ship for love of Señorita Maria Antonia Martinez, daughter of the *comandante* at the Presidio. Richardson was the third Englishman in California. In the 1820's the honeymooners set up housekeeping. Their tented homesite at 823 and 827 Grant Avenue is marked by a plaque placed there by the Northern Federation of Civic Organizations of San Francisco.

After gold was discovered, pioneer forty-niners rushed up a city of 50,000 in a few months—fabulous, golden San Francisco. Fifty-seven years later, in 1906, their descendants saw the metropolis reduced to ashes for lack of water.

The pioneers resolved this must not happen again. After studying water resources, already in 1901 farsighted Mayor James D.

267

Phelan and city engineer M. M. O'Shaugnessy, had decided that the Hetch-Hetchy (Hatchatchie, a Central Miwok grass producing edible seed) system from the Tuolumne River had the purest and greatest volume of water, as well as the most desirable powersites. All those sites, however, were in Yosemite Park and Stanislaus National Forest, presided over by the Department of the Interior. Following a prolonged struggle in Congress, President Woodrow Wilson signed the Reber Act to "serve the pressing needs of the region . . . and yet not impair the usefulness, or materially detract from the beauty of the public domain."

Years of gargantuan toil followed. A 68-mile railroad was built, the O'Shaugnessy Dam was constructed, and the Coast Range bored through. On October 24, 1934, the first Hetch-Hetchy water flowed into the Crystal Springs reservoir on the peninsula and was on its way to San Francisco. While James Rolph, Jr., was mayor the city voted a $45 million bond for Hetch-Hetchy development. The Spring Valley Water Company was purchased for $41 million.

In order to prevent recurrence of the 1906 disaster, an emergency fire-fighting, earthquake-proof, high-pressure salt-water system has been installed at a cost of $7 million that today would require expenditure of between $40 million and $50 million. This system cannot fail unless the Pacific Ocean goes dry. During the term of Mayor Elmer E. Robinson, Pioneers of 1906 voted a $54 million bond issue to expand further the water supply that will serve the city with a population of four millions.

In 1906 four and one-half square miles of the city were burned, with losses estimated at $500 million. Rebuilding began immediately. The Fairmont Hotel, which had been gutted, celebrated the anniversary of the disaster by opening on April 18, 1907. In 1913 Mayor Rolph broke ground for the new City Hall, the first building in the Civic Center. New San Francisco, one year later, created the famed Panama-Pacific Exposition, celebrating completion of the Panama Canal, which brought the city as close commercially to the Atlantic seaboard as Chicago and Mississippi points. All the world visited San Francisco to witness her rise from the ashes.

Forty-niners filled in land from Montgomery Street to the bay, carting away hills to erect dwellings and make parks. Pioneers of 1906 filled in the bay to create a fairyland, the 1915 Panama-

Pacific Exposition. This added a new residential district, the Marina.

An even more amazing feat was the dredging out of the bay of the largest man-made island in the United States, Treasure Island. Here in 1939 was held the Golden Gate International Exposition celebrating completion of the famed bridges. Treasure Island is now occupied, in part, by the U.S. Naval Training Station.

San Francisco erected the beautiful War Memorial Opera House with a seating capacity of 3,285. This building was chosen as the meeting place of the United Nations delegates from April 25 to June 25, 1945, to create a Charter to maintain international peace and security. Here also met the Japanese Peace Conference from September 4 to 8, 1951, to sign the peace treaty, and the United Nations Commemorative Session came together here from June 20 to 26, 1955.

Another great structure is the $9 million Cow Palace, holding more than 22,000 people. On the freeway it is only 12 minutes or 6½ miles from the Civic Center, on the San Francisco-San Mateo County line. Founded by the State Agricultural District, it opened during the depression in 1935. E. J. Tobin was the first president, and today Nye Wilson, secretary-manager, directs the Cow Palace. Here great throngs have been assembled by such diverse attractions as Jehovah's Witnesses, Billy Graham, Barnum and Bailey Circus, the Ringling Brothers, Liberace, Adlai Stevenson. Seventh-day Adventists, and the Russian dancers. The National Republican Convention, which on August 23, 1956, nominated Eisenhower and Nixon, also was held here.

Farther down the peninsula the Pioneers of 1906 have created the San Francisco International Airport, the maxim of which is "Progress or Perish." There is a multimillion-dollar "jet age" expansion program. Envisioned are eight piers; two new terminals to supplement the present terminal; a hangar; three pedestrian overpasses; a three-level parking structure at the center of a quartered "pielike" ground-level parking area; two other ground parking areas; a service court; cargo facilities; office buildings, and a helicopter area. Airport manager Belford Brown says, "The Mills Field Mudhole is the best investment San Francisco ever made."

The city possessed eighteen parks and squares at the time of the Fire. Pioneers of 1906 added thirty-four. McCoppin Park, Mount

Davidson Park, Sutro Heights, Sharp Park, and Coolbrith Park were named for citizens of San Francisco. Begun in 1926, McLaren Park, with 288 acres, lying in the Alemany Boulevard, Bayshore and Mission Street area, honors the creator of Golden Gate Park.

"Uncle John" McLaren's Golden Gate Park has the Academy of Sciences buildings, Zoological Gardens, and the Fleishhacker play field. Women have beautified the city. In Golden Gate Park is the Strybing Arboretum and Botanical Garden, given in 1897 by Mrs. Christian Strybing in memory of her husband. Botanical specimens in the Strybing Arboretum seem to transport visitors to every country in the world. Also in Golden Gate Park is the Morrison Planetarium, given by Mrs. May Treat Morrison. Here is the first planetarium projector ever built in this country.

Another benefactor of San Francisco's parks is Mrs. Sigmund Stern, who memorialized her husband by giving 33 acres of the old Trocadero Ranch at 19th Street and Sloat Boulevard. In this wooded dell, where tall eucalyptus trees have stood for half a century, is a natural amphitheater donated by her with the stipulation that it be used forever by the city for recreation and culture. Here the Sigmund Stern Grove Musical Festival Association annually gives midsummer concerts, symphonies, ballets, and operas for the public without charge.

San Franciscans had done so much to develop the resources of Alaska and Hawaii that in September, 1958, Mayor George Christopher organized a ten-day Pacific Festival to greet Alaska as the forty-ninth state and hailing Hawaii as the assured fiftieth. Governor Mike Stepovich of Alaska and Governor William Quinn of Hawaii were virtually guests of honor.

On October 1, 1959, San Franciscans celebrated the opening of the new 220-acre play field on Angel Island. Lieutenant Don Juan Manuel Ayala sailed the first European ship into the bay in August, 1775, and used the island as an exploration base. Although it was named by him for "Our Lady of the Angels," it later became a dueling ground. During the Civil War it was fortified to protect the city from Confederate vessels, and during both World Wars it became a processing center. A 93-foot flagpole at the base of Ayala Cove is still the mariner's guide on geodetic maps. The army controls 320 acres of the island's 540 and operates a Nike site atop

Mount Ida, Angel's tallest point of 776 feet. Garden societies have seeded the island with vegetation from Australia, Canary Islands, and Rhodesia. Hundreds of deer play in the hills and the cove provides good perch and bass fishing. Outdoor enthusiasts travel by boat from Fisherman's Wharf and Sausalito to the park for $2.50 round trip, making Angel Island a new recreation paradise.

Pioneers of 1906 have included health-giving sports in the city's park development. There are four municipal golf courses: the Harding, Sharp, Lincoln, and the nine-hole course in the northwestern part of the Golden Gate Park. Mrs. Mary Kezar is responsible for the Kezar Municipal Stadium, home of the annual East-West football game, on January 1, for the benefit of the Shriners' Children's Hospital. Here also are played all home games of San Francisco's professional football eleven, the 49ers.

During Mayor Robinson's administration a $5 million bond issue was passed to bring major league baseball to San Francisco. It was accomplished in 1957 during Mayor Christopher's tenure, at the cost of $1.5 million. The Giants were brought to the Seals Stadium and the first year lured 1,272,625 fans to the home games, in comparison with 653,923 during their final year at the New York Polo Grounds. Out-of-towners numbered 509,000 and more than $75 million in financial transactions resulted from visitors' spending.

The Seals Stadium has little room for parking and so, Candlestick Park, less than ten minutes by car from downtown San Francisco, was acquired by the San Francisco Park and Recreation Committee. It has been leased for baseball for thirty-four years to Horace Stoneham, president of the Giants. The pear-shaped park was so named because of an original candelabra rock formation which gave Candlestick Point its name. It nestles in a cove with a breathtaking view of the bay.

The ultramodern, $11 million San Francisco Stadium, built in 1959, has a seating capacity of 40,700. Because many of the Giants' games will be played at night in cool summer weather, a radiant heating system has been installed. Although intended primarily for baseball, the park is suitable for football, boxing, and other outdoor spectacles.

Mayor Christopher's pride is that seventeen new schools have been opened during his tenure and four have been enlarged.

In ten years, from 1946 to 1956, San Francisco had a $289 million expansion for recreation, hospitals, sanitation, public welfare, water, airport, and municipal railways.

Pioneers of 1906 have spent nearly a billion dollars in erecting 196 churches. Many millions have been spent in correcting deporable conditions at the San Francisco Hospital, rebuilding the Laguna Honda Home, closing the old Barbary Coast, clearing slums, moving cemeteries, and building a new sewerage system. Hundreds of worn-out streetcar tracks have been torn up and the streets repaved from curb to curb, to beautify the city. Old firehouses have been rehabilitated and new ones built. Modern fire-fighting equipment has been installed, resulting in an annual reduction to property owners of insurance premiums.

The Atomic Power for Peace Project at Pleasanton shares the distinction of receiving the number one license from the Atomic Energy Commission for Power Reactor, a joint project of San Francisco's Pacific Gas and Electric Company and the General Electric Company. Actual production began August 5, 1957. San Francisco is also an important center of atomic research. The United States Naval Radiological Defense Laboratory—the only research activity in the country solely concerned with defense against the effects of atomic weapons—was constructed at the San Francisco Naval Shipyard at a cost of $8.5 million.

The University of California Medical Center is in San Francisco. The $24 million expansion program begun in 1950 to provide new medical research and treatment facilities is helping to make San Francisco one of the leading cities in the world in this field.

San Francisco had the first street cable car. In 1909 the first National Broadcasting Company was created from the work of San Jose's Charles David Herrold, a classmate of Herbert Hoover. San Francisco is the city in which the principle of television was perfected by Philo T. Farnsworth. San Francisco was the first city in the nation to have a municipal opera house, also to vote municipal support of symphony. Pioneers of 1906 have constructed an ultramodern wholesale Flower Terminal to house a $50 million business, the only one of its kind in the nation. San Francisco is the bridgehead of the world's longest and costliest bridge—San Francisco-Oakland Bay Bridge—and also of the longest single-span bridgehead in the world—Golden Gate Bridge.

Population increased so rapidly that in order to relieve traffic jams Pioneers of 1906 drove a tunnel 2.27 miles through Twin Peaks. The Sunset Tunnel by Duboce Avenue, measuring 4,332 feet; the Stockton tunnel, 1,224; and the $12 million Broadway Tunnel, an artery through Russian Hill—all these expedite traffic. A new freeway system offers a fast route to the downtown area from the peninsula points.

By vision and enterprise Pioneers of 1906 have made San Francisco first in population growth per square mile among major cities of the United States and the city with the highest per capita income among the largest cities in the United States. They have made San Francisco the nation's second most important financial center, the financial capital of the West, headquarters of the world's largest gas and electricity company, and have created the world's largest bank.

Whatever man can envisage man will do—this has always been the working principle of San Francisco's pioneers. In this space age, the San Francisco area is the center of missile construction. Already the youth dream of soaring to the moon or Venus for a holiday. This they may do, but they will gladly return to San Francisco—Magic City.

Index

Date Due